D1297463

# The Wasting of the British Economy

# The Wasting of the British Economy

## British Economic Policy 1945 to the Present

Sidney Pollard

CROOM HELM
London & Canberra

Croom Helm Ltd, 2–10 St John's Road, London SW11

British Library Cataloguing in Publication Data
Pollard, Sidney
   The wasting of the British economy.
   1. Great Britain—Economic conditions—1945-
   I. Title
   330.941'085      HC256.5
ISBN 0-7099-2019-9

Permission granted by the (Sheffield) *Morning Telegraph* and by Mr Bernard Hollowood to reproduce the two cartoons in this volume is gratefully acknowledged.

Printed and bound in Great Britain by
Biddles Ltd, Guildford and King's Lynn

# CONTENTS

# TABLES

# FIGURES

'The fact is that the only demand which will really help the situation is demand from abroad. An artificial stimulation of the home demand will merely mean encouraging people in this country to take in each other's washing and waste their energy in so doing.' (Treasury Memorandum, B.P. Blackett to Chancellor, 1921)

'Without our trade and our finance we sink to the level of a third-class power. Locarno and the unemployed have an intimate connection.' (Foreign Office Memorandum to Sir Austen Chamberlain, April 1926)

'If I were asked to state in a single word the goal to which economic policy should be directed in Great Britain at the present time, I should answer, Balance; balance in. . .the budget, international payments, between savings and investment; but balance also in other matters, between primary and secondary production, in the labour market, and above all between aggregate demand and aggregate supply in the economic system as a whole. Balance in all departments of economic life is an essential condition of attaining a high level of productivity and well-being.' (H.D. Henderson, Rede Lecture, 1947)

'There is, in my opinion, a perfectly simple and attainable remedy for the recurrent difficulties and embarrassments which have afflicted Britain since the war . . . It consists in transforming the country from a relatively low, to a dynamic high investment economy and thus imparting a decisive bias towards expansion. In my opinion we could achieve this aim by relatively small sacrifice in a relatively short time and we should in this way be able to solve most of our domestic and international problems. So long as this objective is not the primary aim of our policy, crises will recur and will force us to take measures. . .which are bound, in the longer run, to aggravate the problem they are supposed to remedy.' (Mr Thomas Balogh, Evidence to Radcliffe Committee, 1959)

'If I cannot afford to buy food, why should anyone else have it?' (Bill Astbury, Chairman, Greater Manchester Lorry Drivers' Strike Committee, quoted in the Observer, 21 January 1979)

# PREFACE

The early appearance of this book has been made possible by a generous grant from the Leverhulme Trust. This has enabled me to enjoy the dedicated, committed and stimulating collaboration of David Moody as Research Assistant. While no doubt too many mistakes still remain, thanks to this aid and assistance there are fewer of them than there otherwise would have been.

After a lifetime of writing learned books, the temptation was great to buttress this volume also with a fortification of sources, statistics and learned footnotes. But for reasons which will become clear to those readers who stay the course and manage to work their way through to the end, my hope has been to reach a wider audience than the purely professional one. In form, therefore, this book has become an uneasy compromise: not enough backing, probably, to satisfy the specialist, and too much to be easily tolerated by the general reader. The aim has been to provide sources for all quotations and all statistics, as well as for all statements and views which may be controversial or not widely known, but for nothing else. One advantage of footnotes is that those who do not want to know their contents can easily omit them.

Many people have given their help and support. The original stimulus came from Nicholas Chapman, then with Associated Business Press, who overcame my first doubts. Others who must be mentioned are: Dr Alan Booth, A.W.P. Fawcett, Dr Gerd Hohorst, Richard Hope, Mrs Beryl Maudling, Prof. R.D.G. Milner, Mrs Irene Wagner, the editor of *Drive* and Secretary and staff of the Society of Motor Manufactures and Traders. Mrs R.A. Duncan drew the graphs with admirable speed and accuracy. None is in any way responsible for the views put forward, and many would no doubt repudiate them. But my thanks to them are none the less deserved and genuine. Any errors and weaknesses that remain are wholly my own responsibility.

In the nature of things, the events with which this book deals are subject to sudden change, and there are several interesting developments in the offing as the last pages are being typed: in detail, some points may therefore be out of date when these pages appear in print. The book is, however, meant to be essentially a history of the past thirty years, rather than an immediate tract for the times. Conclusions may, and are intended, to be drawn for the immediate future as well as for the long-term outlook, but the views put forward here ask to be judged by the developments over one generation, rather than those from one week to the next.

S.P.

# 1  THE FACTS — AND DO THEY MATTER?

## 1 Some Data and Some Unpalatable Facts

This book is about economics, and about economic policy. It is part of an incessant debate which has now been going on for many years, and to an outsider it might possibly seem that the debate is too exclusively concerned with one aspect of life only. Money, after all, is not the only thing that matters, and even if it can be shown, as there will be no difficulty in showing, that the British record of economic policy is one unbroken chain of abysmal failure, Britain is still a fine country to live in. Are the media right to occupy themselves so obsessively with economic affairs, and are we all right to judge governments almost solely by their economic performance? Is this not a sign of a poor sense of values?

There is no doubt that man does not live by bread alone, and that the good life does not depend merely on economic success; yet neither should the pervasive effect of economic performance on other spheres of life be underrated. It affects so many things: not only what we can afford to eat or wear, but also the ability of the medical profession to save lives, the chances of poor children to receive the education their talents deserve, the health of the national theatre, and even the tone, the good temper and the humanity of political and public life. It may even be that the British have accepted meekly the plan to become an atomic dustbin for other countries because as a poor nation we cannot afford to be as choosy as others who are vigorously rejecting such a role. So the state of economic health has very wide implications. That must be, in part, a justification for this book.

How do we measure economic success? There are many different things that people want; the same people want different things at different stages of their lives, and perhaps even on different days of the week. Each society will be better at providing some of these things than others, and again this will vary over time. How can we bring all this on to a single denominator?

There is no perfect measure, but over the years economists have been devising methods for bringing together into a single figure the

1

total of the output of all goods and services of a society in a given period, usually in one year. Adding up apples and oranges or motor cars and theatrical performances does present logical difficulties, but the rationale behind doing it in money terms is that, at any rate in a free society, each person will lay out his or her money in such a way as to get the most benefit out of their disposable income. If £5 will buy a theatre seat or three gallons of petrol, then this must represent, roughly, equivalent values in society's eyes, or else there would be a rush on one or the other, and the alternative would remain unsold.

There are various ways in which these totals of goods and services can be summed. We may include, or exclude, imports and exports; we may include or exclude the capital used up in the year's work. A commonly preferred measure is Gross National Product (GNP), which will mainly be used here. By dividing it by the number of inhabitants, to obtain GNP per head, we have a rough and ready standard. By using an appropriate exchange rate, we can then compare GNP per head in different countries, provided they are not too far away from each other in culture, and by re-calculating everything in constant prices, we can compare different years for the same country.

How does Britain fare in such comparisons? The statistics confirm the national consciousness of a staggering relative decline, such as would have been considered utterly unbelievable only a little over thirty years ago. At the end of the war, when Britain had emerged as one of the victorious great powers helping to shape the peace, she was still among the richest nations of the world, ahead by far of the war-shattered economies of Europe. On the continent, only the neutrals, Sweden and Switzerland, were better off than Britain, and elsewhere only the United States and Canada. Britain was among the technical leaders, especially in the promising high-technology industries of the future: aircraft, electronics, vehicles. The problem that exercised the statesmen of the day was whether the rest of Europe, even its industrialised parts, would ever be able to come within reach of, let alone catch up with, Britain.

Nor was that lead a temporary fluke, a result of the more destructive effects of the war on the Continent. On the contrary, the British lead in 1950 was fully in line with that of 1938:[1] and even more so with that of earlier decades, when the British position had been firmly in the van of Europe. It had a solid and traditional foundation.

Today the picture is startlingly different. British GNP per head is little more than half that of her immediate neighbours and of other countries that are, in their build-up, most like Britain (see Table 1.1).

In this category only Italy is still behind Britain, and even there northern industry has higher productivity; it is just the south, with its almost African backwardness, which brings down the average to below the British level. Since the war, Britain has been successively overtaken by Norway, Iceland, Finland, Denmark, Holland, Belgium, West Germany, France, Luxemburg, Austria, Australia, New Zealand and Japan, not to mention a number of oil-producing states.

After having led the world for two hundred years, Britain is no longer counted among the economically most advanced nations of the world. A wide gap seperates her from the rest of industrialised Europe. The difference as measured in national product per head between Britain and, say, Germany, is now as wide as the difference between Britain and the continent of Africa.[3] One short generation has squandered the inheritance of centuries.

The same point is illustrated graphically in Figure 1.1. It will repay close study. The picture it conveys is that the world has passed Britain by — as if, in a convoy travelling together, all the other ships are sailing serenely on while Britain has gone aground, helplessly

**Table 1.1: GNP per Head and GDP[a] per Man Hour 1977–9, Nine Countries[2]**

|  | GNP per Head 1978 (US$ 000) | GDP per Head 1979 (US$ 000) | GDP per Man Hour 1977 (USA = 100) |
|---|---|---|---|
| Switzerland | 13.32 | 14.97 | 65 |
| Sweden | 10.53 | 12.28 | 79 |
| West Germany | 10.43 | 12.45 | 84 |
| Belgium | 9.81 | 11.26 | 94 |
| Netherlands | 9.36 | 10.62 | 84 |
| France | 8.83 | 10.86 | 79 |
| Japan | 8.53 | 8.72 | 52 |
| UK | 5.51 | 7.16 | 61 |
| Italy | 4.18 | 5.69 | 68 |

Note: a. GDP = Gross Domestic Product.
Source: OECD, *Economic Survey* (November 1979); Angus Maddison, 'Long Run Dynamics of Productivity Growth', *Banca Nazionale del Lavoro Quarterly Review*, no. 128 (1979), p. 4.

watching the rest of the convoy disappearing over the horizon. The captains of the convoy still meet for regular consultation, but while the others represent vessels which are seaworthy and moving towards their destination, the British captain commands a vessel which is little more than a hulk. To drop the metaphor, when British Ministers meet others at their regular conferences, they share the problems of unemployment and business cycles, of currency adjustment and structural change, of defence expenditure and social welfare provisions. Yet these outward similarities hide an underlying fundamental difference: their economies go on growing, providing substantially more resources year by year to deal with it all, while the British economy virtually stagnates. British representatives may behave as if they belonged to the same economic world, but in a very real sense they do not. The British experience is unique.

There used to be talk of a 'German economic miracle', the sheer incredible recovery of Germany out of the depth of the hunger and destruction of her defeat, following the Erhard reforms. Since then the recovery of France has seemed even more miraculous, emerging as it did after a century and a half of stagnation and growing relative backwardness,[4] out of the humiliations of the war and the bloodletting of Algeria and other costly colonial wars. Thereafter it was the turn of Italy to claim attention, a lop-sided economy, defeated in the war, backward and imitative, beset by insoluble social problems — Italy suddenly showed the fastest growth rate in Europe, to build up a powerful industrial complex with great successes in such key sectors as motor cars and domestic consumer durables. Meanwhile, it was realised that the smaller nations, including even Belgium, an old industrialised country too heavily committed to the dying sectors of coal and steel, had done the same; while Switzerland and Sweden, countries without a post-war reconstruction spurt, had likewise kept up. And beyond Europe, Japan peformed the greatest miracle of all. Emerging from total defeat and humiliation, bereft of a vast empire, obliged to feed a densely settled population on insufficient land and lacking in natural resources, she showed year by year rates of growth such as the world had never seen before. Thus she overtook much of Europe — only to be threatened, in turn, by equally 'miraculous' developments in South Korea, Hong Kong, Singapore and elsewhere in the Far East.

Slowly it began to dawn that a 'miracle' which is regularly repeated all round the world is scarcely miraculous, and that there must have been some common or pervasive drive in the world econ-

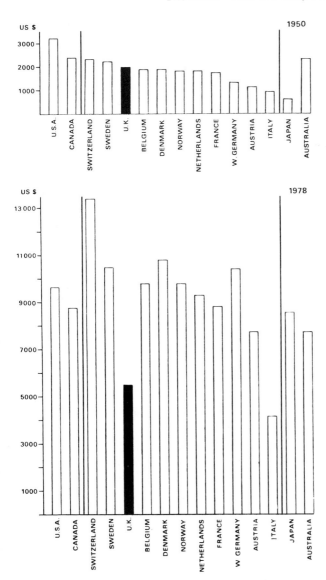

**Figure 1.1: Gross National Product** *per Capita*, **15 Countries, 1950 and 1978**[a]

Note:  a. 1950: In US $ at 1970 prices; 1978: In US $ at current prices.
Source: OECD, International Surveys; A Maddison, 'Phases of Capitalist Development', *Banca Nazionale del Lavoro Quarterly Review* 121 (1977).

omy to make all these successes possible. In the light of this boom, what then required explanation was the British experience: the only economic 'miracle'[5] was the British failure to take part in the progress of the rest of the industrialised world. Surely it must have required a powerful and sustained effort, or most unusual circumstances, to prevent the world boom from spilling over into Britain as well.

Averaged out over the period, growth rates of the EEC and similar countries were all around the 4–5 per cent mark, those of the Scandinavians and North Americans, starting from a very much higher absolute level, and therefore closer to the technology frontier, around the 3–4 per cent mark, and the Japanese, coming up from behind, were around the 9–10 per cent mark.[6] Only the British stayed at 2–3 per cent. Given the power of compound interest rates, it was enough to open up a significant gap.

At annual rates of around 2 per cent compound British economic growth was still faster than at any time in history and led to a widespread rise in prosperity. Nevertheless, measured against what turned out to be possible for others in a competitive, intercommunicating world, it was disappointing to the point of being calamitous. There is no record of any other economic power falling behind at such startling speed.

Within the span of half a lifetime, Britain has descended from the most prosperous major state of Europe to the Western European slum. She is the despair of her friends and the joy of her enemies. She has become the proverbial failure, as all round the Western world an economic proposal has merely to be dubbed as having been tried in Britain to be condemned without further hearing, just as Moscow has been reduced to quoting Britain as the proof that capitalism does not work.

The full extent of this descent may perhaps best be brought home by considering not the advanced rivals in Europe, but the tail-enders. If we continue as we have been doing in 1950–73, Italy will easily have overtaken Britain in the course of the current decade, Spain will have caught up by 1991, Greece by 1987 and Portugal by the year 2008. Since, on the showing of those years, Eastern Europe will also have sailed past Britain, though absolute comparisons are difficult to make with any accuracy in their case, Britain will then, within less than another thirty years, have to settle down to be the poorest country in Europe, with the possible exception of Albania.

If it is felt that the oil crisis has changed all that and we should instead take the five years 1973 – 8 as a guide, we find that the year in which Spain overtakes Britain changes to 1995, Greece to 1998, while Portugal will have caught up only in 2053. Lest this long delay before the drop to the bottom should make one too complacent, it is worth noting that on the same simplistic assumptions, Britain will not have reached the *present* German level until 2051, when all those who are making our present economic policy will be but a distant memory.[7] None of this takes into account the wilful further destruction of British industrial power under Mrs Thatcher's rule.

At this point many readers will rebel. Is not all this too impossibly pessimistic? Surely the country cannot remain so incompetent or so unlucky? Surely, when it comes to it, somebody will do something about it?

Alas, Britain is more than three-quarters of the way there, and no one, neither God nor those who control her economic affairs, has yet seen fit to do anything about it; the latter, indeed, as we shall see, are still on course for speeding her decline. If they managed to bring down a powerful economy such as Britain was in 1946 – 50, enjoying a position in the technical forefront of the day, possessing a powerful world currency and a strong hold over world markets, driven forward by a high morale after her victory in the war while her competitors were in disarray; then it is child's play to continue the downward drift of the decrepit, out-of-date, demoralised economy, with her poor reputation for reliability and quality, which Britain has since become. Today it is the reversal of our fortunes which would need enormous and exceptional efforts.

If it seems inconceivable that countries like Spain or Greece should overtake Britain, let us look at the example of Austria. For at least two hundred years, as far back as the records will go, the Austrian economy had been operating at 50 per cent or less of the British level of output, and there exists a library of books to explain her backwardness. After her involvement on the losing side in the last war, she became the rowing boat that had to carry four elephants (the occupying armies); and the political compromise under which she was given independence included the convention that the overblown state bureaucracy had to fill each important job with two people, one from each of the two main parties. From the viewpoint of, say, 1950, the idea that Austria might catch up with Britain seemed as ludicrous as the notion of Spain rivalling us now. Yet today Austria has long since overtaken us in total output and manufacturing competence. If it has been possible for a country so far behind to pass us with such ease, Spain or Greece will have no difficulty either. Indeed, there is no economy anywhere in the world that will not overtake us, in our weakened state, within thirty or forty years of beginning to industrialise. The industrial belt of Scotland is an example of a formerly leading industrial region which has declined into an area of industrial dereliction, unable in spite of massive regional aid policies to take part fully in the prosperity of her larger neighbour. It is not impossible for Britain as a whole to become the Scotland (if not the Ulster) of Europe.

Yet doubts still remain. Can it be that the GNP figures are wrong, or measure the wrong things? Is there not something they may have left out? It is true that economic welfare depends not only on current output but also on inherited wealth, and here Britain still enjoys some benefits of former prosperity, including a good housing stock. Yet anyone with eyes to see will know that, in spite of it, Britain has dropped a long way behind the other industrialised nations of the Western world.

We can test this general impression by looking at particular sectors where output can be compared directly in actual units or weights. We have chosen two items for comparison, steel and motor vehicles. The choice has been dictated in part by the fact that traditionally these were strong sectors in the British economy, and that they still are, by common consent, both symbols and foundations of modern industrial success. In addition, it is of significance that at the time of writing, the government is actively and savagely *reducing* the size of such segments of both these British industries as happen to be directly under its control.

The picture that emerges is, if anything, even more depressing than that relating to national output as a whole. Whereas in 1950 Britain was far and away the leading producer outside the United States for both products, today she has completely dropped away out of sight: in the case of steel she has been overtaken even by Italy; in motor cars she has been overtaken, unbelievably, even by Spain (see Figures 1.2 and 1.3). It is noteworthy that, just as in the diagram for total output, the rank order of the other countries has not changed very much except for the phenomenal rise of the Japanese economy and the relative decline of the American. The American economy (and, in its tow, the Canadian) has begun to show features altogether remarkably like the British in recent years after following similar economic policies.

Nor can it be argued that steel or motor vehicles were held back in

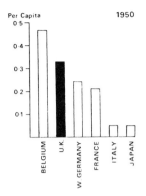

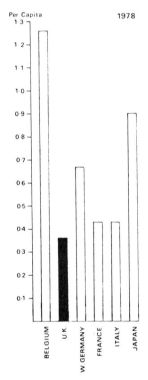

**Figure 1.2: Crude Steel Production *per Capita*, Six Countries, 1950 and 1978**[a]

Note: a. In Tonnes *per Capita.*
Source: B. Mitchell, *European Historical Statistics 1950–1970* (1975), p. 339, Iron and Steel Statistics Bureau, *Monthly Statistics* (December 1979).

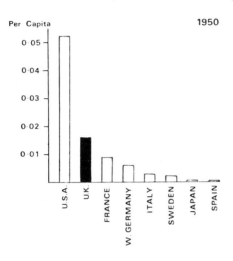

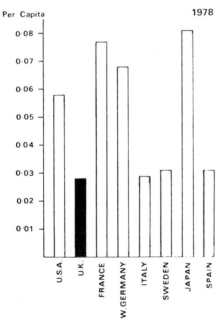

**Figure 1.3: Motor Vehicle Production *per Capita*, Eight Countries, 1950 and 1978[a]**

Note:   a. Cars and Commercial Vehicles produced per Capita.
        Source: *Society of Motor Manufacturers and Traders.*

Britain in order to free resources for other more progressive sectors. The plain fact is that the relative, as well as recently absolute, decline in their output was caused not so much by a reduction in the manpower employed in these industries as by a failure to match the productivity of other countries. Thus in the case of steel, it was the British Steel Corporation's aim in their major reorganisation in 1980 to raise output per man from its current level of 141 tonnes a year, while the French level was in the 180s range, the German lay in the 240 tonnes range, and the Japanese had achieved 364 to 467 tonnes per man four years earlier.[8] A different calculation for 1978, produced by another bipartisan body, a National Economic Development Office expert group, showed that it took 10.9 man hours in Britain to produce a ton of steel, while the European figures ranged from 6.4 for France to 4.8 for Luxembourg.

Motor cars showed similar differences in productivity. Perhaps the most striking were those registered within the same company making identical cars. Within Ford's, the man hours needed to assemble the British Escort and Cortina, as against the German Escort and Belgian Taurus, were 167 and 187 respectively, the Continental plant being 100; in the case of the BL Mini, it was 232 compared with 100 for the Belgian Mini. Taking the national works overall, the number of vehicles produced in 1973 per employee, adjusted for suppliers and product mix, were:

| | |
|---|---|
| Britain | 5.1 |
| France | 6.8 |
| Italy | 6.8 |
| West Germany | 7.3 |
| Japan | 12.2 |
| United States | 14.9 |

By contrast in 1955 British productivity, calculated on the same basis, had been ahead of all other European competitors.[9]

These failures are entirely typical for all manufacturing industry. One recent calculation, made for the Dresdner Bank of Frankfurt am Main in West Germany for the ten leading non-Communist industrial countries, found the actual productivity of the British worker in manufacturing to be the second lowest, with an index of 52, Germany being 100; only Italy, at 51, was still lower, while the USA topped the table with an index of 124.[10] Another one showed that inside 100 multinational manufacturing companies in various industries, British output per employee hour was trailing behind the USA, Germany and France in a similar manner.[11]

Another test for a country's industrial performance is the trend of its shares in world manufacturing exports, and it confirms the sad picture of British decline (Table 1.2). Finally, there is another measure, the 'trade ratio' of exports of manufactures as a proportion of exports plus imports of manufactures, and that dropped from 0.31 to 0.14 in 1966–75.[12] Britain, not so long ago the world's leading manufacturing exporter, will soon turn into a net importer of manufactures.

There is no escaping the enormous and overwhelming weight of the evidence: in a short span of thirty years or so Britain has sunk down from a position of industrial strength and leadership to the level of a second-class industrial nation, her output and her productivity being little more than half of those with whom it would be most reasonable to compare her. But output and productivity are not the only measures of economic success. Every post-war British government has from time to time listed other aims, in various orders of priority. Among them have been:

(1)  full employment;
(2)  stability, in the sense of absence of fluctuations;
(3)  a 'fairer' distribution of incomes;
(4)  good industrial relations;
(5)  stability of home prices;
(6)  stability of the external value of the pound sterling;
(7)  a favourable or stable balance of payments;
(8)  regional balance.

**Table 1.2:   Shares in World Exports of Manufactures (per cent)**

|  | Average of Years 1951–5 | 1973–7 | Change in Terms of World Exports |
|---|---|---|---|
| USA | 25.8 | 16.8 | − 7.0 |
| UK | 20.5 | 9.1 | − 11.4 |
| W. Germany | 13.1 | 21.1 | + 8.0 |
| France | 9.4 | 9.7 | + 0.3 |
| Japan | 4.4 | 14.2 | + 9.8 |
| Italy | 3.5 | 7.1 | + 3.6 |

Source: *National Institute Economic Review* (Various issues), Statistical Appendix.

Other objectives might be added to the list. It may well be that a country showing up badly by the productivity measure might have a much better record in one or more of the others.

Alas, this was not true of Britain in our period. There was not a single objective in which the British performance was better than that of other comparable countries, and in many it was strikingly worse. Taking the period as a whole, her unemployment figure was about average, but has recently risen to among the worst; so was her distribution of incomes[13] and her cyclical stability;[14] indeed, a good case can be made for saying that her lurches from crisis to crisis were more damaging than the fluctuations which accompanied expansion elsewhere. Her industrial relations were distinctly worse than the average, and in the matter of home prices and external value of the pound, she was either bottom or nearly so (see Table 1.3). In the matter of the foreign balance of payments, she fared worst of all by far. None of this is entirely surprising, for a number of these indices are directly or indirectly related to the progress of production and of

**Table 1.3: Some Indicators of Economic Performance**

|  | Consumer Prices | | Average Rate of Unemployment (US definition) 1959-76 | Change in Value of Currency against the US Dollar (market rates, 1950-end 1978, per cent) |
|---|---|---|---|---|
|  | 1975 (1953 = 100) | Sept. 1980 (1975 = 100) |  |  |
| UK | 334 | 201.6 | 3.41 (GB) | − 27 |
| France | 301 | 168.3 | 2.54 | − 17 |
| Italy | 291 | 226.4 | 3.76 | − 25 |
| Netherlands | 273 | 135.9 | — | + 92 |
| Sweden | 270 | 167.3 | 1.86 (1961−76) | + 20 |
| Canada | — | 155.5 | 5.61 | — |
| Belgium | 221 | 137.5 | — | + 74 |
| Switzerland | 217 | 113.3 | — | + 165 |
| USA | 201 | 156.3 | 5.35 | 0 |
| Japan | — | 140.5 | 1.44 | — |
| Germany | 195 | 123.0 | 1.12 | + 130 |

Sources: John Cornwall, *Modern Capitalism* (1977), p. 204; Samuel Brittan and Peter Lilley, *The Delusion of Incomes Policy* (1977), p. 179; Barbara Boner and Arthur Neef, 'Productivity and Unit Labour Cost in 12 Industrial Countries', *Monthly Labour Review* (July 1977); IMF, *International Financial Statistics* (1979); OECD, *Economic Indicators* (1980).

productivity: industrial relations, for example, are easier to maintain on a satisfactory footing when there is a 5 per cent rise to be distributed year by year than when the increase is negligible or nil.

There is thus no consolation to be drawn from these alternative objectives. By all the criteria by which economic performance is judged, Britain's results in the years since the war have been abysmal when measured against the opportunities available to her. She has been the one failure in the Western European economic success story since the war.

## 2 Does it Matter? — Some Arguments For and Against Growth

Yet, perhaps, international comparisons are a poor base for action, and a poor criterion for success. What is wrong with being the slowest economic grower? Would it not be more sensible to feel satisfied that economic growth in Britain in recent years has been faster than in past ages, and leave it at that? In any case, does not change have its own costs?[15]

Now we could indeed in theory develop a strategy of keeping down real wages in line with relative productivity: any backward economy can always compete in world markets by paying its citizens no more than their output is worth. It is a part of the argument of this book that that is precisely what British governments have been attempting to do since the war: in that period virtually all our economic policies and all the major economic and political controversies surrounding them (with a very few exceptions) have not been about how to improve the growth performance of the British economy, but how to slide down gracefully and elegantly rather than in ungainly and demoralising lurches. Deflation, devaluation, tariffs and control of the money supply are all measures designed not to improve productivity or efficiency, but to find means of adjusting to their relative failure to improve. And, as far as that goes, they have succeeded. Britain has managed to keep her necessary imports and exports going by matching her failure to improve her efficiency in line with other countries by a similar failure to raise her real wages and other incomes.

That, however, has not been the objective. On the contrary, it has been the persistent aim of politicians and economists alike to reach an economic performance similar to that of our neighbours, and they have lived in the continuous illusion — which they have never hesitated to communicate to the public at large[16] — that their measures really would bring this about. In terms of their objectives, therefore, their failure is undoubted and abysmal.

Besides, short of a Puritan revolution it would not be unreasonable for the British people to wish to achieve for themselves and their families a standard of comfort, of education and of health which they feel, with some reason, to be within the realm of the possible. There exists today a powerful demonstration effect of the knowledge of what goes on elsewhere, derived from travel, from films and television, not to mention the efforts of the distributive and advertising industries at home. The difference made in this respect by a higher growth rate combined with a higher absolute level can be very powerful and has often been underrated. A simple numerical example will illustrate this.

Assume a British worker's typical income of, say, £80 and an equivalent European income of £150. Assume also a growth rate of 2 per cent a year here and 5 per cent there, and the introduction of a novel consumer good, such as a colour television set at £300, just at the point in the year when the annual real wage increase is due. The European worker can buy the set, leaving the rest of his expenditure unchanged, in 40 weeks (40 × £7.5 = £300); the Briton, on the same assumptions, has to wait two years and nine weeks (52 × £1.6 plus 52 × £3.3 plus 9 × £4.9), by which time his European colleague has accumulated an additional £1,100 towards a new car. With such comparisons before his eyes, it is not perhaps surprising that the stagnation in incomes here has led to a radicalisation of the British worker in recent years.

Yet the argument may be pitched at a different level altogether. Has not growthmanship as a whole been discredited? Is there not a danger of using up the world's resources too quickly, and do we not destroy our own welfare by such by-products of growth as overcrowded cities, traffic jams, polluted beaches and power supplies liable to be cut off at the whim of any of a dozen different trade unions? Is not much of our vaunted technical progress used up merely in the repair of the damage made by the destruction of our environment?[17] Should we therefore not seek to end growth altogether, rather than ponder ways of accelerating it?

Such arguments may have an immediate appeal, but they will not stand up to examination either on economic or on moral grounds. They might perhaps command more attention if they did not emanate, as they usually do, from the better residential areas of

Oxford or north-west London. They have an air of middle-class resentment that one cannot get servants any more, and that working-class incomes are catching up.[18] They forget the survival of widespread hard, grinding, soul-destroying poverty in our midst.

For poverty is still with us, poverty such as no civilised people should be subjected to in this age. If no one actually starves, people at various stages of their lives are still deprived of basic amenities, and millions earn less than even the minimum acceptable level of subsistence as defined by Supplementary Benefit Regulations — a problem for our morals no less than for those who are afraid of the effect on incentives. A recent study found 9 per cent of the population to be living in poverty according to that definition; on alternative definitions, 26 per cent, or 14 million people, could be considered to be deprived.[19] While there are no classic slums left, millions of working people live in the sordid depressing quarters of the old industrial cities of a kind that the rest of the advanced world would no longer tolerate.

There was indeed a time when British health services were among the most advanced, the envy of Europe: they are now among the most starved of funds, using the most antiquated buildings of all. In 1948, 95 per cent of hospitals were originally built before 1891, and there has been very little new construction since. Since Western European societies devote comparable shares of their incomes to health care,[20] and British GNP is so much below the others, British health services inevitably fall behind, and they cannot now install all the technical equipment that recent research has made possible. Meanwhile breakdowns are more common as buildings become older and more in need of repair that cannot be afforded, waiting lists get longer, and the endless bickering over resources and wages lowers morale. Headlines like 'lack of facilities killing 5,000 babies a year'[21] hardly cause a ripple of public interest in a society priding itself on being civilised.

Of course, some of the deprivation could be cured by redistribution, but it is unrealistic to wait for a society of saints, and still more unrealistic to assume that even saints could ever agree on the distribution of fewer resources so as to fulfil as many needs as could be met from a bigger total. In the past, the real relief from poverty has always come from a larger total, not from redistribution. As the National Board for Prices and Incomes concluded in its *General Report on Low Pay*,[22] much the most effective way of improving the real income of low-paid workers more rapidly is. . .to improve the country's rate of economic growth. . . By comparison with this, any conceivable success by wage earners as a whole in securing a larger share of the products of the economy would bring only minor benefits in terms of higher real income.

Between 1953/4 and 1973, while the distribution of lower incomes remained unchanged, actual numbers in poverty fell from 20 per cent to 2 per cent, or by a factor of eight, a fall entirely due to the growth of the economy.[23] Even incomes policies designed to level up wages have failed to do so in anything but the shortest term.[24] In any case, decline and disappointment themselves represent negative welfare.

But there is a more fundamental fallacy in the anti-growth argument, a fallacy extending beyond morals and value systems to the economic base itself. The rustic idyll may have its attractions, but it could only be enjoyed by a maximum population of around 10 million. The British population of 55 million cannot exist without urban concentrations and factories, and these have to be efficient. Cairo is not a suitable ideal for London to aim at.

It is true that the modern age has damaged the environment, but 'pollution. . .is a question of the misallocation of resources' rather than of growth as such.[25] Growth may have led to pollution in the past, but it can also remove it in the future. Britain is full of unsightly slag heaps, polluted rivers and blighted inner-city sites, for which plans for rehabilitation exist but cannot be put into practice for lack of funds, whereas a richer society would have been able to afford them long ago. Again, growth uses up resources; but technology is itself able to turn previously worthless materials into new 'resources'.

Nor does the growth of GNP necessarily mean more things: increasingly it has come to mean better things. Better housing rather than two houses per family; more efficient cars using less fuel, or more efficient heating wasting less energy. It means shorter hours of labour, longer holidays, pleasanter conditions at work, less physical toil. Societies have in the past always converted some of their rising efficiency into methods of expending less effort rather than into making more things; it is an option open only to those who have the resources. To deny oneself the advantages of economic growth means opting deliberately for harder work, for longer hours in worse conditions, for less take-home pay: no one has ever dared to run an election campaign on such a platform.

There is a final objection raised to growth as an object of policy. It comes from those who give a higher priority to political power and influence. In their eyes, economic sacrifices are worth making if they enhance the political standing of Britain in the world. But it is an illusion to think that political power is possible without economic strength. Britain, one of the 'Big Four' at the end of the war and a permanent member of the Security Council of the United Nations in consequence, might have retained her status as a strong second-class power if she had been able to manage her economy as well as did all the other European states. As it is, her influence has declined with her industries. Even a source normally friendly to Britain could not help noting that when the British Prime Minister was invited to the summit meeting of the Great Powers in Guadaloupe in January 1979: 'that exalted company must have been particularly encouraging for a country like Great Britain which nowadays hardly deserves a place in the top League.'[26] It is a comment which may serve as an illustration as to how far Britain has sunk in one generation.

There is, in effect, no way out. There is no merit in being poor or in being incompetent: that way there is neither honour to be had abroad nor gratitude at home. If the slow economic development in Britain has made for a certain stability, that stability has been more than outweighed by the manner in which in recent years one group after another has been willing to disrupt and to do major damage to their fellow citizens in the struggle not to suffer an actual loss in real income. All this is beginning to threaten the very fabric of British society. The revolutions of the past have occurred, not in societies that were in abject poverty, but in those in which some progress occurred but expectations of further advance had been disappointed.[27]

## Notes

1. A. Lamfalussy, *The United Kingdom and the Six* (1963), p. 15. There may be doubts about 1938 as a base year, but the general point remains. Also E.H. Phelps Brown, 'Labour Policies: Productivity, Industrial Relations, Cost Inflation' in Sir Alec Cairncross (ed.), *Britain's Economic Prospects Reconsidered* (1971), p. 102.

2. Part of the spread may be accounted for by the fact that the dollar exchange does not exactly reflect the true price level, but as an alternative it will reflect economic strength. On a different basis, labour costs in manufacturing, based on German rates, Britain has been overtaken by Italy also and has the lowest real wages among ten industrialised nations: Index UK = 100.

|  | 1970 | 1977 |
|---|---|---|
| USA | 270 | 194 |
| Sweden | 190 | 225 |
| Germany | 161 | 231 |
| Belgium | 134 | 231 |
| Switzerland | 132 | 206 |
| Italy | 118 | 138 |
| France | 110 | 138 |
| UK | 100 | 100 |
| Austria | 89 | 150 |
| Japan | 69 | 125 |

Source: G.F. Ray in Frank Blackaby (ed.), *De-industrialisation* (1979), p. 74.
   3. GNP per head, 1977, in US$:

|  |  | Differences |
|---|---|---|
| Germany | 8,406 | 4,033 |
| UK | 4,373 | 3,893 |
| Africa (except South Africa) | 480 |  |

Source: United Nations, *Yearbook* (1978).
These figures are calculated on a different base from Table 1.1, but are equally consistent internally.
   4. 'France [today is] almost strangled by social and economic rigidities,' wrote Gunnar Myrdal in 1956, 'if, by some miracle or exceptionally good luck. . .the French economy were to experience a real spurt of progress' (*An International Economy: Problems and Prospects*, p. 23).
   5. S. Pollard, *The British Economic Miracle* (1976).
   6. All these rates have been much reduced in the world slump beginning in 1973.

| | *GNP, Annual Rates of Growth* | |
|---|---|---|
| | *1951–73* | *1973–8* |
| Japan | 9.5 | 3.7 |
| Germany | 5.7 | 1.9 |
| Italy | 5.1 | 2.1 |
| France | 5.0 | 2.9 |
| Netherlands | 5.0 | 2.4 |
| Canada | 4.6 | 3.4 |
| Denmark | 4.2 | 1.7 |
| Norway | 4.2 | 4.5 |
| USA | 3.7 | 2.4 |
| UK | 2.7 | 0.9 |

Sources: John Cornwall, *Modern Capitalism* (1977), p. 11; OECD, *Economic Survey* (November 1979). Also Angus Maddison, 'Long Run Dynamics of Productivity Growth, *Banca Nazionale del Lavoro Quarterly Review*, no. 128 (1979), p. 4.
   7. Based on OECD, *International Survey* (1974 and 1979); Paul Bairoch, 'Europe's Gross National Product: 1800–1975', *Journal of European Economic History*, no. 5 (1976), pp. 273–340.
   8. From an unpublished report of 1975, by Denis Delay of the TUC Steel Industry Consultative Committee, reported in *The Times*, 17 January 1980. The report was endorsed by the trade union representatives. It has been stated that although 'overall productivity of the BSC is dismal. . .it is not as bad as the figures. . .make out'. Letter in *The Times*, 24 January 1980.

9. Central Policy Review Staff, *The Future of the British Car Industry* (1975), p. 80; also see *The Economist*, 20 December 1975.

10. Report in *The Times*, 6 July 1978.

11. C.F. Pratten, *Labour Productivity Differentials within International Companies* (1976).

12. Ajit Singh, 'U.K. Industry and the World Economy: a Case of Deindustrialization?', *Cambridge Journal of Economics*, no. I (1977), p. 121.

13. One study, using seven different statistical measures for inequality for 12 major economies in the period 1966–74, found the United Kingdom to be rather better than average, but not the most egalitarian: the leading egalitarian countries were Australia, Japan and Sweden, depending on the measure used. Similarly, when calculated on incomes per 'standardized' households, among 11 major countries in 1966–73, the most egalitarian economies were found to be the Netherlands, Norway and Sweden. Malcolm Sawyer, 'Income Distribution in O.E.C.D. Countries', *OECD Economic Outlook, Occasional Studies* (July 1976), Tables 6 (p. 17) and 11 (p. 19). Also see Paolo Roberti, 'Income Distribution: a Time Series and a Cross-Section Study', *Economic Journal*, no. 84 (1974), p. 638; A.B. Atkinson, 'On the Measurement of Inequality', *Journal of Economic Theory*, no. 2 (1970), pp. 244–63.

14. E.g. A. Whiting, 'An International Comparison of the Instability of Economic Growth', *Three Banks Review*, no. 109 (March 1976), pp. 26–46; T. Wilson, 'Instability and Growth: an International Comparison' in D.H. Aldcroft and P. Fearon (eds.), *Economic Growth in 20th Century Britain* (1969), pp. 184–95.

15. Richard Lecomber, 'Economic Growth and Social Welfare' in Wilfred Beckerman (ed.), *Slow Growth in Britain* (1979), p. 29.

16. For a typical example, see Roy Jenkins' Budget speech, *The Times*, 15 April 1970.

17. These arguments are well summarised in E.J. Mishan, *The Economic Growth Debate* (1977); F. Hirsch, *Social Limits to Growth* (1976); H.W. Arndt, *The Rise and Fall of Economic Growth* (1978), Chapters 7–9.

18. 'Affluence is obviously more agreeable when it is a minority condition': C.A.R. Crosland, quoted in Arndt, p. 145. Also H.F.R. Catherwood, 'Major Factors in Economic Growth in the 1970's', *Economics*, no. 8 (1970), pp. 177–8, and W. Beckerman, 'Does Slow Growth Matter?', in *idem, Slow Growth in Britain*.

19. Peter Townsend, *Poverty in the United Kingdom* (1979), p. 896; also *The Poor and the Poorest* (1965); and Frank A. Cowell, 'Income and Incentives for the Working Poor', *Three Banks Review*, no. 122 (1979), pp. 32–48.

20. Alan Maynard, *Health Care in the European Community* (1975), p. 257; OECD, *Public Expenditure on Health* (1977), p. 10.

21. *Guardian*, 1 October 1979. Or the report in *The Times*, 21 March 1980: 'An estimated 1,000 patients died in Britain last year from kidney failure because treatment was not available. . . Britain had fallen behind in providing dialysis or transplantation because of lack of resources. From being a pioneer in the 1960's, it was now behind at least 11 European countries.'

22. Cmnd. 4648 (1971), para. 47 (p. 17) and para. 88 (p. 34). This is confirmed by the longer view of the historian: 'It needs to be said — loudly and clearly — that the greatest and only significant long-run gains for the mass of the nation have come from *enlarging* the national cake rather than redistributing it.' Peter Mathias in Lord Robbins *et al.*, *Trade Unions — Public Goods or Public 'Bads'?* (1978), p. 17. Also Frank Field, 'Poverty Growth and the Redistribution of Income' in Beckerman, *Slow Growth in Britain*, p. 93.

23. G.C. Fiegehen, P.S. Lansley and A.D. Smith, *Poverty and Progress in Britain 1953–73* (1977), pp. 111–14. It is of course possible to see poverty purely in relative terms, as 'relative deprivation' of what some others possess. In that case, 'poverty would be abolished by levelling out incomes, not by increasing their totals,' and this is what Peter Townsend seems to believe and advocate. Curiously enough, in his own

study on which his conclusions are based, only 2 per cent of those asked (plus possibly a further small fraction of the 29 per cent who defined poverty in terms of special groups) saw it in those terms. *Poverty in the United Kingdom*, pp. 240, 915, 926 and *passim*.

24. Britain and Lilley, *The Delusions of Income Policy* (1977), p. 188.
25. W. Beckerman, *In Defence of Economic Growth* (1974), p. 18.
26. *Dagens Nyheter* (Stockholm), 5 January 1979.
27. James C. Davies, 'Towards a Theory of Revolution', *American Sociological Review*, vol. 27, no. 1 (1962).

# 2   FIRST CAUSES

## 1 The Immediate Cause: Shortage of Capacity

The question, then, is the following: why is Britain not more prosperous? Why does she not enjoy an income per head around double the present level, such as she should have been able to enjoy had the British economy grown at the European rate since the war?

Note that the questions about growth rate and about the present absolute level of incomes are questions about the same thing. In the absence of miraculous jumps, unknown to modern economic development, the only method of reaching a high level of income is to grow towards it by annual increments. Note also that in the main industrialised countries of broadly similar culture, high output per worker is associated with high income per head. By both these measures, Britain was far in advance in Europe in 1950 (excepting the neutrals, Sweden and Switzerland); she is now as far behind.

Why, then, does Britain not produce twice the current quantity of goods and services? Put in that form, the answer is blindingly obvious: she does not produce double the current output because she lacks the productive capacity to do so. There are simply not enough steelworks, factories, railway engines and all the other types of productive equipment of the required efficiency, and productivity, to allow British workers to turn out the kind of wealth created in other leading economies. To reach, say, the German steel capacity per head the capacity of the British steel industry would have to double, and increase even more to reach Japanese capacity. Similarly, if Britain wanted to match German car production, she would have to build a whole new set of car factories, and, again, yet more if she were to try to match Japanese output. But it is of course not simply a matter of the number of steelworks, factories or road networks; it is largely a matter of their efficiency.

Even in years of depression, of which the post-war period until recently has seen mercifully few, when some resources are idle and total capacity is greater than total demand, the better plant still wins the orders. It is no coincidence that in the slump years after 1973 foreign manufactures began to drive the British even out of their home markets to an alarming extent.

To build up major industrial complexes of this kind takes time. It may be a matter of two or three years before a plant is up and another year or more before it is running smoothly. Moreover, equipment, once installed, has to be repeatedly renewed and brought up to date by incorporating the latest technology. The raising of the productive capacity of the European countries or of Japan to their current level was therefore not a matter of a single great heave, but of continuing investment in more, and in more efficient, capital and equipment, or, to use the technical terms, in capital widening and capital deepening. Britain also increased her productive potential in this period by investment, but to a lesser extent than other comparable economies. The answer to our question might then be rephrased thus: the immediate cause of the relatively poor British economic performance is that over the recent period she has invested less in productive equipment than have the more rapidly growing economies.

It is worth noting in passing that more productive capital equipment and higher output per worker only mean a higher standard of living; they do not necessarily imply a competitive advantage in the market if other things are not equal. Apart from the cost of its additional capital itself which the technically more advanced country has to bear, it may, and usually does, pay higher wages; it may suffer from an artificially inflated exchange rate; and its manufacturers may suffer discrimination in the matter of tariffs or subsidies. Moreover, quality, delivery dates, ease of replacement of faulty goods and many other qualitative differences may enter into international comparisons. These matters will be discussed further below. Moreover, each country has good and bad plants and the most advanced in Britain may be better than some inferior ones abroad. Nevertheless, the most direct way in which British firms have become aware of their technological inferiority as against their foreign competitors is by the loss of markets to them.

It would be useful to have an exact measure of the extent by which the inferior capital equipment of the British worker reduces his output, but these things are extremely difficult to measure in practice, especially across frontiers. Nevertheless, there are cases where the product mix is so similar and the gap so large that a fair idea of the relationship emerges without claiming a high degree of accuracy. Table 2.1 relates to twelve-month periods ending on various dates in 1976. For the whole of manufacturing industry, in 1976, the same source put assets per employee at £7,000 in Britain, compared with £23,000 in Germany and £30,000 in Japan at then existing exchange

**Table 2.1:   International Comparison of Assets and Value Added per Employee, One Year (1976)**

|  | Assets per Employee (£) | Value Added per Employee (£) |
|---|---|---|
| Motor Industry: |  |  |
| British Leyland | 8,505 | 4,673 |
| 11 Japanese firms | 42,020 | 11,894 |
| Electrical Engineering: |  |  |
| GEC       (UK) | 9,725 | 5,306 |
| Siemens   (Germany) | 16,479 | 10,396 |
| Hitachi   (Japan) | 34,680 | 9,702 |

Source: F.E. Jones, 'Our Manufacturing Industry — the Missing £100,000 Million', *National Westminster Bank Quarterly Review* (May 1978), pp. 8–17.

rates. To have brought Britain up to the level of equipment enjoyed by our competitors in manufacturing alone would have required an investment of £100,000 million.[1] 'Need one say more', added one observer, 'in this year of 1977 save to crawl into a corner and weep for the future of us all?'[2]

There is an alternative way of measuring the extent to which capital investment is associated with higher output. Instead of attempting to calculate the capital *stock* at any one time, we can measure the annual rate of investment as a proportion of the total national product for the year. Whatever the accounting conventions, we are then comparing like with like, and whatever the absolute level of a country's income per head, a larger diversion of its annual income into investment would be expected to result in a faster rate of economic growth. *A priori*, however, one would not expect a stable and close correlation between the two for a number of reasons, of which only the three most important will be mentioned here.[3] The first is that a given sum invested will call forth a greatly varying increase in productivity according to which sector of the economy it benefits. Thus investment with long gestation periods, like roads or railways, will swallow vast immediate sums to be paid for out of cost savings extending over fifty or a hundred years, but yielding relatively very little in the following year or two; by contrast, investment in a consumer goods factory will yield much larger increases in efficiency at once.[4] Different economies will have very different mixes of short-term and long-term yielding investments:

Norway, for example, requires a much heavier investment rate to achieve the same rate of growth as other countries, mainly because so much of her capital is in means of transport, particularly shipping.[5] The second reason is that countries may start with capital of a different age structure,[6] requiring a different rate of replacement. The third is that the 'effects' of higher investment should only become visible in the form of higher output in later years, so that the comparisons between the two series should be made only after a lag of uncertain duration.

In countries of a similar structure, however, we should not expect the ratios to diverge too far from each other, and in fact they turn out to have been remarkably close over some key periods. This is so particularly if we avoid most of the pitfalls of our first difficulty by comparing only industry or manufacturing (see Table 2.2).

Even if we take the whole output, there is still a remarkably close correlation (Table 2.3): the coefficient of correlation among the four larger countries showed almost perfect unity, at R = 0.998.[8] The fit of the smaller countries of the EEC with the larger ones is very much poorer, but they were closely aligned among themselves as a group. The last column shows that the increment in capital required to create an increment in output rises with lower investment and growth, thus giving the fast-growing country a kind of bonus or, looked at from another angle, penalising the slow grower. This sig-

**Table 2.2:   Investment Ratios and Growth of Output in Industry in Three Western European Countries, 1953–60[7]**

| | W. Germany | Italy | UK |
|---|---|---|---|
| All Industry: | | | |
| Gross Investment, % of GNP | 16.6 | 16.3 | 14.5 |
| Net Investment, % of GNP | 14.6 | 14.7 | 8.9 |
| Annual Growth of Output, % | 8.0 | 8.9 | 3.5 |
| Annual Growth of Output per Head, % | 5.0 | 4.0 | 2.6 |
| Manufacturing Industry Only: | | | |
| Gross Investment, % of GNP | 13.3 | 13.8 | 10.7 |
| Net Investment, % of GNP | 11.0 | 11.6 | 5.9 |
| Annual Growth of Output, % | 8.5 | 9.0 | 3.8 |
| Annual Growth of Output, per head, % | 4.8 | 3.9 | 2.7 |

Source: A. Lamfalussy, *The United Kingdom and the Six* (1963), pp. 92 and 94.

**Table 2.3:   Investment Ratios and Growth of Output in Four Western European Countries, 1953–60**

|  | Gross Investment Ratio % of GNP | | Growth of Output % p.a. | Gross Marginal Capital-Output Ratio |
|---|---|---|---|---|
|  | National Prices | Adjusted Prices |  |  |
| W. Germany | 22.0 | 21.9 | 7.0 | 3.1 |
| Italy | 20.5 | 20.5 | 6.1 | 3.4 |
| France | 17.7 | 17.6 | 4.5 | 3.9 |
| UK | 15.0 | 15.0 | 2.8 | 5.4 |

Source: Lamfalussy, *The United Kingdom and the Six*, p. 72.

nificant point will be discussed further below.[9]

If we compare larger numbers of countries, disturbing factors become more numerous, and the correlations are less clear-cut. Nevertheless, in a comparison of the six largest 'Western' economies (Germany, France, Italy, Japan, UK, USA) over the years 1955–67 it was found that 'about 85 per cent of the variation in growth rates is statistically explained by the variation in investment shares'. Excluding Japan, the percentage 'explained' falls to 63 per cent.[10] Another calculation based on the 19 leading industrial countries showed that over the period 1961–72 a drop of 1 per cent in the investment rate led to a fall in the annual growth rate of between 0.13 per cent and 0.23 per cent.[11]

These comparisons of investment ratios are made throughout as a share of GNP so that the richer country will start with higher absolute base figure. However, given a high enough investment ratio, the poorer country may in fact provide more new capital per worker in absolute terms than the richer slow grower, its higher new investment casting the shadow of its ultimate overtaking before it. Thus German new capital investment in absolute terms overtook the British as early as 1951, after which the gap widened rapidly, while her actual output and income per head were still below those of Britain.[12] Since nowadays most advanced countries are both wealthier *and* devote a higher ratio of their income to investment than Britain, the gap in the provision of capital per worker has become very wide indeed. Table 2.4, listing new capital per head, shows the European and other advanced countries falling into two widely separated groups, Britain leading the poorer set. Again, there are certain difficulties about comparing price levels across frontiers, and the figures should therefore be taken as general indications rather than exact statements. Nevertheless, they make it clear that a veritable gulf has now opened up between Britain and the rest of advanced industrialised Europe. They also show how fanciful and utterly devoid of realism are the claims and hopes of British politicians, repeatedly expressed over the years, that they have at last set us on a growth path by one or other of their schemes while ignoring the key quantity of productive investment. The fact is that

> the 'impossible' has happened and a major developed economy is suffering from growing structural unemployment that is the result of too little modern industrial plant to provide work for more than a sharply falling fraction of the labour force. Only more industrial investment can arrest this process.[13]

We have reached the point at which it would seem that no advance-

**Table 2.4:  Gross Capital Formation per Head of Population, 16 Countries, 1974 – 7 ($000)**

|  | 1974 | 1976 | 1977 |
|---|---|---|---|
| Norway | 1.9 | 2.8 | 3.2 |
| Switzerland | 1.9 | 1.8 | 2.0 |
| Denmark | 1.3 | 1.6 | 2.0 |
| Sweden | 1.5 | 1.9 | 1.9 |
| Austria | 1.2 | 1.4 | 1.8 |
| Japan | 1.4 | 1.5 | 1.8 |
| W. Germany | 1.4 | 1.5 | 1.7 |
| Belgium | 1.2 | 1.4 | 1.7 |
| France | 1.3 | 1.5 | 1.6 |
| USA | 1.2 | 1.3 | 1.5 |
| UK | 0.68 | 0.75 | 0.79 |
| Ireland | 0.53 | 0.61 | 0.72 |
| Italy | 0.63 | 0.61 | 0.69 |
| Spain | 0.61 | 0.67 | 0.65 |
| Greece | 0.46 | 0.52 | 0.64 |
| Portugal | 0.26 | 0.39 | 0.30 |

Source: Angus Maddison, 'Long Run Dynamics of Productivity Growth', *Banca Nazionale del Lavoro Quarterly Review*, no. 128 (1979), p. 19.

ment, no forward policy is conceivable unless it rests on the prior build-up of capital equipment.

## 2  Why are there No Plans for Increasing Investment?

In one sense, there has never been any doubt about the key role played by investment in productivity and economic growth. Take a wide enough gap, say between the USA and Britain, or between Britain and India, and it is clear that differences in *per capita* income depend to a decisive degree on the capital equipment provided for the work-force of each country. Such comparisons incidentally draw attention to the fact that such matters as education, company structure or a reliable civil service are also in part a product of investment, the expenditure over one period in order to increase output in the next, though differences in these respects will be small within Western Europe.

Those who have been concerned with concrete plans for economic growth have also taken it for granted that substantially higher output would mean installing more capital. Thus the *National Plan* of 1965, the most consistent official effort made in the past thirty years to get output and incomes to grow in Britain, assumed that to raise GNP by 25 per cent over the years 1964–70 would require additional investment of the order shown in Table 2.5.

These figures may have been questionable in detail, but the principle that there could be no substantial improvement in British production without a preceding appropriate increase in capital formation has never been challenged.

But if that is so, why do we hear so little about it? Why are our economic commentators and forecasters, why are Chancellors of the Exchequer and spokesmen of the Opposition, who have so much to say about the economy, so rarely heard discussing, let alone planning for, increases in investment? How can they hope to make bricks without straw?

A large part of Chapters 4, 6 and 7 will be devoted to answering this question. But some preliminary remarks are in order here and they may help to set the scene for what follows.

The first point to note is that public interest in production and productivity, and with them in investment, has not been constant but has moved through a number of phases. In the immediate post-war years, when the wartime experience that output was the end of the economic machine was still recent, investment and production did receive some attention. There followed the years to the mid-1960s when production, as a problem, receded from the public mind; output was rising, we 'never had it so good', the catching-up process by the rest of Europe was ignored and the lead by the USA was taken for granted. Since then the public has once more become more conscious of Britain's lagging output and of the need for more productive investment. A Chancellor of the Exchequer, though admittedly speaking to the output-conscious National Economic Development Council (NEDC) was even heard to express the view that 'a major lesson of recent years has been the ineffectiveness of overall economic policies that have failed to pay sufficient regard to the problem of supply.'[14] Investment did indeed expand in the mid-1960s and has declined only recently as part of the calamities of the mid-seventies.

The second point is that the neglect of investment had at least two separate causes. One was that politicians, civil servants and even financial journalists are mainly preoccupied with day-to-day matters and crises, and therefore hardly ever get round to more long-term issues such as capital formation. The other is the more paradoxical one, applying particularly to academic economists, that they neglected the obvious precisely because it *was* so obvious. They tended to focus on the next link in the chain of causation, — the surrounding circumstances under which investment might be low, and what sophisticated policies might be pursued to put productive firms in a position where they would raise it. It seemed a reasonable thing for a well established profession to do, yet there is always a danger in taking any link in the chain of reasoning for granted: it might be precisely that link on which actual policies ought to have operated. It is.

**Table 2.5: Additional Investment Required to Raise GNP by 25 per cent, 1964–70**

| | |
|---|---|
| Manufacture and Construction | + 55% |
| Other Private Industry and Services | + 25% |
| Nationalised Industries | + 30% |
| Housing | + 32% |
| Roads (Major Works) | + 74% |
| Other Public Services | + 50% |

Source: *The National Plan*, Cmnd. 2764 (1965), Table 1.1, p. 15.

possible to be too theoretical when faced with giving concrete advice on concrete issues.

Before pursuing these matters further, it will be necessary to proceed more cautiously to the next step in our search for causes. This will be a narration of the chain of events, because somewhere among them must be hidden the causal connections.

## Notes

1. F.E. Jones, 'Our Manufacturing Industry — the Missing £100,000 million', *National Westminster Bank Quarterly Review* (May 1978), pp. 8–17.
2. Montague Calman, letter in *The Times*, 22 April 1977.
3. See further discussion in Chapter 6, section 2, below.
4. T.F. Cripps and R.J. Tarling, *Growth in Advanced Capitalist Economies 1950–1970* (1973), pp. 45–56; J. Carrington and G. Edwards, *Financing Industrial Investment* (1978), p. 82.
5. Colin Clark, *Growthmanship: a Study in the Mythology of Investment* (1964), p. 143.
6. N. Kaldor and J.A. Mirrlees, 'A New Model of Economic Growth', *Review of Economic Studies*, no. 29 (1962), p. 188.
7. For railway investment, figures for 1980 are now available. Here is a comparison of Britain with three countries of similar size, and Belgium and Holland of very much smaller size (in £m):

| West Germany | 918 |
|---|---|
| France | 827 |
| Italy | 774 |
| Britain | 411 |
| Belgium | 346 |
| Netherlands | 191 |

*The Times*, 26 March 1981.
8. A. Lamfalussy, *The United Kingdom and the Six* (1963), pp. 65, 69 and 73.
9. Chapter 6, section 2, below.
10. OECD, *The Growth of Output 1960–1980* (1970), p. 46; also T.P. Hill, 'Growth and Investment According to International Comparisons', *Economic Journal*, no. 74 (1964), pp. 287–304.
11. David Smith, 'Public Consumption and Economic Performance', *National Westminster Bank Review* (November 1975), p. 28.
12. OECD, Economic Surveys. No complete set of data is available. Also see D.K. Stout, 'Capacity Adjustment in a Slowly Growing Economy' in Wilfred Beckerman (ed.), *Slow Growth in Britain* (1979), p. 107; C.J.F. Brown and T.D. Sheriff, 'De-industrialisation: a Background Paper' in F. Blackaby (ed.), *De-industrialisation* (1979), p. 248.
13. Robert Bacon and Walter Eltis, *Britain's Economic Problem: Too Few Producers* (2nd edn, 1978), p. 24. The authors go on: 'but the very process itself squeezes industrial profits and investment so that the economy moves into ever deeper trouble'.
14. Report in *The Times*, 6 December 1979.

# 3 CAUSES BEHIND CAUSES: WHY HAS INVESTMENT BEEN LOW?

## 1 The Stop-Go Period: 1947–c.1973

There was no basic disagreement on economic policy in the immediate post-war years. The need to re-integrate millions of men and women from the armed forces and the war industries into peaceful production, to re-equip industry after years of neglect and run-down, and to do all this smoothly, with as little unemployment and as little disturbance of the foreign balance of payments and the value of the pound sterling as possible, was clear for everyone to see. Tasks relating to real assets on the ground and real output had to take precedence.

Beyond these fundamentals there was, as ever, much controversy on such questions as large-scale socialisation of industry, economic 'planning', redistribution of incomes, and the erection of a 'Welfare State'. This study is concerned with total performance only and does not concern itself with internal distribution, unless it affects the size of the aggregate. We may therefore content ourselves with noting here that nationalisation was considerable, but not very different from that of most other Western countries; that wartime control, perhaps the most powerful apparatus for planning policies inherited by any incoming socialist government, was largely dismantled; and that Keynesian rather than Marxist or other socialist principles came to be firmly entrenched in the Treasury.[1] A general determination to avoid mass unemployment distinguished above all the system within which policy makers operated from that of earlier periods in British history.

As always when the British economy has been given a real economic task, a task to produce and create, such as in the war years and now in the period of post-war reconstruction, it performed magnificently. The target set was a rise in exports of 75 per cent over pre-war to cover the losses of earnings from overseas investments, the adverse prices (terms of trade), and the decline in invisible earnings like shipping freights. To the surprise of many, the economy suc-

31

ceeded in reaching that formidable target with ease and ahead of schedule. At the same time, the rise in total output appeared satisfactory. Production could, of course, be expected to increase quickly by the conversion of existing capacity, but output continued to rise at the unprecedented rate of 4 per cent a year in 1948, 1949 and 1950. Gross domestic fixed investment, fluctuating around 12 per cent of GNP in the pre-war years, stood at 15 per cent. It was noteworthy, however, and ominous for the future, that world industrial production rose by no less than 13 per cent a year during 1948–50, or three times the British rate, largely because of the re-emergence of such old rivals as Germany; domestic capital formation in most other countries ran at well over 20 per cent. There were also problems of readjustment. During the war Britain had been geared to receiving American lend-lease deliveries of vital materials which she did not have to pay for, and their sudden end threw a strain on the foreign currency and gold reserves. What was needed was a temporary loan to cover imports until reconversion was completed, after which Britain might maintain a steady expansion on the basis of a balanced foreign trade and ultimately be in a position to repay the loan.

Such a loan was negotiated in 1946: 3.75 billion dollars from the USA and 1.25 billion dollars from Canada, a total of 5 billion dollars. It was intended to last for a transitional period of three years. However, among the 'strings' attached to it was the dangerous obligation to make sterling convertible within a year, i.e. by July 1947. At that time most countries were still desperately looking for dollars to buy goods in America, almost the only market where they were available. As soon as dollars were to be had for the asking in London on payment of sterling, a rush to London set in to convert sterling holdings into the more desirable dollars, and within a month British reserves were nearing exhaustion and convertibility had to be suspended. In the course of 1947, the gold and dollar reserves had fallen by 600 million dollars, or by one quarter. These drains from a reserve which was in any case diminutive compared with the tasks it had to perform weakened Britain's power to resist outside pressures for many years to come.

Both the collapse of convertibility and the damage this did to Britain had been easily foreseeable, and for that reason Britain had accepted the 'strings' only under bitter protest and because of dire necessity. In retrospect it is hard to resist the conclusion that at least one reason for the American insistence on them had been the belief that Britain was the only potential economic rival in Europe (strange though this may seem today) and that it would not be acceptable to the American taxpayer to finance too generously a competitor out of his tax funds. There was, in other words, some disadvantage for Britain in emerging stronger from the war than other belligerents, and she was penalised in a way that made her more vulnerable later.

There was another important disadvantage that derived from emerging relatively unscathed from the war which was to be of equally fatal long-term significance. Among most other countries the devastation of the war years had removed the landmarks, and it was quite impossible for workers and other income earners to aim at a particular real income; moreover, it was generally understood that a vast reconstruction effort was necessary for survival. The investment rate could therefore be set very high and personal consumption very low, and as long as consumption could be increased year by year, even if from a low absolute base, economic management looked successful while keeping up the investment rate. In Britain, by contrast, real incomes had suffered much less; as victors, income earners expected the spoils in terms of high and rising standards of living. The pressures characterised as 'inflationary' in the early years were in reality pressures to keep up personal incomes, and successive governments were easily tempted to give in and squeeze investment and exports instead. The squeeze on exports took rapid revenge by balance of payments crises which had to be rectified one way or another, but there was no one to defend investment programmes. To cut investment was the easy touch, and thus were taken the first steps on the slippery downward slope. The remaining countries which shared with Britain a set of determinate income levels from which the population expected to rise in the years of peace, including the USA, Canada, Sweden and Switzerland, actually did have sufficient spare capacity to meet their citizens' expectations without having to trench on the vital allocations to capital formation to keep that growth going. Once more, Britain was in a uniquely vulnerable position.

In the convertibility crisis of 1947 the government was still sufficiently under the influence of wartime economic logic to insist that the main economic aim must be to 'devote all our energies to production and more production', and in seeking the inevitable cut-backs, to protect its investment programmes and to cut consumption instead. The trade unions accepted Sir Stafford Cripps' plea for voluntary wage restraint during 1948–50. Even *The Economist* was still inclined to give investment and efficiency pride of place. The Conservatives, to be sure, possibly because so much of the planned investment was to be in the basic industries which were to be (or were already) nationalised, were more concerned to bring the Budget and the foreign balance into equilibrium as the primary objective. R.F. (later Sir Roy) Harrod was of the opinion in December 1947 that 'in the particular case of Britain today, of course, it is in the great capital installation programmes that retrenchments should be made.'[2]

As Marshall Aid began to flow into Europe, there was an improvement in 1948, though the Chancellor still managed to justify a highly restrictive Budget on the grounds of having to bring down inflation. But in the summer of 1949 pressure began to build up against the pound sterling. There were two immediate causes: a weakening in the trade balance of the outer Sterling Area, and a speculative attack in the anticipation of devaluation. There was also a heavy flight of capital abroad which wiped out as much as 40 per cent, by some calculations, of the benefit of the dollar loan acquired at such heavy cost. After all else was tried, including dollar import cuts and an attempt to get another dollar loan, the pound was devalued, from $4.03 to $2.80, in September 1949. By now the balance of payments and the reserves in the Central Bank had become the primary object of policy, and long-term plans about strengthening the productive potential of the economy had to take a back seat. Indeed, in the package of restrictive measures which followed the devaluation, a cut in investment, together with cuts in government spending, took pride of place, and a total of £140 million was to be shorn from the planned investment target, particularly affecting the fuel and power industries, education and housing. 'So far as possible, the necessary cuts will be made at the expense of longer-term projects,' the Prime Minister promised. Government consumption was to be cut by £100 million only, and many of the items cut were in fact capital items.[3]

One further specific point of vulnerability for Britain, not shared by other countries, should be noted here: this was the so-called Sterling Area, consisting mostly of colonies and former colonies. Since its reserve was held in the City the Sterling Area could be a tower of strength to London, but in times of stress it could also be a source of weakness, exaggerating the amplitude of fluctuation to which London was subject. To this must be added the fact that sterling was still a world currency used by many of the oil producers among others, and in order not to let them down or disappoint those who used the City of London as their banking centre, devaluation was ruled out repeatedly and much more harmful measures to the economy preferred instead. The City has, to be sure, throughout this period, contributed large sums in net 'invisible earnings' in the form of dividends, commissions and premiums paid by foreign customers which have helped the British balance of payments; but the periodic restrictive measures made necessary in order to safeguard these earnings have done damage to the economy many times the value of these earnings. It will also be apparent from our argument below that a strengthening of the productive base of Britain instead would have ultimately benefited the City far more even at the expense of a temporary disarray of its international links.

The devaluation was intended to help the faltering balance of payments in two complementary ways: it would discourage imports, by making them more expensive, and encourage exports, by making them cheaper in the eyes of foreigners. However, there were very few luxury imports to be cut, and food and necessary raw materials had to continue to come in. As for exports, the underlying assumption that there was spare capacity, so that an additional quantity could be sold to make up more than the loss of foreign earnings caused by the fall in the value of the pound sterling, was false: the shortage lay precisely in productive capacity, the inability to make rather than the inability to sell. The main reason why the dollar was in such high demand was not that British prices were too high — on the contrary, after devaluation they were much lower than American prices — but that the Americans had goods to sell, while the British had not. Given that there was a ceiling on output in Britian, it would have seemed more logical, if the balance of payments were to be improved, to get the highest prices possible for the limited number of British goods for sale, and thus to up-value[4] the pound rather than to devalue it. Such a course was urged, among others, by Ralph Hawtrey as well as by R.F. Harrod, who commented that the devaluation had led to a 'colossal and unnatural rise in the volume of exports. . .[and] a very heavy strain on the manufacturing capacity of Britain'.[5]

A view of this kind implies an economic understanding which puts production and productive capacity at the centre of the picture. Such understanding was not to be found among British policy makers who looked at the world with traders' and bankers' eyes, and an up-valuation was never seriously considered, either then or later. However, it was understood that the rising costs of imports from the dollar area and all those which had not followed the British devaluation would create a strong upward pressure on home prices that would, unless contained by the strongest measures, sooner or later wipe out the competitive advantages of devaluation while leaving Britain with a self-sustained inflationary cycle. It was for that reason that the devaluation of 1949, far from leading to a breathing space to allow British industry to re-equip itself, as it had done in 1931, was accompanied, to a chorus of approval, by further tough restrictions.

Helped by a strong boom in the USA and the European Continent, as well as a return of the fugitive speculative sums which had toppled the pound in 1949, the measures taken produced a positive balance of payments in 1950. The newly formed European Payments Union further eased the problems of international payments. Official policy was, however, by no means symmetrical. While strongly reducing planned investment activity when the flow was adverse, it did not encourage it when the flow was positive. The Budget of 1950 was still, on balance, 'disinflationary',[6] though *The Economist*, mouthpiece for much of the Economics Establishment,[7] was not satisfied and would have liked even more cuts: 'Most of the so-called Keynesian policies turn out, on examination, to be expedients for keeping an inflation going.'

Whatever hope there might have been of setting the British economy on a more stable course was dashed by the outbreak of the Korean War in June 1950. Costly for all the belligerents, this war turned out to be particularly damaging for the British economy, for at least three reasons. First, it raised the prices of key raw materials far more than the prices of manufactures, so that the British terms of trade turned sharply adverse (though by the same token, some members of the Sterling Area gained substantially). While British export prices rose only by 26 per cent between December 1949 and June 1951, import prices rose by 59 per cent and raw material prices alone by 115 per cent. The balance of payments suffered a swing of £700 million from a surplus of £300 million in 1950 to a deficit of £400 million in 1951.

Second, the large increase in armaments production ordered by the British government hit above all the industries such as engineering that were at the centre both of the export drive and the effort to invest in the expansion of the British economy. Because of the bottlenecks there, particularly as regards skilled labour and machine tools, rearmament took place directly at the expense of exports in the short run, and of technological improvement by new investment in the long run, the two most sensitive and vulnerable aspects of the British economy in comparison with others.

To this has to be added, third, that 'British policy was such that the rearmament burden assumed by the Government was relatively greater than that of any other country in the world.'[8] In consequence, it was precisely in those years that other countries, above all Germany and Japan, could begin to build up a technological lead and start on their process of wresting one export market after another from Britain. While we built tanks and planes, they built the machinery with which to achieve their later successes.

It may be asked why it was necessary for Britain to make sacrifices so much greater than anyone else, including the USA, in what was after all essentially an American war in an American sphere of influence. The question is political, rather than economic, but it is pertinent to note that we have touched here on another liability of Britain, not shared by most other advanced countries: an imperial tradition coupled with a victorious war, to tempt successive governments into politico-military adventures beyond the capacity of the economy.

On this occasion the Chancellor, Hugh Gaitskell, had the grace to affirm that it would have been better to cut consumption in order to pay for the Korean War, but 'with the best will in the world'[9] it could not be done, since the resources required for rearmament were competing directly with those needed for investment goods. While we may deplore that that 'best will' to cut consumption, rather than investment, had not been available in 1947 and 1949, when it might have done some good, it was at least to the credit of the Chancellor, as of others in the debate of 1951, that they examined actual concrete productive facilities on the ground. Henceforth public debate was increasingly to take place in terms of wholly nebulous, if largely Keynesian, concepts such as 'incomes', 'employment' or 'exports' which encouraged forgetfulness as to what these actually implied in the real world. In 1951, at any rate, since deflation would not have benefited the war effort and while exports were meeting resistance for the first time, the easy sellers' market having come to an end, the main burden had to fall on investment. What was particularly damaging in the Budget of 1951 in that respect was the total suspension of 'initial allowances' on new plant, machinery and buildings (one of the most potent encouragements to investment in other countries), with an estimated saving, in a full year, of £170 million. *The Times* deplored the 'starvation of industry',[10] but on the whole, the Budget was well received, criticism turning not on the cutting back of investment, but on the inadequate efforts to contain wage inflation.

The crisis of 1951 was the last one to be handled by a Labour gov-

ernment for some time. The Conservatives won the election of that
year and stayed in office until 1964. We have treated the three crises
of 1947, 1949 and 1951 in some detail, in order to introduce the main
ingredients that went to make up subsequent crises, namely the
balance of payments, the international value of the pound and, to a
lesser extent at that time, internal inflation. We have also outlined
the elements of the particular vulnerability of Britain, including the
burden of the Sterling Area and sterling as a reserve currency, the
quest for a political and military role beyond our means and income
expectations beyond the capacity of the economy except by trench-
ing on investments. They were to form the background against
which the next series of economic crises was to be played out.

There will be no need to treat those crises at similar length, since
their main outlines did not change in essence. All one can say is that
the apparatus for imposing restraints was enormously increased as
the series of crises unfolded. Financial methods were added to fiscal
methods in the very first weeks of 1952, and among the expedients
used were new taxes, curbs on banking and credit, cuts in public
expenditure, protectionist measures and physical controls of various
kinds. All of them were practised in different combinations in
Britain in the long years to 1973, while Europe and the rest of the
advanced world enjoyed an unprecedented secular boom marked
only by the mildest of temporary recessions.

It is time to return to our narrative. From 1952 on the British
balance of payments was aided by the restriction of economic
growth at home, a sharp reversal of world prices, leading to significant falls in import prices and improvements in Britain's terms of
trade, and the eventual end to the fighting in Korea. Since, for once,
there was no crisis in the odd year of 1953, the cycle ran on for four
years until the crisis of 1955. Recovery was slow at first, and there
were no significant Budget or other relaxations until 1953.[11] In that
year initial allowances on investment were restored and taxes cut:
but it was consumption rather than investment which showed significant increases. Even in 1954 no boost was given to the economy, the
Budget being dubbed a 'neutral' or no-change one, the ostensible
reason for this being an expected recession in the United States. The
change to 'investment' rather than 'initial' allowances gave more
tangible benefits to creators of capital.[12] However, by now the
economy was growing fast, and since there had been no capacity
increase to provide the supply for that growth, there were obvious
bottlenecks at home and a sharply rising import bill. Nevertheless,

the Budget of 1955 was expansionary, offering significant tax cuts to fuel the pressure in the economy — a perversity of policy which might not have been entirely unconnected with the impending elections.

The Conservatives duly returned to power, and by the summer a classic crisis had emerged: the balance of payments was out of control and there was a run on the pound. There was an immediate credit squeeze and in an autumn Budget, the last of Mr (later Lord) Butler, taxes were raised, credit was restricted further and, by now almost routine, investment was cut back in nationalised industries and elsewhere.[13] 'The Conservative Chancellor, just like the earlier Labour Chancellors, sacrificed economic growth for the sake of external balance.'[14]

The result was a recession and a virtual ending of growth for three years. In February 1956 the Bank Rate went up to 5½ per cent, there were further squeezes and discouragement of investment. The Budget of 1956 was 'neutral' again and gave no aid, Mr Macmillan, in his Budget speech, stressing that there had been too great a strain on the overstretched investment industries in the preceding year: 'We have had too much too soon.' His remedy was not, however, to enlarge them in order to make trouble-free growth possible in the future, but to go for more savings, for beating inflation, and for greater power for Britain in the Cold War. It was a good thing that businesses were investing less, he told bankers in October, as this helped exports and the balance of payments.[15]

Whatever the chances of recovery later in the year they were dashed by the Suez Canal adventure of October-November. The pound survived the strain only by a loan of £200 million from the International Monetary Fund, and a further stand-by credit of £440 million. In spite of this aid and an only moderately expansionary Budget, together with a fairly sound external balance, a severe speculative run on the pound developed in the autumn of 1957, leading to yet another crisis of classic proportions. Bank Rate was raised to 7 per cent, in those happy days considered a panic rate, and, to no one's surprise, capital investment was again singled out as the particular target of cuts: limitations on bank advances were to reduce private investment, while in the public sector there was to be a ceiling on capital spending. In the interest of curbing inflation, Mr (later Lord) Thorneycroft assured the public, he would 'not hesitate to adjust even the most essential investment programme'.[16]

The 'Suez crisis' might appear as an exogenous factor in this story, a disturbance affecting the system from outside, and it has often been treated as such in the economic literature. But in fact it was symbolic rather than fortuitous. Symbolic, first, of the utter ignorance of politicians and generals of the link between economic power and such military or political muscle as they might dispose of to strut upon the world stage, as well as of their unawareness of how far Britain had sunk in that respect. But it was symbolic also of the constant drain in that period of vital and costly foreign exchange to sustain colonial and military adventures. Year by year, British armies were maintained abroad, in idleness or actually fighting hot wars for the purpose of postponing the independence of such countries as Kenya, Cyprus or South Yemen by one or two years. The costs were to be counted not only in the hundreds of millions of pounds actually spent, but at times in a multiple of these sums in lost output to rectify the original payments gap.[17]

The Budget of 1959 was still cautious, but later in the year credit restrictions and public expenditure limits were gradually relaxed. Sterling, with other currencies, was made convertible. The resultant upswing was further boosted by the Budget of 1959 which, coming as it did before another election, was expansionary and offered, not entirely surprisingly, large tax concessions. The 'stimulus' to the economy, once more, was directed at allowing people to spend more, not at creating greater capacity, though public investment was planned to rise by 11 per cent. A classic case of what came to be called 'overheating' of the economy[18] ensued: rising output, bottlenecks, a sharp increase in imports but not in exports, and a balance of payments shortfall. Bank Rate was raised from 4 per cent to 5 per cent in January, but the Budget in April was still neutral. Crisis measures came only in June: Bank Rate was put up to 6 per cent and there was a credit squeeze including hire-purchase restrictions and the 'special deposit', designed to limit bank lending. The end of another cycle had been reached.

There had been a certain unity about the 1950s. In terms of absolute standards and competitive ability, Britain was still very much a member of the European community of nations. Her power was still one to be reckoned with, the pound sterling was still widely used, her growth faster than ever before in her history and she was not yet inevitably doomed to a different course from that of the rest of Europe. Britain had even resumed her traditional role of exporting capital (Table 3.1) and she was still incurring military expenditure with careless abandon.

**Table 3.1: Balance of Payments, Selected Countries, 1950–60**

| (Annual Average, $m) | | Current Balance (inc. invisibles) | Grants and Donations | Private Capital |
|---|---|---|---|---|
| United Kingdom | 1950–4 | + 256 | + 176 | – 445 |
| | 1955–9 | + 622 | – 168 | – 560 |
| | 1959–60 | – 53 | – 224 | – 554 |
| France | 1950–4 | – 387 | + 429 | + 67 |
| | 1955–9 | – 270 | + 152 | + 215 |
| | 1959–60 | + 628 | + 42 | + 202 |
| Germany | 1950–4 | + 415 | + 185 | – 22 |
| | 1955–9 | + 1,475 | – 374 | – 76 |
| | 1959–60 | + 1,770 | – 632 | – 201 |
| Italy | 1950–4 | – 300 | + 233 | + 72 |
| | 1955–9 | + 44 | + 196 | + 215 |
| | 1959–60 | + 341 | + 211 | + 269 |

Source: A. Lamfalussy, *The United Kingdom and the Six* (1963), p. 36.

As far as growth was concerned, however, a wide gap had opened up. British industrial production (1953 = 100) had risen from 98 in 1951 to 129 in 1960, a rise of 31 per cent; that of Continental Western Europe, on the same basis, from 92 to 171 or by 86 per cent. Mr Butler's oft-quoted expression of hope that the country might double its standard of living in 25 years[19] became a mockery in British ears because it was so far beyond what could be attained; on the Continent it would have been an absurd target: they all managed it in well under twenty years.

At the beginning of the decade after the urgency of the reconstruction drive of the 1940s had worn off, there had seemed to be little concern with growth: the Continentals, building up their shattered economies from very near scratch, seemed to be a part of a different world altogether. Few were prepared to contradict Professor (later Lord) Robbins when he declared, in an influential lecture, that the balance of payments and the value of money should be the supreme test of economic policy: 'Stop the inflation, stop it at all costs: that is the paramount need of the moment in the economic sphere' was his cry in 1951.[20] Similarly, a debate held in Oxford in 1952 which involved a large number of the leading economists of the day spent much of its time discussing whether the recently introduced use of monetary policy would prove to be an effective curb on investment;

what seemed to excite little controversy was the initial assumption that investment should be curbed.[21]

> We can. . .safely contemplate, without any lasting injury to the body economic, a large reduction in the volume of 'widening' investment [was the view of R.F. Harrod]. This reduction will . . .save us from the danger, common to boom periods, of building up what later proves to be excessive manufacturing capacity. It may happen that in the process of reducing the pace of widening, we must lose some deepening. . . If this is much the easiest method — perhaps the only method — of restoring solvency quickly, the net effect on progress over, say, the next five years is likely to be positive.[22]

Gradually, as the cost of the lost opportunities as a result of slow growth began to dawn, there was some inclination to re-admit greater output as a desirable aim of some priority. Another Oxford symposium of February 1955 discussed 'Growth and the Balance of Payments' and their respective compatibility. Despite Thorneycroft's relapse in 1957, when the Treasury seems to have been badly rattled by the speculators and the pound took absolute precedence over all else,[23] there were signs by the end of the decade that even the official policy makers were gradually beginning to incorporate real growth among their more urgent priorities:

> The conclusion I reach [stated the Chancellor, Mr Amory, in his Budget speech of 1958] is that it is impossible to exaggerate the importance of our maintaining and, indeed, improving, our competitive position through efficient investment and lower costs. This is, to my mind, the key to success in the future.[24]

Widespread public disquiet over the poor productive showing was expressed not only by the parliamentary Opposition, as might be expected, or in the leader columns of *The Times*,[25] still staunchly expansionist, but also among economists, whose attitudes had undergone a marked change. In their evidence to the Radcliffe Committee on the Working of the Monetary System (1959) several economists made it clear that they still held to their Keynesian tenet that moderate inflation was an acceptable price to pay for full employment and higher incomes; some went even further and hinted that a high rate of investment would promote growth and the other benefits that had been obtained by our neighbours across the Channel and that it would therefore be worth the sacrifice of other valuable objectives; Thomas (now Lord) Balogh came nearest to the views expressed in this book.[26]

It was in part to meet these widespread criticisms of restrictionism and its attendant damage to the economy that the crisis measures of 1960 were somewhat eased by the incoming Chancellor, Selwyn Lloyd. Bank Rate was reduced in October and December, HP restrictions eased in January 1961. There are indications that the government was willing to take greater risks for the sake of expansion, but that the Treasury, aided as always by the Bank of England, insisted on caution. Thus there were renewed crisis measures even though the balance of payments improved. In the unofficial Budget of July, the Bank Rate went up to 7 per cent, and there was the by now familiar bundle of restrictions on public expenditure, and bank lending. There was also a 'pay pause', the first of a new series of measures for restraining inflation and easing pressures on the balance of payments, by 'incomes policies', i.e. holding wages down below what trade unions could have got in the free market. There also had to be another IMF credit, this time of £714 million. Even in the first half of 1962, when it was clear that Britain was rapidly sliding into a depression, the Treasury was still in favour of restrictions.

At this point there was a widespread revulsion against the obvious futilities of 'stop-go', associated rather unfairly at that time with Mr Selwyn Lloyd. Two alternative approaches emerged. One was the emphasis on 'planning' for growth supported, rather surprisingly, by a remarkable resolution in a Conference of the Federation of British Industries, held in November 1960. It led to a search for better technology and the removal of bottlenecks and other hindrances to expansion, for which the National Economic Development Council (NEDDY) of 1961, and its later specialist groups, were set up. This was extended, under the Labour government of 1964–70, into the formation of a comprehensive 'Plan'[27] of maintaining a 4 per cent growth rate over five years to be supervised by the new Department of Economic Affairs. In practice, neither agency was given any executive power, and the planned targets had no binding force, not even for the nationalised industries. The Treasury, claiming that it was most urgent to impose immediate restrictions, had no difficulty in strangling the DEA at birth.

The other approach, associated particularly with the ebullient Mr Reginald Maudling as the new Chancellor, was to 'drive through' or 'ride out' the immediate adverse balance that was sure to emerge as soon as expansion hit the British supply ceiling and imports came rushing in to fill the gap, until such time as the demand should have called forth the home investment to keep the higher growth going on a self-sustaining course. Astonishing though it may seem, after all the preceding experience, the idea was still that prosperity could be created by giving people money to spend, rather than by making sure there were goods available first on which they could spend their money, but such was the case in the 'profligate years', as termed by their critics, of 1962–4. 'The Maudling boom' noted one observer, 'seems in retrospect rather like a First World War plan for an attack — an assumption that willingness to incur heavy losses was sufficient to ensure success.'[28] There was an expansionary Budget in 1963, and in 1964 even more so — by coincidence, once more an election year. There followed another IMF 'stand-by credit', a massive balance of payments deficit, at £700 million the largest so far, and in October a Labour victory at the polls.

The new government inherited a rampant crisis and almost at once took the expected steps, as well as some new ones, to deal with it. Among the latter was a tariff, thinly disguised as an import surcharge, together with export rebates. Among the former, there were tax increases in Mr Callaghan's first Budget in November, and further substantial foreign credits. In the following April Budget there were yet more tax increases, as well as stricter exchange controls, and there were further credit restrictions accompanied by cuts in government investment in July after Bank Rate had been reduced by 1 per cent. It would be tedious to enumerate the further sorry tale of restrictions, cuts, foreign borrowings and similar expedients of the following two years, in which incomes policies of ever new coloration also played a part. Suffice it to say that it was gradually coming to be realised that the end of an era, the end of 'stop-go' was approaching, since there would in future be ever fewer, if any, 'go' phases: Britain was sliding into near permanent crisis and was being pushed away ever further from any underlying state of balance.

The government, and particularly the Prime Minister, Harold Wilson, were severely criticised later for maintaining these restrictions, so harmful to British output and welfare, in a vain effort to stave off the devaluation of the pound, long after it had become clear that it had become inevitable. A total foreign payments deficit of £1,500 million was thus accumulated, and had to be worked off later at enormous cost. As a result, the cost of devaluation itself was greater than it need have been and it came at the worst possible time.[29] To be sure, the clinging to a particular dollar exchange rate was irrational, as irrational as a great deal else in British economic policy. But it is equally certain that devaluation, when it came, was merely a means of registering the fact that Britain's productivity had fallen far behind that of others while money incomes had risen at about the same rate. Moreover, once it was completed, devaluation would make no fundamental change whatever, since nothing would have been done to arrest the process of relative decline which had made it necessary in the first place. It was merely a typical expression of the wishful thinking of the Economics Establishment to believe that this 'devaluation seems to have rectified the fundamental balance-of-payments disequilibrium'.[30]

This was soon put to the test, since in November 1967 the pound sterling was devalued after all, by 14.3 per cent down to $2.40 to the pound. At the same time Bank Rate was raised to the unprecedented level of 8 per cent, and there were further credit restrictions and foreign stand-by credits on the programme. Crisis measures went on into 1968: public expenditure curbs in January, unprecedented tax increases in the Budget, as well as income curbs and credit squeezes, and further humiliating negotiations with foreign lenders.

The policies were, in principle, exactly those criticised by Harold Wilson when in Opposition: solving the foreign balance problem by cutting production and employment at home, and restraining wage rises by unemployment,[31] though it has to be admitted that there were ever new variants in detail, and ever new twists in language, to describe essentially the same policy — perhaps these semantic innovations were a result of the new, and enlarged, team of economists who were now helping the government.

The most savage deflationary Budget was actually that of 1969, making a combined fiscal as well as monetary policy of unexampled ferocity — nearly eighteen months after devaluation.[32] In consequence, unemployment rose significantly while output stagnated. The danger signs were there, in early 1970: moreover, an election was looming. The Budget of 1970 was therefore one of relief. Taxes were reduced, Bank Rate cut, in two steps, to 7 per cent and even the travel allowance was increased.

These measures availed the government little, for it lost the election, but the Conservatives inherited an economy which had been, in current parlance, 'strengthened': i.e. by producing less, cutting back on investment and on technical improvement schemes (making

British industry much less competitive in real terms), something like a temporary balance in the foreign payments account had been achieved.[33] Output had virtually stagnated during 1968–70, investment had risen very little from its very low level of 1964–7, and price inflation had slightly subsided, to around 5 per cent a year from its earlier levels of above 6 per cent. The pound was by then under-valued in world price terms.[34] But the potential for an enormous wage explosion had been accumulated in the pipeline, following years of restriction and restraint, and wage costs were beginning to push up prices even in the last months of Labour rule in a manner which has become all too familiar in the years since. Under the Heath government of 1970–4, in fact, containing inflation, particularly of wages, was gradually taking over from the foreign balance of payments and the external value of the pound as the main preoccupation of economic policy makers, and the main pretext for restrictive policies.

At first, though, having inherited a healthy foreign balance from the hard slog of the previous years, Mr Barber, the new Chancellor, set the signals to 'go'. Once more, and, it must be recorded here, once more to the surprise of the experts who ran British economic affairs at the time, the encouragement of a spending spree led to a spending spree. Consumption bounded upwards in 1970–2, and, since there had been no antecedent expansion of the British productive apparatus, this led to a massive increase in imports. Potential exports were also sucked into the home market which became an easy touch, and productive capital formation actually fell: such funds as were actually diverted to investment were sunk either in real estate or stock exchange speculation in London, which assumed the proportions of a national scandal, or they were invested abroad. Between 1970 and 1973 net investment in industry fell from 6.2 per cent to 3.6 per cent of industrial production (having fallen from 8.4 per cent in 1967), exports less imports from 11.5 per cent to 6.1 per cent, while net investment outside industry (including also productive investment by the public authorities) rose from 19.4 per cent to 24.8 per cent.[35] It appeared that very few of those who would normally be expected to chance their arm at productive long-term investment at home trusted the new expansionary phase.

It turned out to be a self-fulfilling prophecy. By mid-1972 the turn-round in the balance of payments had mounted to the remarkable sum of £1 billion, and foreign holders and speculators in sterling panicked. This time the lessons of the 1960s had been learned and the pound was floated, in June 1972. It depreciated at once, and continued to lose value as against a weighted average of other currencies in a steady drift to 1976. This fall, however, did not improve the balance of payments which worsened by a further £1 billion between June 1972 and the jump in oil prices towards the end of 1973.

What was most remarkable was that, while the inflation rate was creeping up to 7 per cent and beyond in 1970–3, unemployment was also rising, to a peak of over 800,00 in 1971–2. Restriction now shifted to labour policies. Apart from a disastrous attempt to enforce new restraining legislation on trade unions, there was a wage freeze (strongly condemned by the Conservatives when they had been in Opposition) for three months at the end of 1972, followed by a 'norm' of £1 a week plus 4 per cent and, towards the end of 1973, 7 per cent plus threshold additions when inflation exceeded a certain level. In the summer of 1971, retail price increases had just topped the 10 per cent mark on an annual basis, and had then fallen back, but by that time both wages and prices were rising by annual rates that were soon to exceed not only 10 per cent, but even 20 and 25 per cent — rates which but a few years earlier would have seemed unimaginable nightmares.

This was the state of the British economy when in the later months of 1973 it had to deal with the price rises decreed by the OPEC producers that multiplied the price of crude oil fourfold in four years. Before turning to those years dominated by the oil crisis, we must trace out the underlying pattern in the narrative of the stop-go period.

## 2  A Model of the Stop-Go Cycle

By leaving out individual variations, it is possible to construct a typical or model cycle.[36] Let us follow it through from the end of the 'stop', when, after official discouragement, output was low and resources were less than fully employed. This would not necessarily show up in the unemployment figures, since firms would hoard at least their skilled or loyal labour. At low incomes there was less pressure on imports, and there might also be direct import limitations by the government, all of which would improve the balance of payments. Exports may also have been encouraged by declining sales at home, though here, as we shall see, rising costs had a countervailing effect. In total, the balance was moving into positive figures.

In the preceding 'stop' investment had been cut, but there would be new capacity coming into operation as a result of earlier plans, while the simultaneous reduction in output also contributed to a slack in the economy. The essence of the picture was that there was some spare capacity, say of the order of 5 per cent.

At that point, the signals would be set cautiously to 'go', in part by cutting taxes, which would make more purchasing power available to the public at large, and in part by financial means, making it easier and cheaper for firms and individuals to obtain credit.

On the basis of this easement, orders to businesses would now increase, and be met by the available spare capacity. With fuller usage and rapid growth, real costs would fall and market prices remain steady or rise but little. Expansion of home output, however, was possible only as long as the spare capacity lasted, for the underlying rate of expansion based on *additional* capacity was much lower than that of the purchasing power made available. Indeed, since it takes several years for modern productive capacity in many key industries to come into production, it was likely that the cut-backs decreed in the previous 'stop' would begin to bite just at the point when the extra capacity would have been most welcome to keep the home boom going. But with spare capacity of, say, 5 per cent, an underlying growth rate of capacity of perhaps 2½ per cent, and additional purchasing power allowing a growth of, say, 5 per cent, it is clear that demand would come up against a ceiling of home production in two years.

In practice, there would be particular bottlenecks developing well before that, and they would be met by imports. Raw material imports would also go up with prosperity. At the same time order books and delivery dates would be lengthening, so that exports would tend to fall relative to imports, and a balance of payments deficit would develop. A temporary deficit might be met out of reserves, but in view of their smallness and obvious vulnerability, it was easy for a run on the pound to develop in fear of devaluation. There had, after all, been devaluations in 1949, in 1967 and a continuous fall of the pound in relation to other main currencies after it was 'floated' in the 1970s. Any run further weakened the reserves and panicked the Bank of England and the Treasury.

They would react by decreeing a 'stop'. Fiscal and financial means would then be put into reverse, credit and purchasing power would be reduced, and the government would make attempts to cut its spending. The public then began to be exhorted to tighten its belt and work harder, and to suffer what gradually became a familiar avalanche of clichés: we shall see this thing through, one more pull would get us over the hump, the government alone cannot achieve success, all must do their share, national prosperity is at stake, and so on. No noticeable result has ever emerged from these exhortations, nor have the government's predictions ever turned out to be true, but this did not prevent their re-emergence time and time again. In 1948 and again from the mid-sixties onward, an 'incomes policy', i.e. an attempt to hold down wages, would be part of the package to rectify the unbalance. At times there were also physical controls, tariffs and subsidies. In due course, the package would begin to work. Incomes and output would decline, imports fall, the balance of payments would be righted, speculative 'hot' money flow back, a gap of spare capacity open up once more. The economy was ready for another cycle *da capo* 'to indicate the repetition of everything that had gone before'.[37] The long-term slow British growth path was therefore made up of two components: an expansionary phase, when growth almost reached European levels, and a restrictive phase when it usually stopped altogether.[38]

Note that in spite of government rhetoric it was essentially not consumption that was cut back in the 'stop', but investment. The 'package deal', as the Chief Economic Adviser to the government was to write later, consisted of such measures as restrictions on bank advances, on hire purchase and on capital issues, and of cuts in public investment. 'Monetary policy affects, and is intended to affect, investment much more than consumption,' and in practice this means particularly 'industrial investment' as well as the smaller firms 'because they are more vulnerable than their large competitors'. There is possibly, he added, 'greater power of high interest rates to check investment than of low interest rates to encourage it'.[39] Nor are the effects of a minor nature. Andrew Shonfield described the 'series of attacks on investment' in 'breaking the will to invest' in 1955–7 as including a rise in interest rates; an order to bankers to lend less; the abolition of the investment allowance; and once more an order to the banks, via the Capital Issues Committee of the Treasury, to cut their finance of industrial expansion, which would hit particularly the most progressive firms. Finally in 1957 came a 7 per cent Bank Rate and a cut in the investment programmes of the nationalised industries — and all this within two years.[40] The asymmetry really went deeper: 'The present reliance on the monetary mystique has meant that investment has been repressed whenever there was need for restriction. . .subsequently, as the crisis passed, tax concessions usually stimulated consumption.'[41]

A crisis which began because productive capacity was short and could not sustain the kind of growth rate that was commonplace everywhere else in Europe was therefore 'solved' by reducing that capacity even further through cuts in productive investment. Done shamefacedly at first, it very soon became the normal, and ultimately the preferred, way of 'deflating' whenever an external crisis emerged.

> The cycle is thus complete: failure in productivity led to losses in exports; these led to balance-of-payments difficulties, and these, in turn, led to Government short-term measures which were certain, in the long term, to make the productivity failures worse and start the cycle up again, in less favourable conditions, as soon as restrictions were taken off.[42]

The method, in other words, was the solution of a series of short-term, immediate problems (the balance of payments shortfall) at the expense of the long-term future (the ability to sustain economic growth); but the damage to the future was greater than appears at first sight. It is a commonplace that in order to invest in improved productive capacity, business needs confidence[43] — and it is precisely that long-term confidence that was being undermined by the particular way of handling the recurring crises. Who would invest when he had repeatedly been shown that just when he was at his most vulnerable, his costs of capital would be increased and his prospective markets undermined?

The greatest irony was that the authorities evidently thought that the complex monetary, fiscal and other policies designed to inhibit investment would somehow set the scene in order that growth might at last take place.

We shall return to these points later. Meanwhile we might take note of the immediate costs involved.

> It is surely very irrational indeed [mused Sir Roy Harrod] to tolerate 'stop' measures, lasting two years or more, causing a loss of output of perhaps 3% of national income in the first year and 6% in the second year, merely to correct a deficit amounting to 0.85% of national income.[44]

Samuel Brittan attempted a calculation of the actual costs of

## Whitworth

'He suggested further
investment at the board
meeting, this morning!'

Source: (Sheffield) *Morning Telegraph*, 9 October 1976, the day following the rise of
the Minimum Lending Rate to 15 per cent.

securing an improvement of £600 million in the balance of payments
by means of deflation in 1967. Since for every £100 million a year
reduction in demand, imports would fall £24 million and home output by £76 million, to close the gap of £600 million would need a cut
in total demand by £2,500 million in 1968–9, of which £1,900 million would be in home output. This represented a loss of 5 per cent of
gross domestic product, equivalent to 1½–2 per cent unemployment. The effects on exports could be assumed to be negligible. Even
if the manoeuvre was successful, and growth had got back to the
starting-point in five years, the loss meanwhile would have
amounted to £5,000 million.[45] There is the further point, though the
evidence is less conclusive here, that the methods actually used of
'steering', or managing, the economy around the cyclical peaks and
troughs were likely to have increased the amplitude of fluctuations,
and therefore the costs of containing them.[46] The authorities seemed
to be unperturbed by these grievous losses, incurred for the sake of
balancing the immediate accounts.

There is a further irony to be recorded. Most crises were set off by
a balance of payment deficit: this was the case in the major turning-
points of 1947, 1949, 1951, 1955, 1957, 1961, 1964–7, 1968 and
1973–6. However, there was also often, and increasingly so, the fear
of inflation present as a secondary problem, and it became the

main problem in the 1970s. Inflation was, in any case, related to the problem of the foreign balance, since rising home prices would price our exports out of foreign markets. Moreover, policies of 'deflation', adopted at the peak of every cycle, were, as the name implies, in part policies to keep down prices. The actual experience, however, was the reverse of what the policy makers seemed to assume: prices always rose most in periods of stagnation,[47] and rose least in periods of full employment and high activity (see Table 3.2). Nor is this very surprising, except to those who habitually ignore productive realities. For it is normal for real input costs to fall as output and productivity rise:[48] a rise in productivity is merely another way of expressing a fall in real costs.

The relationship becomes clearer when seen in an international context in those years. Wage rises, it is evident, were remarkably similar in all the main industrial nations, emphasising their institutional element under modern conditions.[49] Where Britain differed from the rest was that she could not make up the increase in money wage rates by parallel increases in productivity, so unit labour costs were not held down as much as by the others (see Table 3.3). British prices therefore rose faster and the UK lost export markets until periodic devaluations would temporarily restore her price level to equality with world prices again. In view of this evident relationship, the unanimous, continuous and vituperative concentration of the British economic literature at the time on the evils of 'excessive' wage demands, which were not in the least out of line, while ignoring the dismal growth performance, which was, is nothing less than breathtaking. This is quite apart from the fact that all the attention was given to wages and other prices which were but symbols, while what

**Table 3.2:    Fluctuations, Prices and Output, 1953—66**

|  | Expansion Periods (1953—5, 1959—60 1962—4) | Stagnation Periods (1955—8, 1960—2, 1964—6) |
|---|---|---|
| Annual Growth Rate of UK Industrial Production | 5.8% | 0.9% |
| Annual Rise in Prices: |  |  |
|     Retail | 2.1 | 4.0 |
|     Manufactures | 1.4 | 2.9 |

Source: Sir Roy Harrod, *Towards a New Economic Policy* (1967), p. 13.

**Table 3.3: Earnings, Wages and Unit Labour Costs in Manufacturing, Seven Major Countries, 1950–77**

| | Total Increase, 1950–62 (percentage) | | | Annual Rate of Increase, percentage | | | | | |
| | | | | 1963–73 | | | 1967–77 | | |
| | All Wages | Production | Unit Labour Costs | Hourly Earnings | Production | Unit Labour Costs | Hourly Earnings | Production | Unit Labour Costs |
|---|---|---|---|---|---|---|---|---|---|
| Japan | 202 | 170 | 9 | 14.5 | 12.8 | 3.3 | 15.9 | 7.3 | 8.1 |
| Germany | 335 | 187 | 48 | 8.6 | 5.7 | 4.4 | 9.0 | 4.6[c] | 5.2[a] |
| France | | | | 9.3 | 5.9 | 3.5 | 13.4 | 4.6[c] | 7.7[b] |
| Italy | | | | 11.0 | 5.4 | 5.4 | 17.6 | 3.5 | 12.8 |
| Canada | 111 | 55 | 35 | 7.0 | 5.8 | 2.6 | 10.3 | 4.3 | 5.8 |
| USA | 98 | 57 | 27 | 5.2 | 4.7 | 2.2 | 7.2 | 3.0 | 4.4 |
| UK | 137 | 41 | 70 | 8.9 | 3.2 | 5.2 | 13.5 | 1.6[c] | 11.5 |

Notes: a. Mining and manufacture. b. Industry. c. Excluding construction.
Sources: J.H. Chandler and P.C. Jackman, 'Unit Labour Costs in 8 Countries Since 1950', *Monthly Labour Review*, no. 87 (1964), pp. 377–84; OECD, *Economic Outlook* (December 1975 and December 1979). See also Walter Galenson, 'The Labour Force and Labour Problems in Europe' in Carlo Cipolla (ed.), *The Fontana Economic History of Europe* (1976), vol. V/1, p. 137; G.F. Ray, 'Labour Costs in OECD Countries 1964–1975', *National Institute Economic Review*, no. 75 (1976), pp. 60–1; F. Cavollari and G. Faustini, 'Labour Costs and Employment in Italy and the E.E.C.', *Banco Nazionale del Lavoro Quarterly Review*, no. 126 (1978), p. 253; N. Kaldor, *Essays on Economic Policy* (1964), vol. 1, pp. 146, 151; Lamfalussy, *The United Kingdom and the Six*, pp. 59–60. Similar relationships can be found *within* British industry also: e.g. R. Wragg and J. Robertson, *Post-War Trends in Employment* (1979), p. 34.

they ignored, the failure to match output growth, was affecting not only prices and foreign balances, but the real economic interest of consumers, the provision of goods and services.

The literature of the day, however, was not merely blinkered regarding reality: it was also curiously faulty in its internal logic. Consider the framework, Keynesian or otherwise, within which the Treasury and other policy makers operated. They believed that in Britain (unlike other countries where high growth rates were proved to be sustainable almost indefinitely) there is something in the internal relationships which ensures that as the economy gets into high gear the foreign balance of payments will turn adverse. In other words, at full blast, call it 100, there is inherently a deficit.[50] This can be cured by going down to less than full employment, call it 95. At 95, the balance is restored and may even become positive. After a suitable interval, the policy then is to go back to 100.

What then? The answer surely is obvious: given our assumptions, who could doubt that 'the old difficulties were likely to arise as soon as expansion was resumed'?[51] As soon as Britain was marched from 95 into 100, she was bound to run once more slap bang into the capacity ceiling and the import excess. Yet that repeated experience seemed to come each time as a complete surprise to the Treasury[52] and those who accepted its advice.

Of course, the same relationship need not hold if the assumptions are varied; in particular, if the inherent deficit at 100 can be modified, things might be different next time round. Had then the relationship been modified from one cycle to the next? As a matter of fact, it had, in at least one important respect. For between each cycle and the next the British position was weakened further by having been artificially held back, while our competitors had actively reduced real costs. Typically, in a period of two years, at an annual rise of productivity of 5 per cent, their real costs had been lowered by 10 per cent by the time we were once more ready to reflate to '100': 'After every crisis Britain's relative position in the world further deteriorated. The attempt to cure balance-of-payments crises by restrictions on investment necessarily further impairs our relative competitive power, and thus perpetuates our weakness.'[53] Indeed, 'the deflationary means adopted in July 1966 to deal with the foreign exchange crisis destroyed not only economic growth and full employment, but the National Plan as well, and the concept of planning, and the DEA as a planning Ministry.'[54] It was therefore natural that Britain's crises should become ever longer, and her 'go' period ever shorter, to disappear altogether in the end, for precisely the reason that the technological gap was widening all the time.

Economics may not be a science, and the discussion on British economic policy since the war has been one of the most controversial topics in the history of the subject. Nevertheless, the failures of the Treasury to anticipate this obvious result and, no matter under which mentors (or none) they operated, to fail to learn from the experience of up to ten similar crises, and go on charging again and again like a bull in the *corrida* in spite of the painful and fruitless consequences each time, must be among the most powerful indictments of our policy makers in modern times.

## 3 Britain under the Oil Bonanza, 1973–9

World economic conditions changed abruptly in the latter months of 1973. The immediate cause was the remarkable rise in oil prices, but this had been preceded by a rising tendency of world prices which had contributed to the decision of the oil producers to exploit their monopoly to the full.

In one sense, the rise in oil prices acted on the West like a natural cost increase, a 'true' economic problem of generating lower incomes for the same productive effort. However, there was at least one additional complication: the oil states were unable to use up all the dollars they were suddenly earning. As one country after another was thus hit by a deterioration in its balance of payments it tended to react in the British manner, creating deflation and unemployment at home while prices, affected by the energy crisis, soared upward. The world was thus plunged into a general depression, from which it has not fully recovered to date, though the stronger economies have long since reverted to low and manageable rates of inflation and unemployment.

Within these generally adverse conditions, Britain occupied a very special place because of the discovery of oil in the North Sea. Though much more expensive to raise than the oil in the Middle East, it came to the aid of the British economy just in time. First turned on in a mere trickle in 1975, it met 12.5 per cent of the British demand by 1976 and practically covered all the home needs by 1980. In 1974, just before the oil began to flow, Britain's expenditure on oil imports, in hard-earned foreign currency, was £3.7 billion; at today's prices and today's rate of consumption, it would be £6 billion. The mind simply boggles at the chaos and destruction which such an import bill would have caused in Britain, given the usual reactions of the Treasury to a payments deficit, had we not been saved by our own oil.

As soon as it became clear that there was oil in large quantities available, a lively public debate set in on how to use Britain's unexpected good fortune. There were, broadly, three views: the right wing of the Conservative Party under Mrs Thatcher thought that it should be used to cut taxes, believing, in the face of at least nine cycles in which the opposite occurred, that to lavish purchasing power on taxpayers would lead to long-term growth. The left wing of the Labour Party saw the oil as an opportunity to take more industries into public ownership. A third school of thought wanted the income to be used directly to create productive investment, to be available when the oil ran out.[55]

In practice, none of these strategies had a chance. The outbreak of the world oil crisis affected British fortunes in two opposite directions. On the one hand, world depression was bound to depress British overseas markets and her fortunes in general, just as the world secular boom since the war had kept her own mild boom afloat. On the other hand, as an oil producer she stood to gain by the price rises, or at least lose far less than the other industrial nations who were large oil importers. The balance of these two contrary effects would have been difficult to predict, but at least it could have been expected that Britain would do immeasurably better than those economies which had to import all their ever dearer oil. Many observers did, indeed, see the windfall of the oil as Britain's last chance. Table 3.4 shows the actual course of events during 1973–9. It will be seen that although the other comparable countries had to devote an ever increasing share of their productivity increases to paying for the ever dearer oil, they still succeeded in adding many times more to their people's incomes than did Britain.

How had this remarkable result come about? How did we, having missed out on the secular boom of the Western world after the war, also come to miss out on the fortunes of the oil-rich countries after 1973?

In 1973, a boom year in Britain, the economy was still at the stage of working into its accumulated idle plant and resources and was growing at a rate of around 5 per cent. However, there was now a persistent and worrying floor of much higher unemployment than before, not falling to much below 3 per cent, even at the peak of the

**Table 3.4: The Years of Britain's Oil Bonanza: Some Major Economies, 1973−9**

|  | Average Annual Increase in GNP 1973−8 (percentage) | GNP per Head, 1973 (US$) | Calculated Increase in GNP per Head, 1973−8 (in US$ of 1973) |
| --- | --- | --- | --- |
| France | 2.9 | 4,900 | 753 |
| Japan | 3.7 | 3,760 | 749 |
| Netherlands | 2.4 | 4,410 | 555 |
| Germany | 1.9 | 5,610 | 553 |
| Belgium | 2.2 | 4,650 | 535 |
| Sweden | 1.2 | 6,140 | 377 |
| Italy | 2.1 | 2,510 | 274 |
| UK | 0.9 | 3,100 | 142 |

Source: OECD, *National Accounts Statistics.*

boom: men were idle even if capital was not. In order to avoid the devastating 'stop' that experience had taught the public to expect, there was a widespread opinion that growth should be eased back gently to 2½ or 3 per cent, which the economy could sustain without overheating, and that efforts should be made, for once, to maintain a high and growing rate of investment:

After 9 years without an investment boom [wrote *The Economist* in February] Britain is littered with outdated plant. Only one in 5 of Britain's metal-cutting machine tools is less than 5 years old, compared with one in 3 in Germany and more than half in Japan. The Chancellor must not 'go slow' in his budget by fearing imports from the investment boom. . . If the British economy is to go on to a virtuous cycle of growth, we must not lose our nerve now, as we have so often done before. . .a vote of confidence in faster growth is not only Mr. Heath's one plausible electoral strategy, but also still the country's greatest social and psychological need.[56]

Some of this attitude persisted into the next year. *The Times* criticised Mr Healey's first Budget since it did not help the 'recent recovery in the still appallingly low level of investment in new plant and machinery. . .the low underlying rate of investment means that

British industry is operating with less efficient plant and machinery than many of its competitors'. In the same issue, Marcus Sieff of Marks & Spencer complained that in all the discussion on the Budget

> no one made the point that to overcome our economic problems and genuinely to improve the nation's standard of living, we need to create more national wealth. . .to create more national wealth we need to produce more.[57]

> There must be many like me in industry [he was echoed by one Sheffield industrialist in September] who are perplexed and angered by the outpourings of gloom and irrelevant, largely academic solutions for solving our national economic crisis. . . nowhere do I see plans outlined for solving the crisis by. . . increasing the output of manufacturing goods, thus maintaining full employment.[58]

By November, *The Economist* was complaining that the Chancellor had not given enough to industry to spark off an investment-led recovery, and that stop-go had been replaced by 'squeeze-easy' of financial flows. By January 1975 it reported that investment plans 'are now being scrapped wholesale', and it continued to emphasise that 'Britain's lack of prosperity springs from (a) low and insufficient investment; (b) even more from the way in which investment, once installed, is not productively used'. 'Politicians should move now', it urged in November, 'to cut government spending and encourage manufacturing investment.[59] It need hardly be said that none of that advice was taken.

The change of policy, and the change of government, were introduced by the dramatic events of the miners' work-to-rule at the end of 1973, followed by a strike which brought down the Heath government and led to a Labour victory at the polls. The three-day week, designed to allow the economy to survive the fuel shortage until the spring, led to only a slight fall in output, and the fact that almost as much was produced in three days as normally in five appeared to prove the case of those who had maintained all along that low British productivity was largely caused by the restrictive practices and deliberately slow pace of work of the labour force.

Having been elected on the ruins of the Conservative statutory wage policy, Stage 3, the Labour government had to begin by allowing 'free' wage bargaining while keeping going the machinery for price control. Trade union power, strengthened by its victories over the Heath government, was now free to create a veritable wage explosion, driving prices up with it. Between March 1974 and July 1975 wages rose by no less than 32 per cent, well ahead of prices, which rose 24.4 per cent in the same period. Once started, the wage-push inflation acquired a momentum of its own. The wage offensive lasted until 1976, by which time it had practically wiped out profits and greatly reduced non-wage incomes; thereafter, wages were hard put to it to keep up with the price rises which the free-for-all of 1974–5 had created.

Almost overnight, inflation became the main preoccupation, even the obsession, of the government, and particularly of the Chancellor, Mr Healey.[60] Those who had hoped that the breathing space created by the windfall of the oil revenues might be used at last to allow a period of uninterrupted growth to proceed without being stifled by the Treasury were in for bitter disappointment. It turned out that no sooner had the Treasury lost one cause for throttling the build-up of British industry, it had more than made up for it by finding another.

Not that the Chancellor was alone in his opinion that inflation had to be cured, as always, 'at all costs'.[61] Thus it was widely maintained, with Latin America as example, that democracy could not survive under a high rate of inflation, in defiance of the evidence of such countries as Israel or Iceland and Japan and France over long periods since the war. Even the history books were ransacked to suggest that it was the great German hyperinflation of 1923 which destroyed democracy there, although in fact the inflation years were followed by the most prosperous and stable of the Weimar Republic, and it was only the deflation measures of Brüning in 1930, looking very like the measures which British governments had been bringing in since the war, which brought on an almost immediate polarisation of politics and above all the fast growth of the Nazi Party.

The preoccupation with inflation becomes more remarkable still when it is viewed against the fact that at the same time that other standing objective of policy, particularly of the Labour Party, full employment, had gone seriously wrong. Generally around 300,000 up to the middle 1960s, unemployment had risen to a base of 600,000 in 1966–70, reached 950,000 before the boom of 1972 and never dropped below 500,000 during it. Thereafter the rise was frighteningly steep: the barrier of 1 million was crossed in 1975 and 1.5 million in 1977. Such figures had been unimaginable only a few years before, when a rise of 100,000 was considered sufficient cause for a major switch in tactics to reverse the trend. It was evident that the public had become inured, by constant failure, to taking ever worse standards as the norm. Meanwhile, the Treasury's scale of priorities was such that it set out deliberately to worsen unemployment even more in an attempt to deal with the price rise as the more important object of policy.

It is true that in some respects the traditional policy makers were in disarray. It had been one of the myths (to be discussed further below) of the dominant Keynesian doctrine that not all desirable objectives could be obtained at the same time, and that, in particular, full employment and stable prices were alternatives: you could have one or the other, but not both. The doctrine was boosted by the so-called Phillips curve, which showed that in the past, unemployment and changes in the wage rate had been closely correlated: the lower the rate of unemployment, the faster the rise in wages.[62] Given the then moderate rate of inflation, and the determination not to return to the miseries of pre-war unemployment, the choice until the early 1970s had generally been in favour of slight inflation to keep up employment, and Keynesians had become rather insouciant over the prospect of a steady, but slow, annual rise in the price level:

> For countries with an advanced economic structure, high incomes, and a fairly free and competitive economic system, most of the [alarmist] assertions usually made in policy arguments about inflation turn out to be not confirmed by the empirical evidence.[63]

The preference for inflation against unemployment was further supported by the belief that unemployment would have to reach quite unacceptable levels of perhaps 10 per cent or more to have any effect on prices.[64] Now it appeared that high employment and high inflation, far from being incompatible, even showed an affinity for each other (see Table 3.5).

The actual coexistence of high, and rising, unemployment with rapid and rising inflation, declared to be impossible by the Keynesians, had served to discredit their advice. Another set of advisers was by then in the offing, the Friedmanite monetarists, and although they also linked unemployment with the containment of inflation, they had been quicker off the mark in disowning the Phillips curve, or rather in adapting it by pointing out that it was real, not money,

**Table 3.5:  Ranking of Stability. Twelve Major Countries**

|  | Annual Inflation Rate Percentage (Third Quarter 1978– Third Quarter 1979) | Unemployment Percentage (Adjusted Figures for Last Quarter 1979) |
|---|---|---|
| Japan | 3.5 | 2.2 |
| Austria | 3.6 | 2.1 |
| Norway | 4.2 | 1.9 |
| Germany | 4.8 | 3.3 |
| Sweden | 7.6 | 2.1 |
| Finland | 7.6 | 5.7 |
| Canada | 8.7 | 7.1 |
| France | 10.8 | 5.2 |
| USA | 11.7 | 5.7 |
| Italy | 14.8 | 8.0 |
| Spain | 15.2 | 9.1 |
| UK | 16.0 | 5.2[a] |

Note: a. Seasonally adjusted figure excluding school leavers.
Source: *International Financial Statistics* (December 1979); OECD, *Labour Force Statistics*.

wages which should be linked with the state of employment, a method which would make the correlation stand up much better. Moreover, they had found a plausible explanation for the disconcerting accelerating wage-price spiral after 1969 that had left the Keynesians rather nonplussed, by a doctrine of expected price rises which would naturally accelerate as long as governments reacted to unemployment by increasing their own expenditure. While they also ultimately saw a high level of unemployment as a cure for inflation, their common remedy for both was to cut government spending.[65] This was widely welcomed for a variety of reasons.

Although Mr Healey never fully accepted the monetarist arguments and solutions (that was to be reserved for the Conservative government which followed), his prescriptions did not differ very greatly from theirs. His own hopeless attempt to square the circle by devising wages policies that the trade unions would accept yet that would also be effective had only limited success and was in ruins by the end of 1978 when a free-for-all helped to bring down the Labour government. He therefore had to resort to other policies to counteract the effects of wage-induced inflation. The reasoning behind his policy was therefore quite different from that current in 1947–73 and that adopted after 1979, but the measures were, distressingly, the same.

Among them were credit squeezes, restrictions and cut-backs in public spending in which, as always, the capital programme suffered most. At constant 1978 survey prices, public authorities' expenditure and plans changed as shown in Table 3.6. In other words, the programme envisaged a vast increase in current expenditure, and a proportionally even vaster cut-back in capital spending. The totals by which actual government expenditure was reduced in 1975/6 to 1978/9 were £3,100 million in current items and the much larger cut of £4,900 million in fixed investment. From 1976 onwards the whole of government expenditure took a sharp downward turn and the thrust of the Healey policies was to reduce incomes and employment. It was, in the end, unemployment which was to be used to neutralise and reverse the wage-price rise,[66] while the government was to play its part by cutting its own expenditure and thus reduce its own contribution to inflation. The symbol and measure of the latter was the annual deficit, now known as the Public Sector Borrowing Requirement (PSBR).

As before, therefore, the crisis was to be solved in monetary and symbolic terms by operating on the price level; the real and competitive efficiency of British industry did not enter into the plan of

**Table 3.6:   Changes in Public Expenditure, 1974–9 (£million of 1978 survey prices)**

|  | 1974/5 | 1978/9 | 1979/80 (plans) | Change 1974/5 – 1978/9 | Change 1974/5 – 1979/80 |
|---|---|---|---|---|---|
| Current expenditure (excl. debt interest) | 49,497 | 53,514 | 55,168 | +4,017 | +5,671 |
| Capital expenditure (excl. transfers) | 11,993 | 9,004 | 9,692 | –2,989 | –2,301 |
| Capital transfers (incl. abroad) | 1,641 | 439 | 196 | –1,202 | –1,445 |
| Debt interest | 1,132 | 2,200 | 2,300 | +1,068 | +1,168 |
| Contingency Reserve | — | 41 | 800 | +41 | +800 |

Source: *Public Expenditure White Paper*, Cmnd. 7439 (1979), Table 13, p. 21. Also see Nick Bosanquet and Peter Townsend (eds.), *Labour and Equality. A Fabian Study of Labour in Power 1974–79* (1980), pp. 233, 254, 53.

campaign. But even within the limited symbolic sphere in which alone the Treasury's policy moved, there was, as before, a fatal logical flaw. This flaw lay in the belief that unemployment, no matter how undesirable for other reasons, at least has the merit of curing inflation. This belief, which we have seen to have been dear to the prejudices of large sections of the Economics Establishment, was sadly lacking in realism in the context of the 1970s.

Let us take as an example a worker at a wage of, say, £60 a week in 1977. His contribution to output will be at least of that order of magnitude, and almost certainly a good deal higher: £20 of his income will go in taxes and contributions to the Exchequer, and his effect on the national price level will tend downwards, since he adds more to the production (transactions) side of the equation than he takes out in consumption. If now, as a result of Treasury action, his firm finds it no longer profitable to employ him, his contribution will become at once negative: for now he contributes nothing to output, but has a social benefit income of, say, £25. Whether he is actually deflationary in the first case and inflationary in the second case in practice will depend on the way in which the government as the intermediary finances the benefit and taxation schemes.

By looking at the government account, the inflationary results of making people unemployed become much clearer at once. Our worker ceases to contribute £20 in taxes, and he begins to draw out £25 a week in benefits. On these figures, which are merely intended to indicate an order of magnitude, the government's accounts (and when these are negative overall, the PSBR) suffer a loss of £45 a week or £2,340 a year, while GNP falls by at least £3,000 in real terms for every man made unemployed. Official estimates valid for the end of 1978 put the cost to the Exchequer at an average of £4,000 a year and the loss in output at £3,000.[67] This does not include the cost of administering the benefit scheme. On a realistic basis, the actual costs involved in Mr Healey's policy to create unemployment in 1978–9 have been estimated at an additional expenditure of £1,500 million in unemployment benefit, £1,500 million in lost tax revenue, and a loss of production of around £4,000 million. Estimates of the costs of unemployment to the PSBR for the whole of the period are given in Table 3.7.

In other words, a policy carried on, at a great and grievous social and economic cost, for the ostensible purpose of lowering the PSBR, actually raised it by a figure growing from £1 billion to £8–10 billion. In the last two years of the series, full employment would

**Table 3.7:   Unemployment and Public Sector Deficits, 1973−9 (£ billion)**

|  | Actual PSBR | Estimated PSBR at Full Employment Level | Effect of Unemployment on PSBR |
|---|---|---|---|
| 1973/4 | − 4.6 | − 3.4 | − 1.2 |
| 1974/5 | − 7.6 | − 4.6 | − 3.0 |
| 1975/6 | − 10.6 | − 3.4 | − 7.2 |
| 1976/7 | − 9.0 | − 2.0 | − 7.0 |
| 1977/8 | − 5.5 | + 2.4 | − 7.9 |
| 1978/9 (est.) | − 8.3 | + 2.4 | − 10.7 |

Source: Bosanquet and Townsend, *Labour and Equality*, pp. 18, 57. The estimates were based on statistics published in the *National Institute Economic Review*.

actually have reversed the PSBR into a surplus. Without accepting these figures at too great a degree of accuracy, the reader may yet become impatient at this point. Surely no government and no government department attempting genuinely to achieve a certain result would deliberately choose a policy so obviously and directly tailored to achieve its opposite? Incompetence, perhaps. But surely not sheer irrationality?

Counter-productive irrationality has, of course, been a hallmark of much Treasury policy since the war. Nevertheless, in this case there may have been an element of rational thought in the belief that there was yet another possible effect of unemployment on inflation which has not been considered so far, and which was powerful enough to outweigh the negative effects estimated above. This was the belief, held from time immemorial and certainly assumed to account for the Phillips effect in the past, that unemployment would demoralise and weaken the trade unions to the point where power in the labour market would shift decisively in the direction of the employers. In some quarters it was held that almost any price was worth paying to achieve that result.

However, the notion that the Labour government of the 1970s, more subservient to the trade unions and more at their mercy than any that has ever gone before, should actually plot for ways in which to emasculate the unions may strike the reader to be as incredible as the notion that the Treasury would go in for counter-productive policies. But it does not follow that the politicians of the day who were pursuing unemployment as a deliberate policy were acquainted with the exact mechanism by which it was supposed to work. Still less does it follow that members of the government, particularly those in the key posts in the Treasury, would think this through for themselves.

Whatever the background, which we cannot know for certain, the hope of terrorising the unions into submission by reducing the number of jobs was clearly utterly unrealistic. The then going rates of unemployment, far from curbing the militancy of union leaders, actually increased union resistance to wages policies and wage reductions, most clearly so perhaps in the steel strike of 1980. It only remains to be added that the concurrent action by the government of maintaining benefits at full indexed levels while national income was actually declining worked as a further powerful aid to trade union intransigence and strike-proneness, thus further undermining the dominant policy.[68]

As if all of that were not enough, the government in 1976 engineered a drastic devaluation of the pound from $2.02 to a final figure of $1.71, or by 15 per cent. The move was designed to help exports, i.e. create employment, though it was accepted that it would boost inflation at home; simultaneously the main line of policy was still to keep down inflation at the cost of employment. The two policies were thus perfectly cancelling each other out, though both worked in the same direction in at least one respect: they were both likely to damage the real British standard of living. In all of this we have ignored, as the government has consistently ignored, the ill-effects of the preferred policy of working at less than full capacity on real incomes, output and real costs of production.

Meanwhile, the oil revenues were beginning to flow strongly and to create not only a welcome new source of real income, but also to give the government much greater potential freedom to carry through desirable policies without being held up by short-term crises as had happened so frequently in the past. Yet the benefits were conspicuous by their absence. Even in the opening-up phase, the weakness and low capacity of British industry meant that a great proportion of the orders for the necessary heavy capital equipment went abroad, thus weakening the balance of payments and failing to boost the British capital goods industry.[69] Thereafter, the fillip which the oil bonanza gave to the level of the pound sterling merely helped to price exports out of their remaining markets. One industry after another found itself unable to compete with foreign firms at home and abroad, motor cars and steel being particularly hard hit.

Meanwhile, entry into the EEC had removed whatever chance of protection there was against the chief potential competitors in these capital and engineering goods markets. Thus the oil created unemployment at home while aiding industries abroad: 'North Sea Oil has provided respite for our balance of payments but may have speeded up the decline of other industries.'[70] We do not even seem to have a secure supply of oil as a result. In July 1979, when panic gripped the British motoring community, and queues and rationing appeared at British filling stations, there was no sign of a shortage among our European neighbours who had no supplies of their own. The reason was that they were able to buy more oil, the responsible British Minister declared lamely in explanation.[71]

Anyone who has read through the literature on British economic policy since the war will have been struck by the consistency with which each author believed the current government, the last to be experienced, to have been the worst to date — only to be proved wrong by the following one. In retrospect, those judgements seem broadly right. As the gap between Britain and other comparable economies and between Britain and her potential opportunities widened, as failure was heaped upon failure without evidently teaching anything to the policy-making authorities, as ever more costly mistakes were made to cover ever wider unbalances, the records of government did indeed get worse.

The Labour government of 1974–9 was no exception. Whereas his predecessors had at least kept to some objectives by sacrificing others, Mr Healey's regime was distinguished by being disastrous for all of them. Unbelievably, at a time when scientific progress was improving potential efficiency year by year and the gap between British technology and the best technology was wider than ever, output failed to go up; incomes, aided by temporarily adverse terms of trade, actually fell for some years after 1973. Unemployment rose to wholly unacceptable levels, as did the rate of inflation[72] and interest rates, while the pound dropped to 57 per cent of its exchange value in a little over ten years.[73] Britain lost much of her remaining world markets and the survival of many of her key industries was put seriously in question. Social and welfare services, including education, that most precious investment for the future, as well as more material investment, were cut back more sharply than ever. In the collapse of morale which accompanied all this, industrial relations became a battle-ground and trade unionists were led into actions of a callous anti-social character unthinkable only a few years earlier.

Even then, the fabric of society was held together only by massive foreign loans which for long periods removed the power of independent action on the part of the British government. While it was saved from further humiliation only by the windfall gain from oil, that source of energy otherwise benefited not us, but our competitors. Given the opportunities, there had never been a total and unmitigated failure like it. It was only meet that in line with the rationality of the policies pursued up to that point, at the end of their period of office Mr Healey was honoured with the CH and one of his principal ministers, Harold Lever, received a peerage.

## Notes

1. The Treasury was not the only body to make economic policy, but since it was by far the most important, it is here and subsequently used as a shorthand term to designate the whole decision-making complex. See further Chapter 7, section 2, below.
2. Sir Stafford Cripps at the Bradford Conference on Production, 22 January 1947; Anthony Eden, broadcast, reported in *The Times*, 21 March 1947; Dalton's Supplementary Budget of 15 November 1947; R.F. Harrod, *And So It Goes On* (1951), p. 117, quoted in T.W. Hutchison, *Economics and Economic Policy in Britain, 1946–1966* (1968), pp. 53–4; *The Economist*, 1 May 1948, leader.
3. *House of Commons Debates*, 24 October 1949, 1016–17. This cut in investment was widely approved among economists at the time.
4. The technical term was to 're-value', but this seems illogical if there has not been a preceding devaluation.
5. Quoted in Hutchison, *Economics and Economic Policy* pp. 75–6.
6. 'Deflation' is a simpler word, but it had a negative connotation and was therefore taboo at the time. The belief that by mincing words you can change things is one of the more engaging aspects of economic literature.
7. A term applied to the opinion creators on economic issues. See Chapter 7, section 1.
8. Joan Mitchell, *Crisis in Britain 1951* (1963), p. 19.
9. *House of Commons Debates*, 15 February 1951, 648.
10. Leader, 11 April 1951.
11. 'The hard, even ominous fact must be faced', noted *The Times* on the occasion of the 1952 Budget, 'that any actual retrenchment, in terms of actual resources, has been in productive capital investment . . . the crisis has been met at the expense of industrial re-equipment, capital wealth and security, while personal consumption and housing have remained exempt' (12 March 1952). *Times* leaders continued in the same strain in subsequent years, e.g. 31 March and 7 April 1954, 18 February 1956. Also *The Economist*, e.g. 20 February and 27 March 1954.
12. Both were replaced by investment grants from 1966 onwards, and these, in turn, were abolished in 1970 in favour of higher depreciation allowances, the rates being biased in favour of the development areas.
13. 'If those concerned with investment programmes', said Mr Butler in introducing his autumn Budget, 'are willing. . .to move rather more slowly for the time being in implementing their projects, they will be contributing directly to the stability of our economy and thus ultimately to their own prosperity' (*House of Commons Debates*, 29 October 1955). 'Because fixed investment has at last increased a small part of the

way towards the level it ought to have achieved several years go', complained *The Economist*, 'it has been found necessary to cut down spending — including some spending on investment itself' (5 November 1955).

14. Sima Lieberman, *The Growth of European Mixed Economies 1945–70* (1977), p. 83.

15. Report in *The Economist*, 13 October 1956.

16. Speech to UK Provident Institution reported in *The Economist*, 13 July 1957.

17. This is discussed further below, section 2.

18. There is a vast economic literature on the meaning, causes and consequences of 'overheating'; the literature as to why the British economy should always overheat at 4 per cent growth, while every other comparable country could grow comfortably at 5 or 6 per cent almost indefinitely, and what should be done to change that curious weakness, is minuscule.

19. See J.C.R. Dow, *The Management of the British Economy 1945–60* (1965), pp. 77–8.

20. L. Robbins, *The Balance of Payments* (1951), p. 32.

21. Fourteen papers of the meeting were reproduced in two numbers of the *Bulletin of the Oxford University Institute of Statistics* (April and August 1952).

22. 'Comment', *Bulletin of the Oxford Institute of Statistics*, no. 14 (1952), p. 172.

23. Samuel Brittan, *Steering the Economy: the Role of the Treasury* (1969), p. 132.

24. Budget Debate, House of Commons, 15 April 1958.

25. E.g. (Sir) Harold Wilson in the Budget Debate of 17 April 1958; *The Times* leader, 17 October 1959.

26. See quotation at the beginning of this volume. Also Hutchison, *Economics and Economic Policy*, pp. 141, 151–4; Radcliffe Committee, *Memoranda of Evidence*, vol. 3 (1960), pp. 40–1.

27. *The National Plan*, Cmnd. 2764 (1965).

28. J.F. Wright, *Britain in the Age of Economic Management. An Economic History since 1939* (1980), p. 157.

29. Callaghan promised the IMF to free £800 million of resources: £500 million to put the foreign balance right and £300 million to meet the now adverse terms of trade. See Michael Stewart, *The Jekyll and Hyde Years* (1977), pp. 85–6.

30. R.C.O. Matthews, 'The Role of Demand Management' in Sir Alec Cairncross (ed.), *British Economic Prospects Reconsidered* (1971), p. 15.

31. Brittan, *Steering*, p. 218.

32. Michael Artis, 'Fiscal Policy for Stabilization' in W. Beckerman (ed.), *The Labour Government's Economic Record: 1964–70* (1972), p. 279.

33. 'In the previous six years [to 1970] the Labour administration had been trying to achieve many goals in theory, but was in practice a victim of its own desire to protect the exchange rate' (W. Keegan and R. Pennant-Rea, *Who Runs the Economy?* (1979), p. 25.

34. David Laidler, 'A Monetarist Viewpoint' in Michael Posner (ed.), *Demand Management* (1978), p. 56.

35. Robert Bacon and Walter Eltis, *Britain's Economic Problem: Too Few Producers* (2nd edn, 1978), pp. 54, 57.

36. Descriptions of the cycle are legion. Two good concise ones from differing points of view will be found in Reginald Maudling, 'Getting the Economy Right Off Square One', *The Times*, 15 May 1973, and Laidler, 'A Monetarist Viewpoint', pp. 42–3.

37. Brittan, *Steering*, p. xv.

38. Lamfalussy, *The United Kingdom and the Six*, pp. 3–6.

39. Sir Alec Cairncross, *Essays in Economic Management* (1971), pp. 99, 119, 98. Also see Brittan, *Steering*, p. 306.

40. Andrew Shonfield, *British Economic Policy Since the War* (1958), pp. 244–5.
41. Thomas Balogh, *Evidence to Committee on the Working of the Monetary System*, vol. 3 (1960), p. 41.
42. S. Pollard, *The Development of the British Economy 1914–1967* (1969), p. 447.
43. 'All the NEDC's researches have shown that the main determinants of investment are confidence and the expectation of high capacity use and a reasonable profit' (Maurice Corina in *The Times*, 3 November 1979). See also J.R. Sargent in *Midland Bank Review* (Autumn 1979), p. 11; W. Beckerman, *The British Economy in 1975* (1965), pp. 47 *et passim*.
44. *Towards a New Economic Policy* (1967), p. 30. W.A.P. Manser spoke of 'swinging a £38,000 million economy about in order to achieve these indistinguishable differences' of plus or minus £200 or £300 million (*Britain in Balance* (1973), p. 207).
45. Brittan, *Steering*, pp. 292–4.
46. R.A. and P.B. Musgrave, 'Fiscal Policy' in Richard E. Caves and Associates, *Britain's Economic Prospects* (1968), p. 44; also Brittan, *Steering*, p. 263.
47. E.g. Bela Balassa, 'Resolving Policy Conflicts for Rapid Growth in the World Economy', *Banca Nazionale del Lavoro Quarterly Review*, no. 126 (1978), p. 278.
48. E.F. Denison, 'Economic Growth' in Caves, *Britain's Economic Prospects*, p. 252.
49. Pollard, *Development of the British Economy*, p. 483; also Brittan, *Steering*, p. 264.
50. 'The British economy is incapable of maintaining high rates of economic growth or continued full employment without *either* import restrictions *or* devaluation' (Nicholas Kaldor, letter to *The Times*, 19 February 1963).
51. Brittan, *Steering*, p. 216. See also Harrod, *New Economic Policy*, p. 22.
52. But not the Department of Economic Affairs (DEA), set up in the vain hope of meeting the short-term negative policies of the Treasury by longer-term positive ones. 'Sterling was in difficulties in five of the last ten years', read its *National Plan* (1965), '[which] were met by sharp checks to economic expansion. This has had adverse effects on productive investment, and hence on our long-term growth potential. . . Part of our difficulties in visible account is to be explained by shortages of capacity resulting from insufficient investment in the past, and from too slow a rate of installing labour-saving machinery and of making use of new techniques' (p. 69–70).
53. Thomas Balogh, *Unequal Partners* (1963), vol. 2, quoted in Hutchison, *Economics and Economic Policy*, pp. 232–3.
54. Roger Opie, 'Economic Planning and Growth' in Beckerman, *The Labour Government's Economic Record*, p. 177.
55. See, for example, the *Observer*, 15 January 1978.
56. *Economist*, 10 February, 7 April 1973. See also *The Times* leaders.
57. *The Times*, 28 March 1974.
58. Letter by B.E. Cotton, *The Times*, 6 September 1974.
59. *The Economist*, 16 November 1974, 11 January, 22 February, 11 October, 22 November 1975. *The Times*, however, believed that the Tribune Group's solution for an investment-led growth in publicly owned industry would be disastrous: 13 June 1975.
60. He also succeeded in making the objective of keeping down inflation a major part of Labour's election programme in 1979.
61. 'Inflation is the overwhelmingly most important problem for Britain at the moment. If this is solved, all the others would at once become more soluble' was a not untypical cry of the day, at a time of high unemployment and declining output and incomes. Its author, F.W. Paish, had been the leading advocate for higher unemployment as a cure for many ills in the high noon of Keynesian ascendancy. 'Short-Term Incomes Policy to Central Labour Monopoly' in IEA, *Catch '76 . . .* (1976). p. 31.

62. A.W. Phillips, 'The Relation Between Unemployment and the Change of Money Wage Rates in the United Kingdom, 1861–1957', *Economica*, no. 25 (1958), pp. 283–99.

63. Harry G. Johnson, *Selected Essays in Monetary Economics* (1978) p. 137; also see N. Kaldor, *Essays on Economic Policy*, vol. 1, (1964), pp. 137, 147, 187 ff; Walter Eltis, 'The Failure of the Keynesian Conventional Wisdom', *Lloyd's Bank Review*, no. 122 (October 1976), p. 18.

64. N. Kaldor, 'Economic Growth and the Problem of Inflation' (1959) in *Essays*.

65. For a short summary, see Milton Friedman, *Unemployment versus Inflation* (1975); also Peter Jay, *Employment, Inflation and Politics* (1976); Laidler, 'A Monetarist Viewpoint'; Samuel Brittan and Peter Lilley, *The Delusions of Incomes Policy* (1977), pp. 20, 53; Michael Parkin in W.A.H. Godley, *Inflation in the United Kingdom* (1978), esp. p. 479.

66. 'More jobs or higher wages', *The Times* summarised his message to trade unionists, 14 January 1975.

67. Martin Timbrell, 'Unemployment in the 1980's', *Lloyd's Bank Review* (April 1980), p. 25.

68. E.g. B.C. Roberts, 'The Government's Challenge to the Unions', *Three Banks Review*, no. 124 (December 1979), esp. p. 20: A.B. Atkinson and J.S. Flemming, 'Unemployment, Social Security and Incentives', *Midland Bank Review* (Autumn 1978).

69. E.g. *The Economist*, 29 January and 27 May 1972, 20 January 1973; Wright, *Britain in the Age of Economic Management*, p. 164.

70. *The Times*, 29 December 1979.

71. *World at One* programme 5 July 1979.

72. The Index of retail prices stood at 102.6 in March 1974 and at 210.6 in March 1979, having thus more than doubled in five years of Mr Healey.

73. Posner, *Demand Management*, tables on pp. 65, 88.

# 4 THE CONTEMPT FOR PRODUCTION

## 1 The Confusion of Ends and Means: Symbols before Reality

In the last chapter we have taken the chain of causation one step further. In our search for a cause of the British failure to invest we have come upon one single overwhelmingly important answer: investment in Britain was low because the whole panoply of government power, as exercised above all by the Treasury, was designed to keep it so. Again and again, in the course of the past thirty years, governments have set out to discourage, cut back and stifle investment, and in the long run they have succeeded. This was done at two levels. There was, on the one hand, a battery of measures to hit investments directly and specifically, but there was also, and perhaps more insidiously, the paralysing effect of the recurring and in the end permanent 'stop' phases on all hopes and plans for the future. It is without doubt a remarkable tribute to the inherent drive of capitalism towards the creation of capital, and to capitalists' urge to invest, that in the face of all the official discouragement, any investment is still taking place at all in Britain.

However, by pointing to government as the immediate cause of low investment we have merely shifted the problem one step backward. For the obvious question that then demands to be answered is why successive governments should wish to go out of their way to inflict such grievous, ever increasing damage to the British economy. One possible impression left by the kaleidoscope of events over the past three decades may well be that the country merely suffered from a chapter of unconnected accidents. Alternatively, we may come to the despairing conclusion that the Treasury will always choose, from any set of options available, the one which will do the most damage — an assumption that will certainly help as a first approximation for putting the events of the past into some logical order and predicting those of the future. Yet both of these explanations would be wrong: an alternative does exist, and in following it in the search for a unifying principle that will make sense of the many apparently contradictory reactions of British policy makers, we are beginning to approach the heart of the matter.

Let us be clear what we are looking for. We are looking for a body of ideas and of principles strong and pervasive enough to make governments continue with their policies even though they have led over a period of three decades, as a matter of experience, to the most devastating economic failure recorded in modern history and do not even make sense in their own terms. For as we have seen in the last chapter, the adopted policies were bound to lead, after every 'go', necessarily and inevitably into another crisis; policies supposedly devised to lead to deflation were bound to lead to rises in costs; and policies supposedly devised to cut the PSBR were bound to lead to its increase. Moreover, we are looking for principles held by British governments and policy makers but not by others — except those, like the United States in recent years, that have shown equally dismal economic results.

There is one and only one principle which will fit the bill: it is the principle of concentrating first and foremost on symbolic figures and quantities, like prices, exchange rates and balances of payment, to the neglect of real quantities, like goods and services produced and traded. In particular, the subordination of one to the other is such that whenever there is a clash of interests, the real must be sacrificed to the symbolic. This scale of values is of course the reverse of that held by ordinary citizens who make up the population of this country, and indeed of every other country in the modern world.

Not that members of British governments have set out to do harm to their economy. On the contrary, they will be found in the past to have supported particular industries, firms or regions, to have supported research and development of new technologies, and in general to have shown all signs of wishing, like the citizens themselves, to ensure the prosperity and full employment of all sections of their country.[1] But these laudable policies have in the majority of post-war years been in direct conflict with the line of high or 'macro-economic' policy pursued by the Treasury, and it has, as a consequence, been a common feature of the period that different departments have worked simultaneously in opposite directions.

No one who has lived through the period and has read or listened to the media will require proof of the single-minded obsession of the Treasury with such issues as balance of payments or inflation: it is the single most consistent thread running through official propaganda and discussion.[2] It is true that for a time the objective of full employment also played a significant part and that British policy zigzagged between the 'Pavlovian responses' of Treasury and Bank officials dreading a 'run on the reserves' and of politicians dreading an unemployment figure over the critical half-million mark.³ But the latter barrier has now been broken. Employment itself has more recently, like production and investment, been used as means with which to get the symbolic balance right, rather than the other way round.

There is no question but that the objectives were in themselves worthy and desirable ones. The point is that they were considered more urgent, and more significant, than real productive power and real goods and services available for consumption which were repeatedly sacrificed for the sake of the symbols. In the last resort, therefore, the attitude of the authorities can only be described as one of contempt for production and of the productive sectors of the economy.

The contempt for production thus stood at the centre of British policy in this period. It informs fundamentally all the actions of the Treasury and other central policy-making bodies. At the same time, it is what most clearly distinguishes the British government from all others.

As a policy principle it also proved to be thoroughly destructive. For it preferred the empty symbol to the living reality, and by utterly confusing ends and means, it lost both. Britain, sacrificing her productive power on the altar of monetary symbols, suffered not only in real welfare, but in the end damaged also the symbols for which it had been sacrificed; whereas the countries that got their priorities right and devoted their efforts to improving the productive base found that their symbols, the value of their currencies and the balance of their payments, also turned out successful and positive.

There is no doubt that much of public opinion supported the official scale of priorities. This was in part because it accepted similar constraints: thus if one gave priority to the balance of payments then according to Wilfred Beckerman it became 'the framework from which policy has to start' and it imposed an immediate constraint on all other desirable ends. 'Everyone agrees that faster growth is important,' but, the financially orthodox would always argue, 'the first priority must be to get the balance of payments right.'⁴ Again, if one set high store by social policies, then the idea

> that consumption should take the brunt of short-term adjustments in demand and that investment should be kept on a steady path [is a] paradoxical prescription from the point of view of wel-

74 *The Wasting of the British Economy*

fare theory [according to Professor R.C.O. Matthews]. To cut down provision for the future in a period of temporary stringency is therefore a rational policy.[5]

Finally, there was the sheer disregard for any alternative. Consider the sentiments behind the philosophy of Hubert Henderson as evidenced in the quotation at the head of this book: it will repay careful study. For here was one of the most perceptive economists among those advising the Treasury, and by no means a simple mouthpiece of 'Treasury views', yet for him the world consisted of a safely ticking-over productive machine, which merely had to be trimmed and 'balanced' to keep it in good shape. There is no inkling here of a dynamic arising in the productive sector that would completely transform modern industrial economies, more than double their output in a few years, require thorough realignment of all other institutions and put Britain before the dilemma of either copying their method, or being wiped out as a leading industrial nation.

Not that there were voices lacking to offer the alternative of transforming the real productive capacity rather than manipulating fiscal and financial policies as a way of breaking out of Britain's vicious circle. While Peter Oppenheimer was perhaps slightly sanguine in his belief that 'nearly everyone would regard the objective (of controlling inflation) as much less important that full employment',[6] the campaigns of such critics as Samuel Brittan, Thomas Balogh[7] or Andrew Shonfield lacked neither in vigour nor cogency. George Brown's creation of the DEA and its National Plan brought such ideas right into Whitehall, and Reginald Maudling actually attempted to pull the Treasury towards what he hoped would be an alternative policy. But it is clear in retrospect that there was never a real chance of shaking the 'balance-of-payments firsters'[8] in the Treasury.

In the country at large it was the capital goods industries which protested most vigorously and repeatedly at being singled out for damage,[9] with the long-term ill-effects that that would have on the economy. Opposition elsewhere is difficult to gauge. Certainly, the alternative of a policy of building up a sound industrial base instead of manipulating the symbols has always been widely canvassed.

[There is an alternative] means of eliminating what you call the Excess Money Supply [commented Philip Allott in the correspondence columns of *The Times*]. The other means is to increase the

Gross Domestic Product. This is the constructive and imaginative challenge which Britain faces.

> The economic argument is simple [according to J.M. Kellett]. Inflation is the result of too much money chasing too few goods. One can correct this by reducing the supply of money or by increasing the production of goods.

> Is it not time [Reginald Maudling asked in reply to Sir Keith Joseph] for all of us to concentrate a little less on reducing demand to match production and a little more on increasing production to match demand?[10]

Examples of such opinions could easily be multiplied. But there was no organised power centre akin to the Treasury in which to focus their combined strength.

It is part of the British insular tradition to take very little notice of opinion abroad, where (apart from the charmed circle of central bankers) our progress in self-destruction was viewed with a mixture of awe, puzzlement and pity.

> In balance of payments crisis after balance of payments crisis [wrote R. Lekachman in 1967] both Labour and Conservative cabinets have reacted in ways distressingly reminiscent of the antediluvian wisdom of the Treasury and the Bank of England. Sometimes it has seemed that the spectre of Lord Norman walks the Westminster battlements, tediously lecturing his countrymen on the need to create as much unemployment and as much business recession as might be required to check and reverse adverse balances in Britain's trading account.[11]

Foreign governments also did, from time to time, apply the kind of restrictive measures that were the stock in trade of the British Treasury and, as noted above, the American government is at the time of writing applying them with a consistency that foreshadows a decline akin to the British one, albeit from a very different absolute level. But a short, sharp application to a healthy economy is something quite different from a long-drawn-out weakening of an emaciated one, just as in medicine, a day's purge may be advisable in the case of a vigorous patient, but is not recommended for one who has been fasting for thirty days. Over the long term, it is clear that among the leading governments the actions of the British government were the most consistently hostile and the least helpful to growth.[12]

There is a delicious irony (and not the first to be recorded in these pages) in the thought that the British Economics Establishment was so certain of its own prescriptions that some voices in it actually criticised foreign governments for preferring productive strength to the economic 'orthodoxy' of looking after the symbols. The first French post-war Plan, for example, which laid the foundations for transforming the battered and decrepit French economy into a modern high-growth one, was questioned because of

> the acceptance of inflation as a consequence of heavy investment programmes and restrictions on consumer goods without adequate control of incomes. It is arguable whether this was a sound policy[!]; but the planners . . . [carried it through] . . . on the grounds that without an expansion of productive capacity and the removal of bottlenecks on the supply side neither growth nor stability would be achieved.[13]

There was no danger of the British Treasury permitting such foolhardy policies.

It was evident that, at least until the oil crisis struck the Western world as a whole and made it react in the Anglo-Saxon manner, the stronger economies all took great care when they suffered drains or unbalances not to damage their productive and growth potential in solving temporary problems. The Japanese, in particular, saw to it that the expansionary stimulus applied in depression went to investment, not consumption or government spending: 'The Japanese economy grows out of a depression through government-assisted investment booms, stimulating the expansion of industrial supply prior to the subsequent consumer demand, and this process leads to high growth with some inflation.'[14] Similarly, in the depth of the depression, in the spring of 1981, France and Germany announced that they would raise 5 billion European units of account, or about 6 billion US dollars, in international money markets to finance new technology, especially in energy saving, and to create jobs, above all among smaller firms.[15]

No one in Britain is inclined to learn from such examples, and the unwillingness to look elsewhere for policy inspirations was undoubtedly a contributory cause of Britain's sorry performance.

For it is difficult to believe that even the Treasury, content though it was to repeat the same mistakes for thirty years in the face of obvious lack of success, could have continued on its blinkered path if it had considered the developments abroad with an open mind.

This lack of intellectual curiosity regarding events elsewhere also lies behind the myth, referred to several times above, that economic policy is a choice of limited numbers of desirable ends: choosing one, one forgoes the chance of another.[16] There is a theoretical basis for this in the curious fallacy with which economists define their own subject,[17] but its survival was due to the failure to look abroad. For if British advisers had done so, they would have noticed that while it was indeed true that Britain could choose only a restricted number of desirable options at the same time, like full employment *or* foreign exchange stability, the others' economies managed to achieve *all* their aims simultaneously. The reason for this was that they had got their productive base right and on an upward curve first, and given high investment and a rising output, it was possible for them to have rising real wages, full employment, fairly stable prices *and* successful exports[18] — but it was precisely that base that the selective blindness of the Treasury refused to recognise as of primary significance.

In recent years the doctrine of balances and alternatives has been dropped even in Britain, somewhat to the discomfiture of the Neo-Keynesians. The reason for this is that we have contrived simultaneously to achieve *none* of our aims, which is as incompatible with the myth of balances as would have been the achievement of *all* the set targets together.

The contempt for production emerged as a hampering or distorting factor in almost everything undertaken by our economic policy makers. Thus, as noted above, they failed to see that the cause of Britain's uncompetitive prices in world markets in the 1950s and 1960s was not that her wages were too high, as official opinion insisted throughout, but her rises in productivity too low (see Table 3.3 p. 53). By the same token, Mr Healey's appeals to the trade unions from 1975 to 1979 to moderate their wage demands in order not to undermine his policies lacked realism because they were couched in terms of two unattached sets of statistics, money wage rates and prices. A reference to real terms, such as that since real output was growing at only 1 per cent, real wages should not grow by more than 1 per cent, might at least have added some credibility, though it is doubtful how far the British trade union movement possessed the maturity and sense of responsibility to work something like the Dutch and Scandinavian wage policy implicit in such an approach. Of course, a reference to such real terms might have also shown up the failure of his overall policies, particularly in years in which national income actually declined.

Again, it is the preoccupation with 'balances' that has predisposed successive governments to spend vast resources on promoting exports by favours to successful exporters ranging from subsidies and other preferences to credit guarantees and Queen's Awards. No one in authority would dream of devoting even a fraction of these resources to developing home production which might substitute often quite easily for the imports paid for at such high cost by the exports. Behind this failure on the part of the authorities to see that there is no benefit in exports as such, that their purpose is merely to buy imports, and that differences in production costs, which alone justify that trade, may often easily be bridged by industry at home, there lies once more the contempt and blindness for production.

This blindness contributed to, as it was certainly made worse by, the British political tradition of fighting over the share-out of the cake rather than considering ways of increasing its size. While such emphasis on distribution is not unknown elsewhere, the conscious-ness that all might gain by enlarging the cake is far more firmly rooted abroad. In Britain, the two main parties, like two fighting boys at a children's tea party, snatch the cake from each other after each election, not noticing that each time another piece drops on the floor thereby, and that neither will gain permanent possession of it.[19] It should be added, however, that there were many in the Labour Party, and not only among the left, who deliberately, and therefore rationally, opted for a fairer distribution at no matter what cost to real output.

The use that Britain made of Marshall Plan funds bears the same character. While all other major recipients were careful to use them, like good husbandmen, for investment purposes in order to build up their economic future,[20] in Britain the Treasury used them, wastrel fashion, to plug temporary holes.

Not that the signs were lacking that the real weakness of the British economy which led to the loss of one export market after another was not so much the weak incentive, or even the price, but the sheer lack of ability to produce enough at an acceptable quality and on time. Yet these signs were consistently ignored, either because they were not noticed at all, or because they were held to be outside the purview of the authorities.

As noted above, there was some understanding of the real problems immediately after the war, when the production drives of the war years were still alive in everyone's mind.[21] Some echo of this was found even in the Korean War boom, and it was widely realised then that Britain's exceptional rearmament drive would injure her investment efforts in other sectors. Thereafter, however, the issue faded from the official agenda, while it increasingly came to dominate the nation's economic fortunes.

Andrew Shonfield produced a graphic account of the problem as it arose in shipbuilding, once one of the most successful and competitive of British industries, and in the years after the war still a potential winner. Emerging from the war with much the largest output capacity outside the USA, Great Britain remained the leading exporter for some years thereafter, trading both on her traditional high reputation reinforced by the naval successes of the war years, and on her large building capacity compared with the shrunken and defective yards of her chief rivals. From 1945 to 1955 world demand overwhelmed potential supply; but while 'Britain achieved the largest shipbuilding order book in the history of man', at 7 million tons, she

> increased actual output by a moderate amount, and lost the first place as the biggest shipbuilding country in the world. . .
>
> The striking thing about the British ship [sic] industry. . .is its stubborn refusal to invest in the creation of more productive capacity. . . During the four crucial years from 1951 – 1954 when first the German yards and later the Japanese were going ahead with large-scale re-equipment, British shipbuilding firms spent £4 million annually on their fixed assets [for] an industry which was producing an average of £120 million a year at this time and employing over 200,000 men.

Replacement alone would have cost £6 million. Altogether, here was

> a British industry with the cards all stacked in its favour, which has strikingly failed to exploit its natural advantage. . . [Its] experience also provides pretty clear proof that it is not any lack of good and profitable business openings which has held up investment in British industry. Rather, there is a climate of opinion which tends to make businessmen invest much or little . . . And the psychological accompaniment of the climate of low investment is a tendency to eschew innovation.[22]

It may be that Mr Shonfield was a little unfair to shipbuilders in belittling the problem of the steel shortage, which was one of the constraints holding them back. But whatever the cause, it was obvious by the early 1950s that 'speed of delivery is beginning to become an increasingly important factor in the shipbuilding industry',[23] and other nations, notably the Germans, the Japanese, the Dutch and the Swedes began to enjoy a marked advantage in this respect. German shipbuilding exports exceeded the British for the first time in 1954 and the Japanese did so in 1955, though both had had to start almost from scratch after the war, and other countries followed one after the other.

Those were the years blighted in Britain by Korean War rearmament, but the problems remained the same even after market conditions were reversed. The next twenty years saw a shrinkage of world demand, and under pressure from foreign competition British shipyards were decimated and their workers hit by large-scale redundancies and unemployment. In such conditions of over-capacity one might have expected at least the problems of delays to have disappeared, but in fact British shipyards were still unable to assure completion and delivery on time. Even in 1978 they were reported to have lost £50 million of orders for that reason, and in 1979 the Cunard Company decided to have its crack liner overhauled in the USA rather than in Southampton, for there it always took so long that the ship would still be sitting in her dock when she could be at sea earning an income.[24] By then the British industry could survive only with a subsidy which had reached around £100 million a year, it had obtained the large Polish order only at a further loss of £40 million, and it had dropped from the largest producer in the world to the *eleventh*, behind such countries as South Korea and Yugoslavia.[25]

As far as that important and once successful industry was concerned, therefore, all the agonising and complex decisions about devaluation and exchange rates, about inflation and the wage level, with which the Treasury and the Bank of England filled their days, and the economics profession filled hundreds of thousands of pages, were beside the point. What it needed was massive injections of capital, such as had benefited the more successful countries abroad, and a secure supply of steel plates and other components from flourishing and expanding supply industries. But far from helping to provide them, the Treasury had on the contrary mainly engaged in a systematic series of measures directly designed to choke both.

This fate was not peculiar to the shipbuilding industry: it was common to all, though it affected particularly the capital goods industries. Thus

> the construction industry provides one-half of the fixed capital
> formation undertaken by the public sector and has suffered the
> greatest damage of all from sharp and massive cuts made in the
> past in capital investment programmes as an expedient response
> to financial constraints, notably at the time of the IMF intervention in 1976.[26]

> Building is investment, not consumption. To put off the proper
> production and maintenance of our building stock is to make a
> future crisis inevitable. . . When the economy recovers, the
> industry will quickly overheat, the costs will inflate and quality
> will be poorer.[27]

Other important capital goods were machine tools, which, unlike shipbuilding, had been a weak point in the British economy for decades, and heavy engineering. A major study of the machine tool industry, covering the years 1956–62 and conducted in econometric terms, found that prices had no influence on ('do not contribute to the explanation of') the flow of orders to the United Kingdom either in real or in money terms. By contrast, 'if the [foreign] customer is quoted a delivery date too far in the future, he may place the order elsewhere, either in his domestic market or with another foreign supplier, and the order is lost'. In consequence, 'the most striking result running through all the regressions is the importance of waiting times in explaining the foreign orders coming to the U.K.'[28]

Once more, the area to which the Treasury devoted its efforts, namely prices, turns out to be of minor significance;[29] what was required was an expansion of capacity, and that is precisely what the Treasury in one measure after another was acting to prevent. As a result, whenever 'go' signals allowed full employment to be approached, the machine tool industry was the location of some of the most serious bottlenecks and contributed its share to the immediate adverse swing in the balance of trade. Its failings in turn hampered other investment plans at home, such as the decision to expand British Leyland in 1975:

> Once again [complained the Chairman of the Machine Tool
> Trade Association] the machine tool industry will be castigated

for failure to supply the very items which for so long the MTTA
has been urging as the true need of British engineering and which
should and could have been supplied in a planned and orderly
fashion over many years.[30]

According to the report of the sector's working party report to the
NEDC in 1980, 'Britain was easily bottom of the international
league table in net turnover per employee, hourly labour costs and
other performance yardsticks' in the gauge and tool industry.[31]

Though British quotations, with the aid of devaluation and low
wages, were frequently still below others in overseas contracts for
heavy engineering, orders were lost because of the reputation of
unreliable delivery dates. Even Sir Freddie Laker, standard-bearer
for British go-ahead enterprise, bought his aero engines from the
USA because the Rolls-Royce engines would not be ready for 1981
when he wanted them.[32]

There would be little point in multiplying examples of lost orders
because of supply failures — they catch the eye in almost every issue
of the trade press and sometimes even the financial press,[33] though it
seems clear that they are kept out of the exalted hands of those who
make our economic policy.

While we have concentrated on capital goods, it will be found that
conditions were no better among consumer durables. We have noted
in Chapter 1 the decline of steel and motor cars, once among the
strongest elements in the post-war British economy,[34] and we may
conclude this topic with a brief reference to motor cars, perhaps the
most important of the industrial products of the twentieth century.

Automobiles are in large part consumer goods, and many consumers develop an emotional relationship to their cars. Since they
represent an important part of the average consumer's outlay, motor
cars are price elastic, but within any given price range it is quality,
reliability, service, availability of spare parts and delivery dates that
matter. This is even more true in the case of business firms, which
buy the majority of new cars. Here lay the weak point of British
manufacturers[35] — but it is one in which it would be vain to have
expected British economic policy makers to have taken any active
interest.

By now the dreary succession of consumer reports which almost
invariably put British cars at the bottom or near it for quality and
realiability are too well known to need repetition. Perhaps the most
comprehensive report in that respect was based on the obligatory

checks carried out on over 7 million vehicles in 350 testing stations by the German official motor testing organisation, TÜV. Their statistics show which cars were rejected at their first test: among the seventy most popular models, there was only one British car, the BL Mini, and it came out worst by a considerable margin.[36] Within the same company making the same models, Ford found British-made cars giving rise to double the number of complaints and repair needs as German.[37] The report of 1975 by the Central Policy Review Staff (Think Tank) on the British motor industry was concerned to play down the 'abysmal' investment record stressed by the Ryder Report and by others,[38] and to emphasise above all the slow pace of work and the endless labour disputes as causes for British failures. Even so, they also had to mention poor quality, unsatisfactory delivery and, among the causes for these failings, low investment, especially on the part of British Leyland. Low quality had lost them many customers, but still the United Kingdom producers were not able to meet demand in the peak year 1972–3. Lost production will 'inevitably lose sales, since many customers are not willing to wait for a car if other models are readily available. . .lost sales lead inevitably to dealer dissatisfaction', and there are 'severe effects on manufacturing costs'. In an enquiry among a sample of 16,000 buyers in mid-1974 relating to the previous 12 months (no longer a peak period), 30 per cent considering a British car decided not to buy one because of unacceptable delivery dates, whereas this was true of fewer than 10 per cent of those considering a foreign car. In the test period, 62 per cent of foreign cars had delivery dates within a week, but only 40 per cent of British cars, whereas dates of over 6 weeks applied to 30 per cent of British cars and only 10 per cent of foreign. 'Long delivery times rank second only to price as a reason for not buying a particular model.'[39]

In considering the economic strategy that would aid industries like the motor car industry, the official assumption is and always has been that the problem is that of finding a market, for which currency manipulation, subsidies, etc. might be appropriate. But as we have seen, the problem over much of the period was the exact opposite: the inability to supply, at least in the quality and time period demanded. The limitation of the British production capacity was particularly harmful in industries like motor manufacture in which economical runs require much larger annual output numbers than are possessed by any British firm, so that low capacity contributed directly to high costs. Whatever the role played in the sorry British performance by the failings of labour in the motor industry (and as we shall see below, some of them are a consequence of a generation of restrictive practices by the Treasury), a large part of the blame must lie with the unwillingness or inability of the industry to meet its potential market and improve the quality of its product by the kind of investment made in other countries by rival makers.

The myth that it was shortage of demand, rather than inability to expand the supply, that lay at the root of the Britain malaise is exposed in this particular industry by the fortunes of the prestige end of the market, by such as Rolls-Royce, Jaguar and the specialist sports model producers. Throughout the whole of the period, these have had waiting lists, sometimes running into years rather than months,[40] without apparently thinking of increasing their capacity to meet, let alone encourage the demand for, their products. Indeed, among several of them it was a cause for evident pride that their customers had to wait for years — an admission which in other countries might have led to the speedy replacement of the executives concerned. Nor will it do to assert that this rationing was necessary in order to keep the premium of a high and exclusive reputation: the output of Mercedes cars was 409,000 in 1977 and this has not in the least diminished the reputation of that product, but rather the contrary.

Only a small sample of industries has been mentioned here, but deficient investment holding back quantity and quality of output has been common to most, particularly the manufacturing export industries. In steel, 'the main reason for the high import share in most. . . products has been the poor delivery and reliability in the past.'[41] Basically, the 'deficiencies [were] on the supply side'[42] in every single sector.

The problems of these industries do not end with immediate losses of sales, for the effects on markets are cumulative. Once a car buyer has left one model for another, he will not easily return next time, and so the market for British makers is reduced by attrition. Even more fatally, the loss of a reputation, like its gain, is cumulative. The former British reputation for high quality, reliability and technical excellence was an enormous asset which has been squandered like so much else inherited from the past by the policies of the last generation. Today, according to an enquiry among over 2,000 upper-middle-class citizens of five Western European nations, the reputation of British goods was the second worst, only Italy being lower (and Italians were not among those asked), coming below

German, American, Dutch, French and Belgian goods in that order. British products were considered to be expensive and technically out of date and British manufacturers had the reputation of paying little attention to the wishes of their customers and falling behind with their deliveries. The belief that British goods are of high technical quality was held only in Britain.[43]

The callousness on the part of the authorities towards the real problems of British productive industry was in sharp contrast to the constant care and concern which they lavished on trade and finance. There was never any question of harming them in the interest of short-term adjustments, still less would it have been conceivable that currency or trade might have been sacrificed in the interests of the productive industry on which the prosperity of Britain ultimately depended.

Nor was this emphasis accidental. The Treasury works in an atmosphere in which the voice of industry is heard but weakly, while the voice of the banks, particularly the Bank of England, and of the overseas trade 'lobby'[44] reverberates daily around its corridors. As all of them clamoured and pushed for their one-sided and finance-orientated priorities, one is left wondering sometimes if there was anyone there who spoke up for Britain.[45]

The contacts with the Bank were naturally the closest of all. Among the Bank's main functions were the management of the foreign exchanges and the marketing of government securities and, like all other institutions, it viewed its own activities as of quite overriding importance in relation to all others; unlike other institutions, however, it was in a position to get its self-centred views largely accepted. The exact relations between the Treasury and the Bank of England were and are complex and shifting, and depend from time to time on personalities, particularly of those of the Chancellor of the Exchequer and the Governor, and since in recent years their objectives have been so similar, Governors do not now, as they did in some post-war years, air their disagreements in public over the heads of their nominal superiors in the government. However, it is clear that the constitutional authority of the government over the Bank, which is there to fulfil certain technical duties on behalf of the Treasury, has never been fully or even approximately implemented.

It is the Bank and the banking community that has been largely responsible for fixing the absolute constraints within which the Treasury has assumed that it has to work:

Expansion which is bought at the cost of the exchange reserves and the stability of the currency can only harm us in the long run; to 'put sterling second' and go all out for expansion is not a possible policy for Britain.[46]

The harm done 'in the long run' by saving the exchanges at the expense of productive investment appears to have received less powerful advocacy.

The bankers were, of course, pushing against open doors: the Treasury's own immediate interest was also with such matters as balancing the budget, maintaining the external value of sterling, and conducting the affairs of the 'Sterling Area' while monitoring and steering the movements of the so-called sterling balances, the funds held by other countries in London. This constellation of forces, at any rate in such pure form, is almost unique to Britain. Elsewhere, central banks as well as economic policy makers and planners see themselves as responsible for the welfare of the whole of the national economy; if they have any particular interests, then frequently, as in Germany, Italy and Japan for example, they are likely to lie in home productive industry.[47] The danger of mistaking the foreign balance as an overriding policy goal and the currency as a 'kind of national virility symbol'[48] would therefore hardly arise.

In Britain, the tradition was otherwise. Traditionally United Kingdom banks do not generally acknowledge the need to be more integrated with industry.[49] The City and merchant banks have placed their main interest in trade and overseas investment. These are important, but it is bound to lead policy making astray if the special concerns of a narrow section of the economy, refracted by the distorting mirror in which everyone sees his own role in society, are allowed to dictate national priorities. The egocentric views arising therefrom might have appeared amusing in the past. The quotation from the Treasury at the head of the book has raised many a smile, by the sheer ignorant confidence with which the productive activity of the greater part of the nation, the basis of all Britain's prosperity and strength, is dismissed contemptuously as 'taking in each other's washing'.[50] Moreover, there will be little doubt in most people's mind that that one particular official's blinkered attitude, typical for the Treasury at the time, arises essentially because the foreign trade balance happens to be his concern, and industrial production is not. But the tragedy is that there has at no point been a major change of direction in the Treasury obliging it to change its priorities, and the

*'It's like this. You're the dollar, I'm the pound and I'm
looking you in the face'.*

Source: Bernard Hollowood MA, MSC (Econ.) (London) *Times*, 4 January 1978.

same sentiments, no doubt overlaid by Keynesian theory, still hold
sway. Industry has every time to be sacrificed on the altar of the
City's and the financial system's primacy: 'How much this has cost
Britain in terms of lost economic growth it is impossible to say. But it
far outweighs whatever benefit has come from the invisible earnings
which the policy has generated.'[51]

Again, this is not only a highly dubious scale of priorities; it is also
self-defeating. By confusing ends and means, base and superstruc-
ture, grievous damage was done to both. The fortunes of British
industry have never depended on the soundness of the finance
sector; it has always been the other way round. London's original
rise as a financial centre was grounded firmly on the strength of the
British economy as a whole, and the growing industrial power of,
successively, the USA, Germany and Japan, has brought them
financial power and helped to undermine London's premier position. In the end Britain's productive weakness contributed to the
waning power of the City itself, and to its falling net earnings.[52]

Similarly, the benefits of the Sterling Area to a small sector of the
banking community (which therefore become vociferous in its support) look less impressive when measured against the costs of having
to hold additional reserves and suffering exaggerated fluctuations as
a result.[53] The foreign funds, attracted by one of the Treasury's
favourite weapons, high interest rates, may have helped one or other

temporary balance, but they brought with them the obligation to pay large sums every year in interest to foreign holders that had to be earned by real exports first. In the 1950s and 1960s, the reserves always fell and rose faster than the trade balance (leaving out countervailing government action), showing to what extent international speculators added volatility to the British balance — the very thing which financial policy was intended to avoid. And at every step it has to be remembered that because of the ratio of the 'propensity to import', the losses in home output, incomes and investment were always several times as large as the financial disturbance which had made the rectification necessary. In the end, one stronghold after another so dear to the City, including the exchange value of the pound, had to be given up because of the inability of British export industry to produce enough of the right things at acceptable qualities, prices and delivery dates: the primacy of the productive base thus reasserted itself in a negative form.

Perhaps nowhere else is the Treasury's mistaken set of priorities as clear as in the field of foreign investment. The export of British capital in our period at a time when the home economy was starved of new investment, and at a level much higher than in the case of all other comparable countries,[54] is surely one of the most astonishing features of this period. To have banned capital exports altogether was hardly practical, but it need not have been encouraged quite so much in the belief that accumulating funds abroad would help the British economy. In one way, this was part of a vain search for past glories. In the nineteenth century British capital exports emanating from a position of strength were an eminently sensible method on the part of the dominant economy forming the major source of capital in the world for opening up markets and natural resources abroad in regions that were not competitive but complementary. But in the second half of the twentieth century the real drive behind capital exports was essentially the same faulty scale of priorities that informed the rest of macro-economic policy.

The defence of foreign investment was that it must have yielded higher returns than home investment if investors preferred it. In fact the returns were no higher[55] unless they are seen as a flight from the declining pound sterling, thus having a lower risk premium element. Even if they had been, there is all the difference in the world between home investment, improving the productivity of home workers (and if there is unemployed labour, actually setting people to work in Britain) and therefore adding to output at home, and doing the same thing abroad. The loss is the same as the loss arising if a multi-national closes its British branch and opens one abroad — a loss the nature of which is clearly and widely understood; it is the loss of the extra value added, instead of retaining only that small part of it that becomes interest or profit (less tax). Surely the contempt for home production can go no further than to restrict home output and investment in order to create a balance out of which such capital exports to equip potential competitors abroad could be financed.

## 2 Live Now, Pay Later

There is a strongly moralistic element in the Treasury predilection for cuts. It contains an appeal to the bourgeois/Puritan streak in all of us which believes that it is somehow wrong to spend and virtuous to refrain from spending. The barrage of propaganda which has been let loose on the British public in the past thirty years has constantly and habitually contrasted the efforts by an apparently economical Treasury to hold to its good housekeeping with the irresponsible wastefulness of an allegedly spendthrift public. 'We' must spend less, it is proclaimed from every Whitehall rooftop, 'we' must practise restraint now, in order that we may build for the future.

There is also something of the superstition of primitive medicine in that appeal, the notion that a medicine cannot be much good unless it tastes awful; and indeed there is much in common between the pre-scientific medicine of the past and the pre-scientific economics of the present. However that may be, there will surely be much instinctive support for the view on recent cuts expressed by Mr John Grugeon, policy committee chairman of the Association of County Councils: 'Of course we expect the cuts to hurt. If they did not cause any pain, they would not be effective,' or for Sir John Musker's 'It is only by taking unpleasant medicine that there is any likelihood of survival for the United Kingdom.'[56] It is in vain that such as Reginald Maudling complain that it is a

> delusion . . . that there is something inherently wicked about a consumer boom. I must confess that I have never really understood this moral attitude. What is the point of an economy if it is not to provide more goods for consumption? There is no joy or profit in production for its own sake; the only purpose of production is consumption.[57]

The general feeling is that there is something self-indulgent about consumption, and that the moral weakness shown by it will bring its own nemesis, whereas only ultimate good can come from suffering cuts and hardships. Andrew Shonfield had made the acute remark that the British public was willing to suffer rationing and the pretty tyrannies of shopkeepers much longer than citizens of other countries, including those who lost the war, for the sake of some moral comfort and perhaps a feeling of security.[58]

It is the traditional task of the Treasury to cut back the programmes of the spending departments as part of the annual exercise of budgetary planning. Economy in (public) expenditure is therefore its most deeply held conviction, and the typical official has risen within the Department by his skill in enforcing it.[59] It is an easy and natural next step for him to be filled with the conviction that spending is undesirable in principle, and that abstemiousness equates with good housekeeping and will ultimately bring its own reward. The traditional saving of candle-ends at the Treasury itself has now changed, one gathers, into a certain moralistic pride that high officials on whose decisions the livelihood of millions may depend do their work in cramped and out-of-date offices, with inadequate equipment.

Keynes spent a large part of his later years fighting this attitude and showing that a modern national economy is not quite like a household, and that there are occasions when cuts will make things worse for the present and the future, while spending, though it may actually give pleasure, will also turn out to have been economically sensible in the long run. The Treasury was, after the war, allegedly dominated by Keynesian thinking, but it never quite took to that comforting part of the doctrine. Instinctively, it preferred cuts to the freedom to spend, and the Paul Ormerod's bitter comment rings true: that under the Labour government of 1964–9 the 'targets' set varied from time to time between PSBR, money supply or domestic credit expansion, 'seemingly according to which target financial opinion thought would lead to the most restrictive policies'.[60] British devaluations since the war have always been too severe, deflations too savage: 'the chance of screwing a margin of excess capacity, in accordance with a recurrent intellectual fashion, was too tempting for some Treasury officials to resist, whatever the circumstances in which this came about.'[61] It was almost as if they liked inflicting hardship on the British public for the good of their souls.

The same attitude also emerges from the way in which, until fairly recently, national income, trading, financial and similar official statistics were always presented in the most adverse way. Those which appear as approximations in their first version (to be corrected later when more details are available) normally — and one is almost inclined to say systematically — err on the side of presenting a blacker picture than reality warrants, sometimes by quite substantial margins. Again, sterling balance liabilities were always grossly exaggerated, assets as greatly under-valued. The apotheosis of this tendency occurred in the 1960s, when it was discovered that from 1963 to 1969 exports had been systematically under-recorded, and there was thus a substantially better real trading position year by year than appeared from the figures. If we remember that adverse trade balances require very much larger cuts in income to be rectified (that there is a 'multiplier' at work), a part at least of the savage deflation of 1968–9 could be credited to the responsible officials.[62] Of course, what had occurred was a genuine mistake; but it is hard to believe that in the Department's atmosphere a mistake of an opposite tendency, making the balance appear as too rosy, would have been missed for six critical years.

Yet that solid and well established picture of the Treasury as the frugal keeper of our collective purse was false; for while it is indeed the case that in dealing with annual departmental budgets, its role is that of saving the taxpayer's money, in its capacity as the formulator of macro-economic policy, the Treasury acts in exactly the opposite direction. Here it plays the part of the wastrel, the spendthrift and the unregenerate rake, for as we have seen, its standard and systematic method of solving the immediate and 'urgent' problems of the day was to cut investment every time — in other words at the expense of the future. 'Live today, pay tomorrow' — it has been the rake's motto throughout the ages, and it has been the Treasury's gospel for the past thirty years.[63]

Since the end of dynastic government, politicians of all ages in every country have shown a well attested tendency to use the economy freely for their own immediate ends and to raid whatever resources they may find, leaving future generations to bear the costs: after all, they get the benefits now and it is someone else who will have to cope tomorrow.[64] This contrasts with the normal tendency for fathers of families and even boards of joint-stock companies to build for the future, and has always formed one of the most respectable arguments against public ownership. One might have expected the Treasury as the keeper of the nation's continuing fortunes to safeguard the future against this known weakness of politicians: but far from doing so, it has frequently led the move to raid the future for the sake of the present and to meet the current bills out of sums that should have gone to investment.

After thirty years of this rake's progress the bills, inevitably, have come in to be paid. We have found increasingly over the years that in crisis after crisis after crisis we were desperately short of the productive equipment that should have been there to carry us over into a virtuous cycle of higher output, higher exports, higher demand and higher output in turn, but that had been sacrificed to a temporary need some years earlier; and each time the new crisis was solved only by making yet another, even deeper raid into provisions for the future.

The tragedy is that this rake's progress was not confined to the public sector, deplorable though that would have been on its own. Nowadays the Treasury enjoys overriding powers and controls over general demand, employment and investment, and as a result the baneful effects of its disregard for our long-term welfare have been almost as great in the remainder of the economy. On each occasion when the nation has come to the Treasury (with the Bank of England), like a client farmer to his bank, admitting that it could not make ends meet, it has received the same answer: 'Work less and eat up your seedcorn,' and has been given no option but to do just that. And, not surprisingly, after we have been forced to work less and eat up our seedcorn season after season over thirty years, the farm has gradually fallen into decay.

Our major problem has throughout been our inability to produce enough, based on our inability to invest enough, yet 'the only advice ever received from the City, the Bank of England and the Economics Establishment in times of stress was the perverse one to cut production and investment still further.'[65] Nor can it be wondered at that such treatment has over the years demoralised the whole community. In Britain, unlike any other country west of the iron curtain, it has become the unspoken and therefore particularly potent and insidious assumption that shortages are met, not by plans to produce more, but by plans to ensure that people consume less. Thus if houses are in short supply, the reaction is not to build more houses, but merely to restrict the rights of owners, so that before long, still fewer come on the market to let and meanwhile the mobility of labour is reduced;[66] or if there are not enough engineering students, the British reaction is to reduce the size of the staffs, rather than seek ways of attracting more students. Once more, the most dangerous aspect of this is that inevitably the same attitudes have begun to pervade productive industry as well.[67]

The policy, to repeat, is not only mistaken from a national welfare point of view: it is also inherently counter-productive. For frequently the 'savings' secured on capital account are more than balanced by additional running costs, but since the 'savings' may loom large in the public accounts while costs are dispersed elsewhere, our rake is encouraged to indulge himself in his ill-advised career now at the expense of the future.

Out of many examples, two which have recently come prominently before the public must suffice. One relates to London Transport, who were forced to forgo automatic ticketing, at a cost of £90 million, which would bring in £5–10 million a year in additional fares, beside further millions in staff savings: the Chairman of London Transport, admitting the inferiority to the Paris RATP, explained it by the fact that 'over the past 10 years, Paris, a smaller city than London, has invested more than three times as much as London in its public transport.'[68] The other relates to the well known fact that the British failure to invest in technology has saddled the country with very much higher fuel costs per unit of output;[69] at present, in the face of the energy crisis, Britain is 'saving' money by abandoning or curtailing support for building insulation and energy conservation. Although 'our programme is likely to come under increasing scrutiny in both the EEC and the International Energy Agency. . .Conservation is. . .now well down the list of the priorities of. . .[Government] Departments, if it is on their lists at all.'[70]

In addition, there is the perennial problem of railway and telephone costs raised because of investment squeezes and of buildings constructed too shoddily by following government guidelines, and then becoming a constant drain on resources. Council housing, particularly of the high-rise variety, is potential slum property almost from the start in many cases, though 'industrial systems' and prefabricated building are not much better.[71] Among the more spectacular examples, Oak and Elder Gardens in Birkenhead attracted a great deal of nation-wide attention in October 1979. Built in 1958 at a cost of £750,000, no rent had been collected for five years, and £620,000 loan and interest charges were still outstanding. It was estimated that its demolition would cost another £200,000. It was an extreme example of a tale that could, with variants, be told many times over.

Perhaps there should be a technical term introduced to describe the phenomenon: 'Treasury-style saving', to mean savings on capital account which are in a few short years counter-balanced by losses on current account, leaving society with both an inferior asset and higher running costs thereafter.

## 3 The Pontius Pilate Posture

It may be that there is an answer to all this. It may be that the policy makers in the Treasury, the Bank of England and elsewhere are correct in their assumptions that the 'disasters' that have hit us, the 'awful balance of payments, the rapidly worsening competitiveness and profitability of British industry, company failures, deepening import penetration — in a word, de-industrialisation' — that these were 'acts of God'.[72]

That certainly seems to be the assumption of many of those who make or defend official policy. Thus Sir Alec Cairncross, for many years Chief Economic Adviser to the Government, complained:

> Governments are constantly being admonished to go for a policy 'of sustained economic growth' as if it were open to them by some simple set of enactments to raise the rate of economic growth. Nobody is obliging enough to explain how. Is there something that Governments can do to improve output per man-hour in the average factory — something which remains a secret from the employers who stand to gain most from knowing?

> I believe that the direct influence of governments on economic growth is relatively modest and that the common belief to the contrary in this country has been actually pernicious, tempting governments into policies which had the very reverse of the effects for which they were designed. . . We have suffered on the national scale from a 'get-rich-quick' mentality that is still with us.[73]

As if to emphasise his regret at having strayed into the real world of production even for an instant, Sir Alec went on at once to say that all that governments could do was to cause demand to rise, and that would merely produce inflation.

Many even of the critics started with the concept of an 'underlying' real growth rate as a datum, and went on to urge the government to find it and adjust demand to it so as neither to exceed nor undershoot its mark.[74] Similarly, agencies like the NEDC and the National Plan of 1962–5, which appeared outwardly to have been designed to raise that underlying rate, assumed a constellation of factors which allowed at best a marginal increase in it. Again, the 'structuralists', the term applied to the minority of critics who were considering the reform of the real economic structure instead of tinkering with fiscal and financial ratios, were met with the argument that while one might reform the structure, one could not alter attitudes[75] — as if government policy had not had a profound effect on the attitudes of businessmen.

That line of defence may be paraphrased as follows: government has no role or function in the productive sphere of the economy as such. Its task is to set the scene, to provide the best possible conditions by demand management, by a favourable fiscal and financial system and by general legislation, and let business, including nationalised industry, flourish within them. The primary economic tasks of any modern government are 'to regulate demand and to keep the economy in external balance'.[76] Thus the scene may be set — but the play has to be written and acted out by someone else.

This may be a comforting doctrine in the corridors of Whitehall, but it bears no relation to the real world. In the real world, the influence and impact of government on the economy are overwhelming, and they affect all sectors, including those of real production, distribution and exchange. This is so not only in the way in which the overall economic 'steering' impinges on the fortunes of business,[77] but also by direct action on trade, industry, location, technical training, safety regulations, redundancy payments, trade union legislation, the prices of fuel, power and other products of nationalised industries, and a thousand more.[78] 'Our industry today is the creation of a national system over which government exerts as much general control as does a master chef over the creations of his kitchen.'[79] Even that arch-critic of the idea of influential government, Sir Alec Cairncross, had to admit that the government, by 1970, was spending hundreds of millions on investment grants and on other assistance, and was 'in contact with industry on a very wide front': 'The activities of government are themselves part of what we call 'the economy' and. . .it is increasingly difficult to offer useful explanations of the working of the economy without simultaneously trying to explain the working of its management.'[80]

Sir Alec's modified Whitehall view therefore is that the role of government is of overwhelming significance in the economy, but at the same time it cannot be blamed if matters go seriously wrong. This also won't do. The fact is that 'The role of government in the direction and management of the economy [has] become paramount', and

> the onus of proof is surely on those who believe that the frequent checks on output imposed by the balance of payments had no effect on underlying performance. The Brookings Institution had no doubt that 'efficiency of business investment was reduced in a setting when businessmen were uncertain about the future size of their markets because of recurrent squeezes imposed as a result of the balance of payments, and that these forced British business into hand-to-mouth investment policies which perpetuated old and inefficient plant layouts'.[81]

There may be a case, in theory, for saying that the best way to run an economy is for the government to set the scene and provide a framework, leaving productive industry (including perhaps also nationalised concerns) to get on working the system as best they may. There may even be a case for believing that the inherent expansionism of capitalist economies is so strong that if it had been left to its own devices, British industry would have taken off on an expansion path similar to that chosen by all other comparable countries. But the fact is that the British government was at no point neutral as regards production, and it did at no point limit itself to setting the scene. On the contrary, far from keeping industry at arm's length, the government has repeatedly, deliberately and directly acted on it, above all by enforcing cuts in its investment programmes and thus making its relative stagnation and competitive decline inevitable.

These actions were carried out largely within the framework of Keynesian macro-economics, and it is true that Keynes himself was largely interested in short-term problems and virtually ignored growth.[82] Investment for him was largely a matter of balancing savings within the national income accounts. However, it has been possible for Harrod-Domar and other theorists to develop out of that framework a body of doctrine to describe long-term economic expansion. Investment is there seen as a delicate mechanism which equates the surplus as the potential capital supply with growth potential and future production plans based on it. The investment flow is like a gland in the human body, and a disturbance of this function will have damaging repercussions quite out of proportion to the impulse that triggered it off. In consequence, economic theory in this field demands the most careful and sensitive monitoring and stabilisation of those key ratios. What the investment ratio received at the hands of the government, however, was a repeated brutal battering with total unconcern for the finely tuned relationships involved and for the immediate costs and the long-run damage that were bound to arise. Real investment has been used as a regulator for the temporary balances of purely symbolic quantities, an expendable item in the national accounts: 'Whenever the Government has faced an economic emergency since the war, it has reached out, like a blind man with a single automatic gesture at his command, and taken a smack at investment.'[83]

It need hardly be added that at no time did the government make up for the damage it did to industrial investment by a high rate of investment on its own account: indeed, the infrastructure for which it is responsible was usually the first victim of the cuts. Nor has it contributed much to savings, as was the case in Scandinavia or Germany, for example,[84] where an egalitarian tax policy reduced the number of private fortunes out of which savings might be expected. The British government's small positive account in the early years of our period has recently turned into deficit, mopping up the savings originating in other sectors of the economy for plugging temporary holes.

It cannot therefore be argued that the government bears no responsibility for the failings of the productive sector, and that it is correct in excluding it from its range of policy options. In reality, far from being neutral, the government was vitally and repeatedly concerned with it, even if only for the purpose of doing it grievous damage.

There is a final defence possible. It is that, good or bad, government influence on the decisions, calculations and attitudes of businessmen on whom decisions to invest must depend is insignificant, so that any ill effects, if they did arise, were bound to be negligible. It is an attractive idea: all these speeches by the Chancellors, all these highly paid civil servants, economists and City editors, these bank chairmen and IMF experts, passing legislation, writing regulations, planning, debating, explaining the many facets of their economic policies, for cutting back this or steering that — all this in vain and to no effect? Was it all but shadow boxing? Should we then sack all the macro-economic policy makers, and return to a Victorian Treasury in which the only thing worthy of consideration is to find enough taxes to pay for government expenditure? The prospect may be pleasing, but we have to conclude regretfully that the Treasury cannot be exonerated on the grounds that its actions have no significant effect: Britain is littered with the very real derelict victims of its policies.

Giving the Treasury the job of setting the scene in the belief that only when they get it right can business flourish and take off is rather like an attempt to learn to ride a bicycle by first learning to balance on it while stationary, and only then daring to ride it forward. As in the case of the bicycle, the actions taken by the Treasury to get things right, to get balances balanced and the currency rectified, included precisely those measures which made it impossible for the vehicle to move at all.

## Notes

1. Even when cutting investment, they have attempted from time to time, and not too successfully, to protect at least certain priority sectors of manufacturing. Cf. R.C.O. Matthews, 'The Role of Demand Management' in Sir Alec Cairncross (ed.), *Britain's Economic Prospects Reconsidered* (1971), p. 18.

2. Even the DEA's *National Plan* of 1965 began with the statement that 'an essential of the Plan is a solution to Britain's balance of payments problem: for growth cannot be maintained unless we pay our way in the world' (p. 1).

3. Samuel Brittan, *Steering the Economy: the Role of the Treasury* (1969), pp. 226–7.

4. 'Introduction', pp. 13, 16, Roger Opie, 'Economic Planning and Growth', pp. 171–2, both in W. Beckerman (ed.), *The Labour Government's Economic Record: 1964–70* (1972).

5. 'The Role of Demand Management', pp. 17–18. 'There have always been at least as many good reasons produced on the Left as on the Right for cutting investment first in any emergency,' as Andrew Shonfield commented in *British Economic Policy since the War* (1958), pp. 244–5.

6. 'Muddling Through: the Economy 1951–1964', in Vernon Bogdanor and Robert Skidelsky, *The Age of Affluence 1951–1964* (1970), p. 139.

7. See the quotation at the head of the book, by Balogh; Brittan, who was a more consistent critic in the early 1960s, would even in 1969 'still put growth and a high level of employment and economic activity above any numerical ratios such as exchange ratios and price increases', *Steering the Economy*, p. xvii.

8. Opie, 'Economic Planning and Growth', p. 56.

9. E.g. Letters in *The Times* by R.W. Wild, 13 October 1977, Derek Gaulter, 29 January 1980, G.T. Bodkin, 5 February 1980, and report on speech by Peter Galliford, *The Times*, 12 April 1978. See also footnote 26 below.

10. *The Times*, 17 July 1976, 29 February 1980, 19 March 1977.

11. Quoted in Opie, 'Economic Planning and Growth', p. 58.

12. E.g. J.-P. Mockers, *Croissances économiques comparées: Allemagne, France, Royaume-Uni 1950–1967* (1969), pp. 117 and *passim*; also D.H. Aldcroft,

*The European Economy 1914–1970* (1978), pp. 195–7; PEP, *Growth in the British Economy* (1960), pp. 124, 201, 210.

13. Geoffrey Denton, Murray Forsyth and Malcolm MacLennan, *Economic Planning and Policies in Britain, France and Germany* (1968), p. 82.

14. J. Carrington and G. Edwards, *Financing Industrial Investment* (1978), p. 210.

15. *Financial Times*, 9 April 1981; *Frankfurter Allgemeine Zeitung*, 4 and 24 April 1981.

16. E.g. Paul Streeten, 'The Objectives of Economic Policy' in P.D. Henderson (ed.), *Economic Growth in Britain* (1966), pp. 29–53; Sir Alec Cairncross, *Essays in Economic Management* (1971), pp. 84–5; Richard N. Cooper, 'The Balance of Payments' in Richard E. Caves and Associates, *Britain's Economic Prospects* (1968), p. 147.

17. See Chapter 7, section 1, below.

18. R. Lubitz, 'Export-led Growth in Industrial Economies', *Kyklos*, no. 27 (1973).

19. E.g. Paul Johnson, 'Are Socialists interested in *creating* wealth?', *Daily Telegraph*, 1 October 1979.

20. E.g. Denton, Forsyth and MacLennan, *Economic Planning*, pp. 73–4, 343.

21. 'Few countries', Hubert Henderson had written optimistically in 1943, 'would be willing in future to make the volume of their internal purchasing power depend on the magnitude of their gold reserve' (*The Inter-War Years*, (1955) p. 291).

22. *British Economic Policy*, pp. 41, 42, 48.

23. 'Frustration for Shipbuilders', *The Economist*, 27 December 1952.

24. News items, 4 October 1978, 16 May 1979.

25. *Lloyd's Register of Shipping*.

26. Letter by Mr Jamie Stevenson of the National Federation of Building Trades Employers in *The Times*, 10 January 1980. Mr Stevenson had been alerted by a report that 'capital projects are [the] next likely targets for public spending cuts. . .it seems likely that the government's desperate search for more savings will lead it to cut investment programmes in the time-honoured fashion.'

27. Letter by Ray Moxley, Chairman, Association of Consultant Architects, *The Times*, 14 March 1977.

28. M.D. Steuer, R.J. Ball and J.R. Eaton, 'The Effect of Waiting Times on Foreign Orders for Machine Tools', *Economica*, new series, no. 33 (1966), pp. 387, 395 and 397.

29. It has been found that even in the case of metals and materials that can be standardised, prices alone do not account for successful exports: large price differences between markets can continue for many years on end. I.B. Kravis and R.E. Lipsey, *Comparative Prices of Non-Ferrous Metals* (1966), pp. 32 and 40, and 'Export Prices and the Transmission of Inflation', *American Economic Review*, Supplement 67 (1977), pp. 156–7; I.B. Kravis, R.E. Lipsey and P.J. Bourque, *Measuring International Price Competitiveness* (New York, 1964), pp. 16, 17 and 25; D.K. Stout, NEDO, *International Price Competition, Non-Price Factors and Export Performance* (1977).

30. *The Times*, 22 May 1975.

31. Report in *The Times*, 24 January 1980.

32. On the Chinese rolling mills contract as an example, *Welt am Sonntag*, 15 October 1978; on supplying high-technology Cern machines, *Times Higher Education Supplement*, 9 May 1980; on Laker, news item, 27 September 1978.

33. For an amusing example, at a time of mass unemployment, see the letter 'Who buys a foreign razor blade?' by Peter W. Wood, *The Times*, 5 March 1980.

34. See especially Figures 1.2 and 1.3.

35. Entirely typical is the report of the introduction of the Chrysler Sunbeam car, made at Linwood, into the German market. It was the cheapest available, conceded

the experts, but it was five years behind the times. The greatest problems would be the low-quality finish and the unreliable delivery which one had come to expect from British cars. *Frankfurter Allgemeine Zeitung,* 10 January 1979.

36. Report in *Stern,* 11 April 1979, from the *TÜV Auto-Report 1979.* Also report, 'Design Chief slams BL', *Observer,* 13 January 1980.

37. Krish Bhaskar, *The Future of the UK Motor Industry* (1979), p. 144.,

38. Ibid., pp. 5, 63, 85.

39. Central Policy Review Staff, *The Future of the British Car Industry* (1975), esp. pp. v and 94–6.

40. In 1980, a time of massive unemployment and heavy losses  by British Leyland, delivery time for the Land-Rover was 14–17 months. 'BL's inability to find the funds necessary to increase production at a time when it had a virtual monopoly of world-wide "four-by-four". . .vehicles, had never ceased to amaze its competitors. More than one had likened it to. . .a "licence to print money".' Toyota's Landcruiser, it has been stated, would not have been launched but for this continually unfilled demand for Land-Rovers. Bancroft Clark, letter in *The Times,* 2 April 1980; W.R.M. Michel, *The Times,* 15 December 1980; report in *The Times,* 8 December 1980.

41. D.V. Atterton, Chairman, NEDO Steel Working Party, letter to *The Times,* 21 April 1980.

42. Ajit Singh, 'U.K. Industry and the World Economy: a Case of De-industrialisation?' *Cambridge Journal of Economics,* no. 1 (1977), p. 131.

43. News item, 8 June 1979, reporting on an enquiry by Market and Opinion Research International.

44. Opie, 'Making of Economic Policy', p. 63.

45. If the memoirs are to be believed, it was usually left to the non-expert politicians to urge some consideration of the British population in policy discussions — but such retrospective writings are not always reliable. Mr Maudling's 'There is no virtue in unemployment. It must be a sign of mismanagement if hundreds of thousands of able bodied men and women seeking work can find no use for their talent or their labour' (letter in *The Times,* 22 January 1977) recalls the qualms of Winston Churchill on returning to gold in 1925.

46. Sir Oliver Franks, Chairman's report to Lloyds Bank, 1961.

47. Carrington and Edwards, *Financing Industrial Investment,* pp. 149–51.

48. Michael Stewart, *The Jekyll and Hyde Years* (1977), p. 27.

49. Carrington and Edwards, *Financing Industrial Investment,* p. 151.

50. For the inter-war years as a whole, see S. Pollard, 'Introduction' to *The Gold Standard and Employment Policies between the Wars* (1970).

51. C. Gordon Tether, *Observer,* 17 October 1976.

52. J.R. Sargent, 'U.K. Performance in Services' in F. Blackaby (ed.), *De-industrialisation* (1979), p. 104.

53. E.g. Richard N. Cooper, in Caves, *Britain's Economic Prospects,* pp. 153, 181 and *passim.*

54. Table 3.1 above. Also Ann D. Morgan, 'Foreign Manufacturing by U.K. Firms' in Blackaby, *De-industrialisation,* and Stuart Holland, ibid., p. 95.

55. W.B. Reddaway, *Effects of U.K. Direct Investment Overseas, Final Report* (1968), esp. Chapter 17; Cooper, 'Balance of Payments', pp. 175–6.

56. Report in the *Guardian,* 2 October 1979: 'Tory MP rebels over council cuts'; letter to *The Times,* 3 March 1980.

57. *The Times,* 31 May 1978.

58. *British Economic Policy,* p. 30.

59. Hugh Heclo and Aaron Wildavsky, *The Private Government of Public Money* (1974).

60. 'The Economic Record' in Nick Bosanquet and Peter Townsend, *Labour and Equality. A Fabian Study of Labour in Power 1974–79* (1980), p. 61.

61. Brittan, *Steering*, p. 160.

62. See accounts, e.g. in W. Beckerman (ed.) *The Labour Government's Economic Record: 1964–70* (1972), p. 24; Cairncross, *Essays*, p. 57; Shonfield, *British Economic Policy*, p. 268.

63. Curiously enough, foreign central bankers thought of Britain's borrowings to tide over temporary unbalances as 'a rake's progress at someone else's expense', S. Brittan, *The Treasury Under the Tories 1951–1964* (1964), p. 63.

64. Michael Pinto-Duschinsky has called this the policy of 'bread and circuses': 'the sacrifice of policies desirable for a long-term well-being of a country in favour of over-lenient measures and temporary palliatives bringing in immediate political return' (in Bogdanor and Skidelsky, *The Age of Affluence*, p. 59).

65. Letter in *The Times*, 14 January 1975.

66. There are some who delight in this result: 'It would now be generally agreed', wrote David Webster, 'that the death of the private rented [housing] sector is to be welcomed and that long-term policy need not include provision for it' (Bosanquet and Townsend, *Labour and Equality*, p. 250).

67. See Chapter 5, section 1, below.

68. *The Times*, 26 February 1980; letter by Ralph Bennett in *The Times*, 13 March 1980; Anthony Sampson, 'Dotty decay of the London Tube', *Observer*, 6 April 1980.

69. E.g. Colin Clark, *Growthmanship* (1964), p. 147.

70. Confidential Civil Service document quoted in *Observer*, 30 March 1980.

71. E.g. *Guardian*, 20 and 29 August 1979; *New Civil Engineering*, 5 July 1977; *The Times*, 4 and 31 July 1980.

72. Bryan Gould, 'Bankers' Blight on Industry', *Guardian*, 10 October 1979.

73. 'Economic Growth', *Economics*, no. 9 (1971–2), p. 149, and *Essays in Economic Management*, p. 21.

74. E.g. W.A.H. Godley and J.R. Shepherd, 'Long-term Growth and Short-term Policy', *National Institute Economic Review*, no. 29 (1964), pp. 26–30; P.D. Henderson, 'Introduction' in *Economic Growth in Britain* (1966), pp. 18–19.

75. Brittan, *Steering*, p. 250.

76. Ibid., p. 319.

77. E.g. J.C.R. Dow, *The Management of the British Economy 1945–60* (1965).

78. There is now a very large literature, and it is the standard assumption of every textbook. E.g. J.W. Grove, *Government and Industry in Britain* (1962); C.T. Sandford, M.S. Bradbury and Associates, *Case Studies in Economics: Economic Policy* (1977), Ch. 5; Geoffrey K. Fry, *The Growth of Government (1980)*.

79. Sir Alan Cottrell, *The Undermining of British Industry* (1979), p. 4.

80. *Essays in Economic Management*, pp. 18, 33.

81. Peter Calvocoressi, *The British Experience 1945–75* (1978), p. 105; Brittan, *Steering*, p. 269.

82. Walter Eltis, 'The Failure of the Keynesian Conventional Wisdom', *Lloyds Bank Review* no. 122 (October 1976), pp. 14–16.

83. Shonfield, *British Economic Policy*, p. 49.

84. Mockers, *Croissances économiques comparées*, pp. 142–4.

# 5   THE LEARNING PROCESS

## 1  Businessmen

The last chapter referred several times to the cumulative effect of repeated experiences, in this case the repetition of restrictive economic phases. Such recurrences will teach people to anticipate and bring into their calculations what at first they thought to be random and unexpected, and they may thus be said to be undergoing a learning process. This is part of a more general pattern of behaviour which distinguishes human sciences from physical sciences and mars so many econometric studies which assume the constancy of ratios that change with repetition. Further, once behaviour has come to be transformed by the new expectations, it becomes a factor in its own right and affects other variables: what began as a consequence turns into a cause.

Seen in this light, it is not entirely surprising that the repeated restriction phases should have changed in a fundamental way the attitudes of businessmen, particularly of those who make decisions on investment and other long-term plans. In a predominantly capitalist economy decision-making must rest on the hope for future profit; nationalised industry also bases its decisions on its view of the future. Technical efficiency is the result of a mass of such decisions, and while at the beginning of our period Britain was in this respect ahead of most other countries mentioned in this book, British enterprise and willingness to innovate were distinctly inferior towards its end. In the interim there had occurred a sharp deterioration in British entrepreneurship. Many would, indeed, see here the main cause of the relative decline of the British economy.

The notion that the bustling, competitive cut-throat world of British business lacks enterprise might seem far-fetched at first sight. We know that in some areas, like banking, insurance and international finance, the British have fully held their own in international competition. Given half a chance at every 'go' phase, there was no lack of enterprise in making the most of the market opportunities: even in the last boom of 1971–2 there was plenty of risk-taking and initiative in such activities as speculation in London properties and real estate.[1] Where enterprise was conspicuously lacking was in the productive sector. There it had been corroded in thirty years of discouragement.

Industrial investment in new plant and machinery nowadays involves preparation and planning years ahead and then committing large sums in the expectation of a long-term profitable market. What Treasury policy did was to undermine precisely these kinds of expectation and 'the public appears gradually to have adjusted its expectations to a continuation of perpetual squeeze and perpetual inflation.'[2]

Official discouragement used the worst possible method: not only did it inhibit the expectations of an expanding market, such as had generated the rising output in other countries, but it did so in unpredictable fits and starts in an atmosphere of uncertainty. Moreover, given the normal lag within which capital formation programmes can be changed or halted, spending had to go on as the market was being squeezed away, so that the new plant became uneconomic at the date of its opening; by the same lag, the cancellation of future plans came into operation just as the imminent upturn of the economy would have required greater capacity. Consumer durables, and above all the motor industry, were hit particularly hard by the frequent changes in hire-purchase regulations, in purchase tax and VAT, which wrecked all their expansion plans in the most damaging manner;[3] but the panic lurches of Treasury policy were bound to damage business in all sectors by spreading uncertainty about future markets.

After a number of such cycles, managers will have learnt their lesson:

> Private industry will not invest, even if money is poured into its pockets, for it knows by bitter experience that long before any new capacity is at work, the Treasury will have engineered another 'stop' period, so that it has been quite rational for people with money to invest to put it into assets in Brussels or Hamburg, or in property speculation at home, rather than into productive plant.

Quite apart from the fluctuations, the overall effect was bound to be depressing.

Memories of these payments crises exerted a pessimistic influence on expectations even in the upward phases. For in laying down new plant businessmen were very well aware that whatever politicians said the growth of the British market was likely to be slow. Frequent short-term investment restraints imposed by the British Government tended to limit investment demand as well as investment supply.

[In] capital goods subject to import competition, an NEDC study came to the conclusion that 'industry's willingness to undertake investment sufficient to avoid recurrent capital shortages would depend heavily on confidence being established that future growth would be a reasonably steady process'. . . An experiment in raising expectations is doomed from the start if businessmen do not believe that the Government will allow demand to rise by anything like the projected rate, for balance of payments reasons.

For this reason the disappointment over the National Plan of 1965, drawn up and sponsored with such enthusiasm by a senior Cabinet Minister, George Brown, but scrapped unceremoniously at the first sign of balance of payments trouble, was particularly destructive: 'the burnt child avoids the fire.'[4] 'The recent suspension of the "National Plan" for external balance of payments reasons will have been a fatal blow to confidence for a number of years.' Moreover:

[When] immediate and overwhelming exigencies have enforced discouragement, there is a danger that the measures calculated to restrain investment, partly intentionally and partly unintentionally, will have been relaxed too late so that natural momentum — so slow in getting built up in the first place — will carry the discouragement deeper in degree and further in time than is intended by the authorities. The planning of investment is a lengthy process. And businessmen's spirits, remarkably resilient though they have shown themselves, cannot just be turned on and off at will.[5]

While the rewards for enterprise to modernise or expand industry were thus continuously hit on the head,[6] curiously enough the penalties for failure to invest were continuously kept down by maintaining a generally buoyant and inflationary market framework, and by encouraging consumption in the 'go' phases. Thus the typical reaction to a labour scarcity was a price rise rather than labour-saving devices, and the typical reaction to deflation was a cut in output rather than an effort to seek new markets:[7] these were the exact opposite of the reactions to French 'indicative planning'. It has been a ' "reverse-carrot-and-stick" policy. Stick for the winners and carrots for the losers.'[8]

The cumulative effect of these disappointed hopes was to ensure that, other things being equal, British business would require a higher expected rate of profit before it would sanction a planned investment, in order to compensate for the years of non-full capacity working engineered by the government.[9] In these circumstances, the drastic decline of the British profit rate between 1950 and the late 1970s,[10] matched as it was by a higher rate of capital consumption,[11] was particularly devastating.

Long periods of stagnation have a depressing effect on others besides business executives. Engineers, for example, can learn and keep up to date only by being given ever more ambitious tasks to do, design offices need expanding plans to let their imaginations roam. The very atmosphere in an expanding concern is worlds apart from a stagnating one, in job satisfaction as well as in achievement. Without growth expectations even accountants will make calculations to exaggerate the risks and diminish the hopes of new ventures. The market will come to expect no change, and its resulting sluggishness will make this into a self-fulfilling prophecy. The most active spirits, those who propel a society forward and are never adequately compensated for what they contribute, will atrophy — or they will join the brain drain.

> People respond to the stimulus of economic growth. There is a profound contrast in spirit between a country which is going places and one which is stuck, a company which is expanding and one which is standing still, an industry which is exploiting the frontiers of technology and one which is routinely administering a technology fully developed a hundred years ago. The one is exciting and worthwhile, the other is dull and listless. The one brings out and develops the human character and enables the most unexpected people to make a contribution, the other turns us all into cows who eat and breed and die.[12]

The point to be stressed throughout is the cumulative effect, the learning process. While business responded to market opportunities in the 1940s and early 1950s with a burst of investment that was almost comparable with European rates, the response of the 1960s, though higher in absolute terms, was much less adequate in relation to needs, and in the 1970s the fall was even more marked. Business had begun to adjust to a low-growth, low-investment economy. It had learned that initiative and innovation would be punished, and sitting still would be rewarded. It had learned to expect sudden lurches in policy, sudden increases in the costs of capital and the sudden wrecking of markets, particularly in capital goods and in consumer goods requiring credit or having a price-elastic demand. Those who opted for investment knew that they would be singled out for punishment next time there was a restriction, and that it would never be very long between one such period and another.

How can one blame businessmen for their response? How can one speak of a 'strike by capital', a phrase made familiar by Jack Jones of the Transport and General Workers' Union, in those conditions? The fact is that businessmen's reactions were the cumulative result of thirty years' battering. They acted sensibly, logically and rationally in the conditions provided for them. In holding back investment, innovation and enterprise they not only did what the government expected them to do; they did what the government expressly wanted them to do — even though it may well be that the government was quite ignorant of the long-term consequences of the policies which it forced on the business community and on the productive industry of Britain.

## 2  Labour and the Trade Unions

In their long history British trade unions have contributed to the raising of the incomes of their members and of other workers, they have brought order into a chaotic labour market, and by insisting on reasonable conditions they have helped to civilise and humanise life at work. They became a model to many other countries by the steady common-sense methods, tempered by militancy, courage and self-sacrifice when the occasion demanded, by which they achieved their gains.

All that lies in the past. In recent years they have had to be counted among the most irresponsible and destructive unions in Europe, and they have had a material share of the responsibility for keeping down the incomes of their members and other workers, for increasing unemployment, and for barbarising industrial relations and with them the quality of life at work. It is worthwhile to trace out in some detail how this remarkable transformation has come about.

British unions have probably always been more resistant than others to technological innovation, and the memories of the unemployment of the 1930s seem to have remained more alive for them, possibly because there were fewer intervening experiences to shatter them. Immediately after the war, it is true, they were willing to co-operate officially in the productivity campaigns, even though with some misgivings,[13] but that enthusiasm has long since waned. In the motor industry,

> managers in the three multinational firms operating in Britain generally expect that continental plants will have a lead of up to three years on British plants in introducing sophisticated new equipment to raise productivity, simply because of the problems of gaining acceptance of new manning levels and work practices in Britain.[14]

Three years is a long time in the life of a car, and that resistance alone cost the British car worker a large proportion of his wage. British trade unionists are frequently willing to lose income and jobs rather than accept new technology: the resistance of dockers to barge containers, which drove the trade to Holland, is a well known example, but others, like the closure of the Goodyear Tyre plant with 700 jobs for similar reasons,[15] are not hard to find: 'The latest TUC document, "Employment and Technology" presents technology as a kind of capitalist ramp, or malignant disease, to be inoculated against and quarantined.'[16]

Even if the trade unions accept the new technology, they will often do so only after bitter struggles, at great loss to themselves and their firms. Any innovation, like British Rail's Advanced Passenger Train, becomes a sitting target for pace-making claims while its progress is held up literally for many years.[17] Alternatively unions will claim the whole or practically so of the resulting increase in productivity even though it was entirely due to the new piece of capital equipment, as in the case of the Llanwern No. 3 Blast Furnace, where the dispute lasted a year, or in the *Times* strike, also of a year's duration. In the case of the Hunterston deep-water port, built at a cost to the British Steel Corporation £100 million of its limited capital funds, a demarcation dispute between two unions led to months of heartbreaking and costly standstill, and threatened the very survival of the Shotton Steel Works.[18] Such demarcation squabbles are not entirely unknown elsewhere, but what is unique in Britain is the equanimity with which trade unions view the loss of output and potential earnings from them.

There is, in fact, a tradition in Britain that it is part of the trade union's task to reduce the output rate of their members, in direct conflict with the employer who wants to maximise it.[19] This attitude, which would strike most foreign trade unionists as absurd,[20] is sometimes rationalised by the expectation that limitation of output would lead to more overtime at higher rates. Americans and Continentals prefer to make the same money by working properly for shorter hours.

Behind the British tradition there sometimes lies the belief fostered by ideology that under capitalism workers are 'alienated' from their work which until the day of revolution can only be pure drudgery. But in fact, as for example National Opinion Polls showed in 1978, many workers, particularly in skilled and white-collar occupations, enjoy their work, are proud of their skills and are aware of their own importance within their firm or department. This pride and awareness is part of their humanity, and to drill it into them that they are merely being exploited and that their work is basically meaningless does immense and immeasurable damage to their psyche. To a visitor, at least, one of the most striking outward differences between workers in other advanced countries and in Britain is the self-assurance and self-respect of the former compared with the social inferiority complex of the British worker — though, to be sure, there are numerous exceptions of those who successfully defy the prevailing doctrine. The comparative reluctance of the British worker to acquire any theoretical knowledge regarding his job[21] is another aspect of the same tradition.

Since the war, the tenets of American 'business trade unionism' have been widely accepted in most other advanced countries where unions start with the assumption that they cannot prosper unless their employer prospers first: their wage negotiations are almost automatically linked to productivity negotiations. In Britain, it is true, the shop-floor workers, if not always their leaders,[22] will abstain from damaging their firm after they have battered it within an inch of its life, as in the case of British Leyland in the winter of 1979–80, but they will resume battering it again as soon as it shows signs of life[23] instead of, as abroad, making sure that the firm can afford large wage payments, and then obtaining them. There are obvious risks in this brinkmanship policy and little experience so far in the fine tuning required. Altogether these attitudes do large, if immeasurable, damage both to national prosperity and to the real wage level in Britain.

British trade unions, it is nowadays widely asserted, are too powerful for the good of the economy, and public opinion polls show that the view is even held by very large numbers of trade unionists.[24] This view is borne out by the need for an incomes policy which would not arise if trade union power were counter-balanced by the power of employers. Even then, some trade unions were strong enough to bulldoze down incomes policy by sham 'productivity deals' which further widened the gap between the powerfully unionised trades and the rest.

Exactly when union power became 'too great' it is difficult to say. British wages have for many decades now been higher as a proportion of national income than those of other countries.[25] There is obviously a point beyond which, given that wage earners do not save much, wage increases will kill off the goose that lays the golden eggs. The point had been reached around 1969 if not earlier, when wage increases vastly began to exceed price increases and thus both accelerated a cost-push inflation and drove profits towards zero.[26] By that time the gap between the wages of strongly unionised labour and the rest had also been widened,[27] and there were therefore no further distributional gains the unions could make for themselves at the expense of other classes. They could therefore no longer determine their real wages, but merely the rate of inflation. At the same time output and productivity were held down by an interplay of trade union and Treasury action — the one causing unbalances by excessive wage gains which were 'solved' by the other by cutting employment and investment — so that the scene was set for the confrontational strikes of the 1970s.

These modern strikes are very unlike the strikes of trade union tradition. The latter attempted to apply force to the actual employer, sometimes by striking against a single firm, the remainder of the members at work providing strike pay for the limited numbers of men out. In the modern strike, the attack is not so much on the employer as on third parties, and preferably on the community in general. Its origins have to be sought in the nationalised industries where in the last analysis the government is the employer and frequently, as in the case of the steel strike of 1980, has itself forced the union to attack the national economy. The issue is clearest in Civil

Service strikes, as in that of the spring of 1981: the government's hand is to be forced by inconveniencing, *inter alia*, the travelling public at ports and airports. The logic behind such strikes is that trade unionists can be counted on to be sufficiently ruthless not to care how much damage they do to the rest of the community (also mostly consisting of trade unionists and their families), whereas there would exist a public authority with enough sense of responsibility to find the damage done to substantial parts of the nation intolerable, and supply the means to give in to the union demand. Clearly, if strikers had as much social conscience as the public authority, the blackmail effect of such strikes could not operate.

A neat case study was provided by the Sheffield bus strike in the winter of 1977–8. Here the crews struck for only one day every week — but kept the actual day secret until the last minute. Since it could make no difference to the employer, the South Yorkshire Transport Authority, whether the strike day was announced beforehand or not, the people intended to be hit were the early shifts of workers, mostly also trade unionists, and mostly the poorer group among them using public transport. The logic must have been the hope that the public authority could not stand by and see the hardships inflicted by one group of trade unionists on another continue indefinitely.

Possibly the classic strike of this nature was the steel strike of 1980. Confused as it was from the beginning by trade union opposition to the large-scale redundancies (over 50,000 jobs) foreshadowed at about the time the wage dispute began, there was no doubt that the nominal employer, the British Steel Corporation, hardly came into the issue: the strike was directed at the government. Hence instead of isolating the BSC, by supporting the private steel producers with whom there was no dispute and possibly levying the men at work to maintain the rest, as well as encouraging imports, the strategy was from the beginning to stop *all* steel production and sale, including that of the competitors of the BSC, and to damage as many people as possible who were not concerned and had no means of influencing a settlement, such as the engineering firms that had not yet recovered from their own strike some months earlier, and the food canning industry. As Mr Williams Sirs, General Secretary to the steel workers' union, said at the outset, the objective was 'a short, sharp strike intended to cripple British industry and achieve its aims within days', and Mr Edward Thorne, secretary of the South Yorkshire strike committee, explained: 'Our objective right from the beginning has been to shut all engineering industry down in this country.' The early failure to do this brought other unions into play. Thus Mr Moss Evans, Secretary of the largest trade union in the country, the Transport and General Workers' Union:

> the best strategy is to look at B.S.C.'s biggest customers and ask how it is possible to continue at 100 per cent levels when no steel has been produced for nine weeks. The intention will be to have pickets at those companies in order to prevent production.[28]

In these circumstances, it is difficult to quarrel with Mr Jo Grimond's view that 'Strikes are now aimed not by down-trodden workers against wicked employers but by reasonably well-off interest groups against the public. The mentality behind them is the same as that behind kidnappings.' To which Charles K. Rowley added: 'The terms "extortion" refers to such an act of obtaining payments in return for not imposing harmful effects on other citizens.'[29]

Perhaps what is most remarkable about this development is that at times it is supported even by some of the victims.[30] In the steel strike, for example, the miners stood to lose in three ways: (a) as taxpayers if the wage increase were to come out of higher subsidies; (b) if it were to be met by higher prices, the closure of more steelworks would also lead to the loss of many miners' jobs; and (c) at the least, the miners' next pay claim would have to be pitched that much higher to keep up with the steelmen's gain. Yet there were many miners ready to join in the violence of mass picketing for a cause that could only do them harm.[31] Similarly, the TUC gave its support to the civil servants' disruption campaign in April 1981 even though it was clear that their claim for 15 per cent would either come out of the pockets of workers who were by then settling for far less, or would, in the circumstances of existing Treasury policy, lead to further unemployment among those less sheltered than the civil servants themselves.

The cost of these strikes are frequently calculated on the limited basis of losses to the strikers themselves: in those terms it is generally asserted that if a strike lasts less than three weeks, as most of them do, the strikers will recoup their loss in wages within the year for which the settlement will run and will register a 'gain' overall. But this omits the loss of wages of other workers laid off which must be included if the cost/benefit analysis is extended to the working class as a whole. It further omits the losses suffered by firms which affect their ability to pay wages in the future: in these terms the engineering

strike of 1979 was calculated to have cost £2,000 million in lost production, or over £100 for every family in Britain, the Vauxhall strike
£120 million, and the steel strike of 1980 some £200 million.[32] The
quaintly named TUC 'Day of Action' on 14 May 1980 was set to cost
£315 million in lost output, or £15 for every family in the land.[33]
Beyond these are the losses of orders and markets for the future, as
well as delayed bankruptcies originating in the dispute and delays in
investment: thus BL are forced to freeze investment expenditure
whenever a strike deprives them of cash.[34] What is frightening is that
not only do these calculations not enter into the decision when a
strike is called, but they are omitted when unions count the cost of
their militancy afterwards. Most steelworkers, for example, have
been left unaware by their unions of how their wages will suffer and
how many jobs will go as a result of the likely loss of 1.5 million
tonnes of orders in 1980 because of their strike, and when the effects
are brought home to them they may well be tempted to react in the
usual manner — by yet more strikes.

Official statistics show that the incidence of strikes as measured by
numbers of working days lost was no greater in Britain than elsewhere, at least before 1979.[35] However, this not only omits short,
unofficial strikes in which British workers specialise,[36] but is also
misleading as to the costs. For there is all the difference in the world
between, say an American auto workers' strike called fairly rou-
tinely at the time of the re-signing of the contract, once in three
years, in which the whole labour force is out, but the factories are
closed and incur no costs, and the British statistics, in which the same
numbers of days lost are made up by a constant drain of unexpected
interruptions, each of which affects the output of a multiple of the
people actually in dispute. Thus for the motor industry, it was found
that two-thirds of the lower production of British plants compared
with Continental plants were due to labour disputes of that kind. On
any given day in 1973, 15 of Chrysler's (UK) suppliers were on strike.
In BL, during the 33 months in which Mr Derek Robinson held
office as convenor, there were 523 disputes — only 4 per cent of
days being free of them, and the company lost 62,000 cars and
113,000 engines.[37] In the nature of things, the overall losses as they
finally affect the real wages of British workers cannot be calculated,
but are substantial.[38]

There was damage also to the image and the ideals for which trade
unionism has stood in the past. In recent years trade unions have
acquired unparalleled power in the state: they have toppled govern-

ments,[39] prevented the passage of laws they dislike, defied successfully those that were passed, neutralised the right and freedom to
work and have forced others to break formal contracts without
redress.[40] If we start with the assumption that in modern British
society the trade unions are the only social institution truly to represent the working classes, since even the Labour Party is dominated
by middle-class leaders or by those leading middle-class lives, then
their new-found political as well as economic power is the nearest
thing to the Dictatorship of the Proletariat that the country has yet
seen.

What has the proletariat done with its power, limited though it be?
The ideology that has informed the trade union movement is based
on a criticism of capitalism as being harsh and anarchic, favouring
the strong against the weak, generating selfishness and a fight of
each against all, and pandering to the lower instincts of human
nature. The tragedy is that the power that trade union leaders have
lately achieved has been used not only to retain all these negative
attributes, but also add a few more besides. They have created a collective bargaining framework that is anarchic, irrational and favours
the strong as against the weak. In place of altruism it fosters selfishness, and in place of self-sacrifice it offers utter ruthlessness, even
towards one's own fellow members.[41] Moreover, while the much
maligned capitalist was at least progressive in technology and in
raising overall output, trade union power has been used to hold back
progress; and while the capitalist mentality may be criticised as that
of a huckster and profiteer, the trade union mentality is now that of
the highwayman.

Instead of civilising the labour process, the unions have barbarised
it. They have shown that there is now no dependence of one human
being on another, and where there are the sick waiting to be healed,
the bereaved waiting to have their loved ones buried, motorists risking
their lives on icy roads, the British workman will put his boot in to
secure some extra percentage on his wages. In a few short years,
British trade unions have destroyed the moral basis of trade unionism built up over generations.[42] They also, perhaps most tragically of
all, made a victory of their own Labour Party impossible in 1979.

Social science knows many examples of collective traps in which
each pursuing his own rational self-interest contributes to harming
everyone, himself included, and in which no individual way out is
possible. With annual wage claims reaching figures of 20 and 30 per
cent or more, no union could afford to be left behind in the scramble

to keep abreast not only of the known current claims, but also the estimated increased future claims of others who would put them forward in the same expectation of escalation. Everyone knew that they would do better to gain 3 per cent if everyone else gained 2 per cent, than to gain 23 per cent if the rest had 22 per cent, yet as they all clamoured for over 20 per cent, they all suffered inflation while harming each other by bitter disputes and losses of output and jobs. It appeared like

> a Greek tragedy. . . Somehow workers in some sectors have found themselves destroying their firm, fully aware of what they were doing, yet unable to stop. They found themselves answering strike calls. . .in the full awareness that. . .the result could only be ruin for all concerned.[43]

Yet the unions were more fortunate than most: they were offered a way out. Successive governments and especially the Labour administration of 1974–9 decided on incomes policies tailored to trade union demands that would provide exactly the assurance to each that all the others would keep to the rules. It was a godsend that one might have expected the unions to accept with alacrity. Instead, they met it with the bitterest hostility; and each year the nation was treated to the spectacle of seeing the union leadership deliberately damaging the economy, the working class and not least their own members by whittling down, cheating on and bypassing wages policies from which they obviously stood to gain. Ultimately they overthrew all control in 1978–9.

Thus the unions not only destroyed all hopes of planning, a firm plank in every Socialist platform; they also took to breaking their own agreements[44] which once were the foundation of their policy, just as it came to be accepted that any promise solemnly made by the TUC itself was not worth the paper it was written on, as witness the 'Social Contract' or 'Statement of Intent'. Further, the leaders increasingly distanced themselves from their own former democratic methods. The case of Mr Derek Robinson, shop steward convenor at Longbridge whose dismissal received much publicity, brought to light an indicative straw in the wind. Members had voted in the ratio 7:1 for a certain course of action. What was remarkable thereafter was not only that it had clearly not occurred to the leaders to take any notice of that vote but on the contrary they immediately proceeded to make plans in the exactly opposite sense; even more significant is the fact that that attitude was widely taken for granted and excited little, if any, comment. The bitter opposition shown by many union leaders to proposals for balloting before strikes fits the same trend.

While there will be little dissent from the view that a major change in the character of trade unionism has occurred in recent years, there is wide disagreement as to its causes. One school of thought puts it down to the accretion of power to trade union bureaucrats, whose self-interest is served by struggles and confrontations rather than by getting the objectively best terms for their members. Thus in the miners' dispute that led to the fall of Mr Heath, 1973–4, the government's offer was rejected not because it was unacceptable *per se*, but because having been made in full from the start, it left the leadership no chance of showing that their bargaining had improved the offer. A similar cause, a full offer from the start that left no room for the union leadership to gain any glory by bettering it, is believed to have lain behind the vote of the General Council of the TUC to reject the Labour government's package in the winter of 1978–9 which brought on the 'Winter of Discontent' that toppled Mr Callaghan. Again, at the beginning of the 1980 steel strike, Mr William Sirs, the steel workers' leader, hoped for a short dispute and terms which were defined not as being fair, but in 'which we can feel that honour has been satisfied'.[45] It is thus arguable that these costly disputes, among others, were fought not for wages as such, but mainly to satisfy the political needs of the leadership, pointing to a gap between the interests of leaders and members. The truth of these allegations is hard to judge, but their weakness as an explanation is that potentially they apply with similar force abroad, yet in other advanced countries trade unions act as responsibly and are as mindful of their members' interests as ever.

The forms of organisation of British unions also come in for frequent criticism. It is argued that the decision-making process gives the greatest immediate power to shop stewards and delegate conferences, who are always the most militant section of the membership,[46] and that the ordinary member thus 'mis'-represented by his delegates finds it hard to stand up to the resulting initiative, once the bandwagon rolls. Further:

[i]n Germany, in Scandinavia, in Austria — wherever there has been a commitment both to wealth creation and to welfare there has been prosperity, far greater than in Britain and in conditions of assured freedom. . . [But] the approach so successful wherever

it has been tried will not be allowed to be tried here. The trade unions will see to that. . . . Their commitment to competitive collective bargaining, their vested interests in declining industries and over-manned plant, and their inability to reform themselves or effectively lead their members are seemingly insuperable barriers to the adoption of a wealth-creating Social Democratic approach.[47]

The messy craft/industry organisation of British unions also leads to poor co-ordination and costly demarcation disputes. Yet with all these handicaps British unions acted differently in the past, and the union world in America or France, for example, is just as illogically organised without leading to the same chaos. Such causes can therefore at best be contributory.

A third set of explanations blames the law that allegedly favours unions, as well as the social security benefits and tax rebates which cut the costs of strikes to the members. While the effects of the social security system have in any case been exaggerated,[48] the fact is that some support from the tax/insurance system applies abroad also, and the law also is favourable to trade unions in most other advanced countries, though with differences of emphasis: thus in many countries the closed shop is outlawed, but some have made the lock-out illegal as undermining the right to work.[49] The difference therefore is not that abroad the unions' legal or economic powers are more restricted: the difference is that unlike the British they do not *wish* to use them in ways damaging to the nation in general and their members in particular.

What, then, is the explanation? Let us begin with one central fact: the long list presented here (and it could easily be lengthened) of actions by which trade unions damage the incomes of their members, though true as far as it goes, is but a half-truth, and like all half-truths is grossly misleading. It is above all misleading to hold trade union leaders responsible for initiating what look like aggressive and destructive campaigns when it seems to them, out of their own experience, that they are merely defending their members' standard of living and conditions of work in time-honoured fashion against encroachments by inflation, taxation, incomes policies[50] and the erosion (respectively the widening) of differentials.[51] Virtually all Treasury policies, whatever the immediate objective and whatever the other details, have included a pay curb as a major ingredient.

There has been a variety of trade union responses but a single thread has been running through them, and it is the same thread that we found in the history of Treasury action: it is the contempt for production, the disregard for the need to create wealth before it can be distributed: 'Our present trade union leaders. . .display no perceptible concern for the long-term improvement of their members' living standards or for the creation of. . .wealth.'[52] The contempt for production is found in the blithe hostility to innovation, in the ease of striking and in the tactics of 'closing down' whole industries for one or two per cent in wages. The union world thus forms an almost perfect mirror image of the world of the Treasury and of the other policy makers to whom the share-out is always more important than the size of the cake. Judging by their actions, it seems that it would occur to trade union leaders as little as it would to Treasury policy makers that the only way to reach the income of our Continental neighbours is first to reach their level of output.

The contrast between Britain and the other countries may be put another way. While it was normal for trade unions abroad to take into account the growth of output and therefore to bargain for as great as possible a share of that growth, in Britain growth was so minimal as not to enter substantially into calculations, particularly in the stagnant last decade.

The presumption of an unchanging total leads directly to a fight over shares. It also leads back to restrictive attitudes, some of which were initially responsible for the slow growth. A splendid example is the prolonged hostility of British unions to the tachograph ('spy in the cab') which others had accepted years earlier. For while it seemed normal for Continental unions to view it as a means of cutting costs and increasing efficiency, for which they could claim higher wages, British lorry drivers, or at least their leaders, seemingly ignored that aspect and could see only the limited and limiting advantages of cutting corners, breaking the law and petty cheating that the freedom from surveillance gave them.

Minimal growth in Britain caused not only blindness towards the possibilities of gain by greater efficiency, it was also directly responsible for the growing deterioration of the temper of industrial relations which, significantly, occurred only towards the end of the period after twenty years of frustration. As seen by one acute German observer:

Wage negotiations in the Federal Republic were carried out for decades against a background of a steady high rate of growth with very little inflation. Britain had in the same period a miser-able growth rate and a rate of inflation several times as high as the German one. Growth was throttled there time and again by Government intervention, inflation stoked up time and again by public expenditure and paper money. In many branches of industry the employees reached the view that since there was no natural growth, they should take as much as possible out of their firm.[53]

Conversely, since German workers received real wage increases year by year, there was less reason to press for inflationary ones. What aggravated British frustration especially from the middle of the 1960s onwards was the fact that owing to the inflexibility of the tax system, inflationary wage gains brought workers into higher marginal tax rates, that social security contributions were increasing, and that the wage bargaining system ensured that money wage increases spread fairly equally between those who had increased their productivity and those who had not. Therefore to capture some of the gains from their rising output and from their bargaining strength, unions had to run ever faster and become ever more militant and a rational selection process favoured the most militant leaders.[54]

By instinct, trade unions would want to exist in a world of progressive, efficient firms. Above all, they can be trusted to fight for full employment and against the closing down of productive industry. But an environment of cuts and stagnation has turned them into reactionary and destructive bodies. It is not the least indictment of Treasury policy that it has converted the potentially positive force of British trade unionism into an agency that inhibits growth, embitters social relations and brings long-established working-class ideals into disrepute.

## Notes

1. Increases in bank advances, November 1971–May 1974, per cent:

| | |
|---|---|
| Manufacturing | 115 |
| Other production | 166 |
| Financial (incl. property companies) | 327 |
| Services | 186 |
| Personal | 178 |
| Total advances | 178 |

A.D. Bain, 'Monetary Policy and the Recent Inflation' in Peter Maunders and

Raymond Ryba (eds.), *Studies in Inflation* (1975), p. 4.

2. R.C.O. Matthews, 'The Role of Demand Management' in Sir Alec Cairncross (ed.), *British Economic Prospects Reconsidered* (1971), p. 16.

3. In the years 1961–9, there were nine changes in HP regulations and four in purchase tax; in 1970–4 there were two more of HP regulations and two in VAT. CPRS, *The Future of the British Car Industry* (1975), pp. 123–5; J.C.R. Dow, *The Management of the British Economy* (1965), pp. 275–82; George Maxcy and Aubrey Silberston, *The Motor Industry* (1954), pp. 44–5, 48–51; NEDC for the Motor Manufacturing Industry, *The Effect of Government Economic Policy on the Motor Industry* (1968) and *Industrial Report: Economic Assessment to 1972* (1970) p. 37, para. D. 12; Krish Bhaskar, *The Future of the UK Motor Industry* (1979), p. 10.

4. Letter in *The Times*, 8 September 1974; Samuel Brittan, *Steering the Economy: the Role of the Treasury* (1969), pp. 268–9, 281–2; Sima Lieberman, *The Growth of European Mixed Economies, 1945–76* (1977), p. 91; Sir Roy Harrod, *Towards a New Economic Policy* (1967), p. 49.

5. R.F. (later Lord) Kahn, Radcliffe Commission, *Memoranda of Evidence*, vol. 3, para. 13.

6. This is quite apart from such other measures as a steeply raked taxation system, redundancy payments and other measures introduced by Labour governments for perfectly good social reasons, but in a form dictated by a dislike of capitalist business in general. It was part of the British tragedy that her socialists were too weak to seize power, but too strong to let a capitalist economy function properly.

7. Tibor Barna, *Investment and Growth Policies in British Industrial Firms* (1962), p. 60, also pp. 50–1.

8. Sir Alan Cottrell, *The Undermining of British Industry* (1979), p. 7.

9. See PEP, *Attitudes in British Management* (1966), p. 124.

10. For a good summary, see J.R. Sargent, 'Productivity and Profits in U.K. Manufacturing', *Midland Bank Review* (Autumn 1979); J.S. Flemming, 'Rate of Return to Capital . . . 1960–74', *Bank of England Bulletin* (March 1976), esp. pp. 37, 42; A. Glyn and Bob Sutcliffe, 'The Collapse of U.K. Profits', *New Left Review*, no. 66 (March/April 1971), p. 5, Table A.

11. Robert Bacon and Walter Eltis, *Britain's Economic Problem: Too Few Producers* (2nd edn, 1978), pp. 224–7.

12. H.F.R. Catherwood, 'Major Factors in Economic Growth in the 1970's', *Economics*, no. 8 (1970), p. 179.

13. J.E. Mortimer, *Trade Unions and Technological Change* (1971), pp. 25–8.

14. CPRS, *The Future of the British Car Industry*, p. 120; also report in *The Times*, 31 July 1980.

15. News item, 20 February 1979.

16. Paul Johnson, 'Are Socialists interested in *creating* wealth?', *Daily Telegraph*, 1 October 1979.

17. At the time of writing, APT is six years behind(!), of which 2–2½ years are due to strikes and blackings. *Railway Gazette International* (December 1978), pp. 467–9 and radio interview, Richard Hope, 26 March 1979.

18. For another typical, less publicised, example, see the opposition of the Civil Service unions to Whitehall's most advanced computer project: *The Times*, 14 November 1979.

19. J. Pencavel's example, in which a unionised coalfield produced 22 per cent less output than a non-unionised one, may be apocryphal but it is not implausible. 'The Distributional and Efficiency Effects of Trade Unions in Britain', *British Journal of Industrial Relations*, no. 15 (July 1977).

20. 'It would be unthinkable in Japan for workers to damage their plants,' said Kouji Yanada, of Toyota. 'It is difficult for us to comprehend what is happening in British Leyland.' Report in *The Times*, 30 December 1980.

21. Paul Willis, 'Shop Floor Culture, Masculinity and the Wage Form' in John Clarke, Charles Critcher and Richard Johnson (eds.), *Working Class Culture; Studies in History and Theory* (1979), esp. pp. 194 and 197.

22. *Morning Telegraph* (Sheffield), 24 November 1979; *The Times*, 10 December 1979; *Daily Telegraph* 24 April 1980.

23. In April 1980, it was only the workers in the still profitable plants at BL who came out on strike against the new working conditions, including those making Rovers, Land-Rovers, Sherpas, Jaguars and TR7 vehicles, and later also those on Mini production.

24. E.g. *The Times*, 21 January 1980; Stephen Milligan, *The New Barons. Union Power in the 1970s* (1976), pp. 221–2.

25. This ratio is not as easy to measure as was thought at first, for it depends on the proportion of wage-earners in the total, and on the distribution of non-wage incomes above and below average wages. An elaborate attempt at an international comparison was made by Brown and Browne who chose the ratio of the average wage to the average income as the index, with the following result:

| Wage/Income ratios: | 1913 | 1924 or 1925 | 1953 |
| --- | --- | --- | --- |
| France | – | – | 65 |
| Germany | 59 | 59 | 73 |
| Sweden | 60 | 59 | 60 |
| UK | 63 | 63 | 80 |
| USA | 58 | 72 | 75 |

E.H. Phelps Brown and Margaret H. Browne, *A Century of Pay* (1968), pp. 224 and 275.

26. See note 10, above. Also Milligan, *The New Barons*, p. 32 and *passim*.

27. Though the gap is sometimes exaggerated: Ralph Turvey, 'Counter-inflationary Policies' in M. Posner (ed.), *Demand Management* (1978), pp. 195–6; Charles Mulvay, 'Estimating the Union-Non-Union Wage Differential: A Statistical Issue', *Univ. of Glasgow Discussion Papers in Economics*, no. 24 (n.d.); Nick Bosanquet, 'Labour and Public Expenditure', in Nick Bosanquet and Peter Townsend, *Labour and Equality. A Fabian Study of Labour in Power 1974–79* (1980), p. 26; National Board for Prices and Incomes, Report No. 169; *General Problems of Low Pay*, Cmnd. 4648 (1971), pp. 39–40.

28. Reports in *The Times*, 16 February, 8 March and 20 May 1980.

29. Both in Lord Robbins *et al.*, *Trade Unions: Public Goods or Public 'Bads'?* (1978), pp. 91, 130.

30. Not as a rule: thus in the steel strike of 1980 there was opposition by workers and union leaders in engineering and private steel firms affected.

31. It might be argued that the miners, being among the main beneficiaries of the blackmail type of strike, had to secure the success of that example in order to maintain the credibility of the method as a whole. But such argument rests on a very uncertain base, for it seemed at least equally likely that the steel strike would contribute to the determination of governments to enact legislation to minimise the blackmail effect in the future.

32. News item, 4 October 1979; *The Times*, 29 January 1980; *Guardian*, 10 March 1979; *Morning Telegraph* (Sheffield), 26 March 1980. On the Isle of Grain, a strike by 27 laggers materially contributed to shutting down a power station on which £450 million had been spent. *Daily Telegraph*, 24 April 1980.

33. *Observer*, 4 May 1980.

34. Bhaskar, *Future of the UK Motor Industry*, p. 167.

35. For problems of international comparisons, see Malcolm Fisher, *Measurement of Labour Disputes and their Economic Effect* (1973).

36. In the 1960s, unofficial strikes formed 90 per cent of stoppages, 70 per cent of total time lost in disputes. Lloyd Ulman in Richard E. Caves and Associates, *Britain's Economic Prospects* (1968), p. 334.

37. CPRS, *The Future of the British Car Industry*, pp. 84, 96–8; *The Times*, 1 February 1980.

38. The latter have been estimated at 6 per cent of GNP — a likely exaggeration but showing the order of magnitude. John Burton in Robbins, *Trade Unions*, p. 50.

39. B.C. Roberts, 'The Government's Challenge to the Unions', *Three Banks Review*, no. 124 (1979), p. 5; Gerard A. Dorfman, *Government versus Trade Unionism in British Politics since 1968* (1979).

40. On a local scale they also assume the right to determine promotions, to decide whether maintenance man should work, to blackmail civil servants carrying out their duties, and to prevent hospital complaints, to quote some typical examples. See *Morning Telegraph* (Sheffield), 1, 8 and 27 October 1979; *Guardian* letter, 7 November 1979.

41. Witness the attempts of the striking steelworkers in 1980 to force the men in private firms to strike, even though they had nothing to gain by it, they were frequently worse paid, and they stood to risk their employment by bankrupting their firm, while the men in BSC assumed, erroneously as it turned out, that the bankruptcy of their own firm would be staved off by limitless payments from the public purse.

42. Typically, they have accused the media of being responsible: TUC, *A Cause for Concern* (1979). See also the quotation at the front of this book.

43. S.G. Checkland, *The Upas Tree, Glasgow 1875–1975* (1977), p. 60.

44. The Ford strike of 1978 was a classic example; it was also an example of a strike called long before negotiating or grievance procedure was exhausted.

45. Interview, BBC Nine o'clock News, 29 December 1979.

46. Thus in the steel strike of 1980 it was the delegates and local strike committees that repeatedly called for safety men to be withdrawn and thus cause damage of up to £200 million and plant closures of up to two years. They were opposed by the men who refused to carry out these orders, and by the union leadership (*The Times*, 6 and 29 February, 15 and 17 March 1980).

47. Peter Jenkins in the *Guardian*, 1 October 1979.

48. Milligan, *The New Barons*, pp. 42–3; J.W. Duncan and W.E.J. McCarthy, 'The State Subsidy Theory of Strikes. An Examination of Statistical Data for the Period 1956–1970', *British Journal of Industrial Relations*, no. 12 (1974), pp. 26–47.

49. Entirely typically, Britain differs from most others by leaning in both cases in the direction of caring little for the right to produce, but much more for the right *not* to work.

50. In the motor industry, tax and HP changes on average every ten months 'in the 1950's and 1960's created cyclical employment. . .and helped to stoke the inherent insecurity of the labour force. The resulting insecurity partly explains the horrendous industrial relations and trench warfare attitudes' (Bhaskar, *Future of the UK Motor Industry*, p. 15).

51. 'Our people feel they are under attack on the industrial front, economic front and the legislation front': Len Murray, reported in *The Times*, 4 February 1980.

52. Johnson, 'Are Socialists interested in *creating* wealth?'

53. Jochen Rudolph, *Frankfurter Allgemeine Zeitung*, 20 November 1978.

54. E.g. David Jackson, H.A. Turner and Frank Wilkinson, *Do Trade Unions Cause Inflation?* (1972), pp. 88 and 98–100; Bacon and Eltis, *Britain's Economic Problem*, pp. 6–8; F.W. Paish, 'Personal Incomes and Taxation', *Lloyds Bank Review*, no. 116 (1975); J.F. Wright, *Britain in the Age of Economic Management. An Economic History since 1939* (1980), p. 171; Samuel Brittan and Peter Lilley, *The Delusion of Incomes Policy* (1977), pp. 66–7; Hugh Clegg, *How to Run an Incomes Policy* (1971), pp. 60–6.

# 6  ALTERNATIVE CAUSES

## 1 False Trails

We have seen that the British economic problem was anchored in a cycle which begins with a balance of payments problem or with inflation, leading to government action to cut investment which makes inevitable future balance of payments problems, stagnation, inflation and social strife. This cycle will by itself fully explain the poor economic performance of Great Britain, but other explanations have been offered and we must examine them. We shall find some of them to have no validity, but others to draw attention to factors that have undoubtedly aggravated various aspects of British economic weakness.

A number of explanations are historical in nature. For example, among those who blame poor entrepreneurship there are some who allege that it has been a traditional failing for a long time. In its more bizarre form the allegation harks back to the 1860's or even earlier,[1] leaving one to wonder at the respective quality of the Japanese, the French[2] or even the German entrepreneurs in the mid-nineteenth century that made their successors so efficient 120 years later. More common is the belief that poor entrepreneurship began to hold back British progress only in the late nineteenth century, itself caused by the third-generation syndrome or the education and social habits of the British upper classes. This explanation too has problems, particularly of definition, and it is not difficult to show that British entrepreneurs did what was objectively right for them, even though it may have caused slower growth in the long run — and no entrepreneurs ever did more.[3] Applied to the post-Second World War period, the explanation has to assume not only that some 10,000 or 20,000 British business executives (except of course those in banking, finance or real estate speculation) were suddenly struck by debilitating lethargy, but that the even larger numbers of young men pushing to take over jobs in their companies were equally smitten. But that is totally unscientific in social terms:[4] thousands of people do not suddenly all change in the same way — *unless* there is a specific external reason to make them. The blame on poor entrepreneurship thus resolves itself into a search for the external cause operating *on* entrepreneurs, and this is precisely what the earlier chapters have attempted to provide.

There is a variant which concentrates on the British failure to assimilate technological innovations, especially those of American origin — the lack of so-called 'innovative dynamism'. This is in part a re-definition of the problem rather than an answer; inasmuch as it is linked to such social failures as poor technical education or the contempt of the British elite for engineering, it is contradicted by the data. Thus in 1971 only Britain, apart from the USA, had an export surplus on the 'Technological Balance of Payments', all others being mainly buyers rather than developers and exporters of technology. Again, among the countries supplying technology to Japanese companies from 1950 to March 1979, Britain came third, behind the USA and Germany but ahead of all others.[5]

Another historical explanation bases itself on idle labour hostile to technical innovation which allegedy plagued even the Victorians.[6] The trouble with this explanation is that in the early post-war years, at least, output per head of the British worker was higher than that of his contemporaries abroad. This changed thereafter, but as the last chapter has tried to show, that change was a direct result of government policy.

We are on firmer ground with the explanation that slow growth itself has a historical dimension. Britain registered a slower rate of growth than the other industrial countries from at least 1870 onwards, if not earlier, and whether we put this down to some mystical and circular reason such as that she was 'mature' first and had exhausted her growth potential,[7] or that the late-comers were catching up, or yet that Britain turned into a consumption economy prematurely, it is clear that it is harder to switch from a slow to a fast rate than to stay on a fast rate once it has got going. However, the post-war rate was completely out of line with any past rates of growth among all countries in the West. They all describe a sharp 'kink', and it is not easy to see why it should be possible to jump from, say, 1 per cent to 5 per cent, but not from ½ per cent to 4½ per cent. In any case, in the lead-in period of the 1930s, not to mention the war years, Britain's output did better than that of most of the others, and this should surely have had more weight at the post-war take-off point than a growth rate lying further back.

It has also been argued that Britain was historically burdened by an unfavourable industrial structure, with its main weight in such industries as textiles and other consumer goods, which were growing

**Table 6.1:   Rates of Growth, Eight Countries, 1913−50 (Annual average compound growth rates)**

|  | Total Output 1920−9 | 1929−38 | GDP per Man-hour 1913−50 |
|---|---|---|---|
| Belgium | 3.5 | 0.0 | 1.5 |
| France | 4.9 | −0.5 | 1.7 |
| Germany | 4.5 | 3.9 | 1.2 |
| Italy | 3.0 | 1.4 | 1.8 |
| Netherlands | 4.2 | 0.3 | 1.5 |
| UK | 1.9 | 1.9 | 1.5 |
| Average Western Europe | 3.6 | 1.2 | — |
| USA | — | — | 2.5 |
| Japan | — | — | 1.4 |

Source: Angus Maddison, 'Economic Policy and Performance in Europe 1913–1970', *Fontana Economic History of Europe*, volume 5/2 (1976), p. 451; and *idem*, 'Long-Run Dynamics of Productivity Growth', in W. Beckerman (ed.), *Slow Growth in Britain* (1979), p. 195.

more slowly the world over, rather than machinery and other capital goods which were about to take off on a very fast expansion path. There was certainly some truth in this in the inter-war years, but by the mid-forties Britain had acquired great strength in some of the most promising sectors like vehicles, aircraft and electronics, while the distribution in some of the fastest growers like Japan or Italy was far more unfavourable. It is therefore unlikely that the earlier distribution of industry could have mattered very much. In the orientation of her exports, Britain was better placed than any of her main rivals except Germany (see Table 6.2).

Nor can it be shown that it was a handicap for Britain to be geared to the more slowly growing colonial or Commonwealth markets since the fast-growing European Continent was as open to Britain at the beginning of the period as to any of the others and was in fact crying out for British goods. It was our failure to supply that lost us the markets.

Another set of explanations focuses on the slow growth of the industrial labour force in Britain. It is alleged that elsewhere the large influx of labour either from agriculture, where its income had been low, or from abroad (especially the flight from the East into

**Table 6.2:   The Distribution of Exports, Four Countries, 1955 – 73 (percentage of total exports)**

| Product Groups | UK 1955 | UK 1973 | France 1955 | France 1973 | Germany 1955 | Germany 1973 | Japan 1955 | Japan 1973 |
|---|---|---|---|---|---|---|---|---|
| Faster-growing | 52 | 68 | 37 | 60 | 57 | 68 | 25 | 64 |
| Slower-growing | 48 | 32 | 63 | 40 | 43 | 32 | 75 | 36 |

Source: D.K. Stout, 'De-industrialisation and Industrial Policy' in F. Blackaby (ed.) *De-industrialisation* (1979), p. 177. Also see Lawrence A. Krause, 'British Trade Performance' in Richard E. Caves and Associates, *Britain's Economic Prospects* (1968), p. 215; ASTMS, *The Crisis in British Economic Planning* (n.d. ?1976), p. 14; T. Barna, 'Industrial Investment in Britain and Germany', *The Banker*, no. 108 (1958), pp. 12–23; H. Tyszyinski, 'World Trade in Manufactured Commodities 1899 – 1950', *Manchester School*, no. 19 (1951), pp. 272–304; 'Fast and Slow-Growing Products in World Trade', *National Institute Economic Review*, no. 25 (August 1963), pp. 22–39; M. Panic and A.H. Rajan, *Product Changes in Industrial Countries' Trade 1955–68* (1971); NEDO, *The UK and West German Manufacturing Industry 1954–72* (1975).

Germany) not only aided economic growth simply by shifting people from low- to high-output sectors, but also imparted a dynamic and a flexibility to industry that were sorely lacking in Britain.[8]

Although this explanation has been very popular, there are at least four objections to it. The first is that it does not quite fit the facts: the labour supply to French manufactures was no greater than to the British, yet France made one of the most dramatic economic recoveries. Second, it seems to confuse cause and effect: many of the immigrant workers from the poorer countries, such as Yugoslavia, Spain, Portugal and Italy came to the Continental countries because they were growing fast and more would have come to Britain if there had been more jobs on offer. Third, it is not clear that the influx of labour, without capital, is an unmixed blessing: it would certainly not have been so in the case of the British economy suffering from a shortage of investment. In Third World countries such as India it is a commonplace that it is the constant additions to the labour force that have to be supplied with capital at a low level that prevents the better equipment of the existing labour force: ever more spades instead of replacing spades by tractors. Finally, while it is true that Britain lacked an agricultural labour reservoir, she had plenty of low-productivity labour in other sectors which could have moved if high-productivity opportunities had been available. Nor is the argument that labour mobility was lower here than elsewhere very convincing: inter-sectoral labour mobility in manufacturing industry was a more powerful positive factor in Britain than in Germany from 1954 to 1976,[9] and if it fell rapidly in the course of the post-war period that was clearly a consequence of slow growth and adaptation rather than a cause.[10] In any case, there was high mobility into the service industries.[11]

In a more sophisticated version, the explanation starts with the well known relationship of a high rate of growth of production with a high rate of growth of productivity, especially in manufacturing: there seems to be a gain, in other words, if the size of the whole economy is expanding. This is sometimes known as Verdoorn's Law,[12] and it depends in the end on a growing labour force as one of its basic conditions. While it seems to be well established that fast rises of production and productivity go together,[13] this does not necessarily imply that a rise in the size of the labour force is the cause.

Some explanations turn on the alleged absence of a fast-growing demand in Britain.[14] It is an argument that is often implied, rather than put directly, and it runs the risk of being circular.[15] One could more easily posit the opposite, that compared with Britain and her high prestige and control of markets at the outset, the obstacles facing German exporters who had to overcome hostility and discrimination, not to mention the Japanese who additionally had to live down a reputation of imitative and shoddy manufacturing, must have seemed overwhelming. At that time, the British home market also offered a much firmer base than the home markets of others and gave her the favourite's position on the starting grid. Still less persuasive is the view that British war destruction was too light, or alternatively too heavy (depending on which economy one is using as the standard) to trigger a response of fast growth. Countries with roughly similar records of war losses, like Denmark or Holland, had no difficulty in keeping near the normal European rate of growth.

There is also the doctrine (which we have already met in one guise as the underlying Treasury assumption) that somehow British key ratios were wrong: in one important version it is argued that while other countries might benefit from an export-led growth, the ratios were against Britain, so that, for example as industrial productivity increased, imports grew faster than exports, and the better the productivity, the worse the balance of payments.[16] But this kind of explanation merely pushes the question one step back, for it still has to be explained why this should be so: and the reasoning offered here, as indeed elsewhere, was that it was the lack of previously prepared capacity in Britain which converted the expansionary impetus into imports.

All these explanations go back, in some way or other, to origins that lie in the past and therefore tend to suggest that it was not so much what was done since 1945 as the inherited weaknesses which were the root of the trouble. As we have seen, none of them is very convincing.[17] Let us therefore turn to explanations that concentrate solely or mainly on post-war actions.

A favourite one is the high level of taxation and government expenditure and/or the high level of social services, which were alleged to have removed incentives to work and to take risks. However, since the level of taxation and the share of the public sector in Britain was in fact lower than in some of the countries that did so much better it cannot easily be taken as a reason for slow growth (see Table 6.3).

It will be noted that British transfer payments (i.e. the difference between the first and third columns) are particularly low by international standards, and 'social charges' as a proportion of earnings are lower by far in Britain than elsewhere: her 21 per cent compares with 88 per cent in Italy, 69 per cent in the Netherlands, 64 per cent in France, 54 per cent in Germany and 27 per cent even in the USA. British social service expenditure measured in absolute figures is now abysmal by European standards.

It is in any case by no means certain whether higher taxation is a stimulus or disincentive to effort: the issue has been debated in this country at least since the eighteenth century without any agreed conclusions. It may be comforting to some people to believe that taxes act as an incentive to low income earners, but as a disincentive to the rich,[19] but it is hardly likely that such a proposition would enjoy widespread support. It may be that it is not so much the level as the distribution of taxation that works negatively in Britain, but in fact the system is not very different from that of the Continent.

A more complex version of this explanation which has enjoyed some popularity focuses on the rise in the share of public and other 'non-marketable' activities at the expense of marketable goods and services. In the shrinking private sector, according to this doctrine, even high investment in modern labour-saving capital will not help: it will simply create more technological unemployment that can be cured only by still further expansion in the already overblown public

**Table 6.3:  Proportion of Disposable National Income Spent on Total Public Expenditure, Nine Countries, 1961–72**

| | Excluding Transfer Payments | | Including Transfer Payments | |
|---|---|---|---|---|
| | 1972 (per cent) | Increase in Percentage 1961–72 | 1972 (per cent) | Increase in Percentage |
| Sweden | 25.6 | + 8.1 | 45.3 | + 15.4 |
| USA | 23.2 | + 2.3 | 35.0 | + 3.7 |
| UK | 20.7 | + 2.7 | 41.9 | + 7.9 |
| West Germany | 20.4 | + 4.9 | 44.8 | + 4.4 |
| Netherlands | 18.3 | + 3.1 | 52.0 | n.a. |
| Belgium | 16.5 | + 3.1 | 39.4 | + 8.2 |
| Italy | 16.0 | + 3.2 | 37.6 | + 6.1 |
| France | 14.0 | − 0.7 | 43.1 | + 3.3 |
| Japan | 10.4 | + 0.8 | 25.9 | + 1.9 |

Source:  David Smith, 'Public Consumption and Economic Performance', *National Westminster Bank Review* (November 1975), p. 23. Also see diagram in Bent Hansen, *Fiscal Policy in Seven Countries 1955–1965* (1978), p. 87; William G. Shepherd, 'Alternatives for Public Expenditure' in Richard E. Caves and Associates, *Britain's Economic Prospects* (1968), pp. 381–2; Sir Henry Phelps Brown, 'What is the British Predicament?', *Three Banks Review*, no. 116 (1977), p. 11. The percentage of total tax revenue in GDP in 1979 was as follows:

| | |
|---|---|
| Sweden | 52.9 |
| Netherlands | 47.2 |
| Belgium | 44.5 |
| France | 41.0 |
| West Germany | 37.2 |
| UK | 33.8 |
| Italy | 32.8 |
| USA | 31.3 |

*Economic Trends.*

sector. Britain is thus locked in a vicious circle of an ever-shrinking productive industrial base, which either has low productivity, or high productivity and high unemployment, but which cannot grow.[20]

In so far as the emphasis on the failure to invest ahead of expansion is central to the argument, it shows a welcome degree of realism, but the analysis as a whole is not very convincing. It omits the 1950s, when the share of the public sector was declining, yet Britain was clearly launched on her downward path; nor can it easily explain away the successful growth in such progressive countries as Sweden or Germany, where the non-market economy expanded as fast as in Britain. Moreover, the figures for the public sector are unduly inflated by including nationalised industry, but it is not clear why the growth of, say, the railways or the coal industry should be a bad thing for the economy or their decline a good thing. Measured conventionally, employment in manufacturing, though declining, was still proportionately greater in Britain than in most other countries. Altogether, there is no particular merit in having a large manufacturing sector, any more than there is in having a large agricultural sector, as the Physiocrats once thought. Shrinking manufacturing, as against a growing tertiary (including government) sector, simply reflects the fact that as societies become richer, they spend proportionately less on manufactures and that more production activity consists of design, pre-planning or transport. Of course, waste in the public sector is undesirable, but no more so than in the market sector.

Finally, there is the so-called 'New Cambridge School'. Its members use the same basic concepts as the Neo-Keynesians but have radically different views on certain key relationships. In particular, it believes that the 'private acquisition of financial assets' and private investment are stable and/or predictable, and that the government is the only potential destabiliser. An injection of incomes, such as the British government has practised in the past in order to move out of a trough, would therefore flow directly into imports and upset the trade balance. In this view, the Treasury has in the past consistently played on the wrong variables, aggravating crises and fluctuations.[21]

Assuming, as does so much of modern theory, that ratios of macro-economic quantities remain constant, the school has time and again put forward a tariff as the best means of solving Britain's problems. This solution is not exactly new, and protectionist policies have been debated, in different contexts, for three centuries. It is difficult to believe that anyone looking round British industry today would think that a tariff is what it needs, though it would certainly fit the pattern of the other measures tried over the past thirty years, which have all been basically designed to live with failure rather than to remedy it. What is evident is that protectionist countries have not done notably better in recent decades, nor has the EEC, with its internal free trade, done any great damage to its six original members. A tariff specifically to protect a massive investment programme would of course be a different matter.

Each of these explanations and suggestions for remedies focuses on some important aspect of reality and none can be entirely ignored. But they all fail the final test: they fail to explain adequately, though they all contribute to an explanation, why Britain's fate has been so different from that of all other comparable countries except, significantly, the United States in the past ten years. They fail to account for Britain's relative decline for the past thirty years despite her initially favourable position at a time when the rest of the industrialised world economies registered such remarkable successes.

## 2  The Failure to Invest Reconsidered

Those who have other explanations have naturally criticised the notion of the lack of adequate investment as the first stage in the causation of the poor British performance. This criticism has been broadly of two kinds: it has been said that the statistics do not show a clear correlation between output growth and investment,[22] and that there are general theoretical considerations why that should be so.

We have seen in Chapter 2, section 1 above that even if growth rates depended wholly on investment, no simple and stable correlation between them across space or across time could be expected. This lays the theory open to the objection that it cannot be proved or disproved and that it therefore cannot be much use as an explanation. Certainly, the proof cannot be wholly in statistical terms (which may not be altogether a disadvantage), but its explanatory power may perhaps best be upheld by analogy. We may look upon investment as basis for growth rather like we look upon food as a necessity for human survival. It would not be true to say that health improves in proportion to the food intake, still less would it be true to say that we can improve health indefinitely by increasing the food supply indefinitely; yet there is a relationship between nutrition and health and if we do not get enough to eat, we cannot remained healthy, and below a certain point we die. In the same way, more investment will not lead to exactly proportionate growth, and ever higher investment will not lead to an indefinite rise in the growth rate; but there is a relationship between them which is derived from internal logic as well as from the statistics. 'High investment does not guarantee rapid growth, but low investment does constitute a bar to rapid economic growth.'[23] More precisely, inadequate investment will beyond a certain point stop an economy growing altogether.

Moreover, the divergences of the investment from the growth figures are not wholly random. On the contrary, there is a fairly clear trend within similar economies for growth to go up more than proportionately with a higher investment rate: there is a kind of 'bonus' in fast growing. In technical terms, the marginal capital-output ratio and, with it, the average capital-output ratio, fall in line with a higher rate of investment.[24] Britain, as the slowest grower, was particularly adversely affected by this and it meant that in Britain a given quantum of investment would result in a lower increment of growth than the same quantity of investment made somewhere else.

As it happened, the British investment ratio, measured as a proportion of national income, rose quite substantially from the early 1950s to the late 1960s, yet at the same time the growth rate was slightly lower in the 1960s than in the earlier decade. This led to widespread disillusionment with investment as a solution to Britain's slow growth rate and by the mid-seventies the government and others had become convinced that it was not the lack of new capital, but the poor use made of what there was that was responsible for low productivity and slow growth.[25]

It is clear that unless good and convincing reasons can be found for the discrepancies, the rate of investment will not bear much weight as an explanation of poor productivity and poor growth in Britain.

No problem arises in the case of net investment, or in other words additional capital only, for Britain's net capital-output ratio was not dissimilar from that of others.[26] The explanation we seek relates only to gross investment and is essentially this: why should a country with a relatively low level of additional investment get less benefit from its new capital than one with a higher level? Why did Britain get such a poor return for her efforts?

In searching for a reply we must bear in mind that Britain was not simply a low-investment country. British citizens would have preferred to invest as much as others, but their investment was, as it were, artificially pruned back in repeated 'stop' phases below its desired level by government fiat. The government's method was pruning in one form or another to make investment less attractive by making it less profitable. While a part of the answer may be that in those 'stop' phases the capital was not fully employed and thus failed to yield an adequate return on investment, our explanation must be concerned less with absolute yields than with growth.

The most obvious disadvantage of an artificially truncated capital programme is that it often becomes, in Lamfalussy's phrase, a 'patching' programme, or a form of 'defensive' investment.[27] In those conditions firms will prefer to keep the existing capital stock going rather than scrap it, and to make do with minor improvements only. For a while, increased output can be achieved by such means,

> but if *all* the economy (or a large part of it) has been working under a continuous pressure on profit rates, the adoption of more explicitly growth-oriented investment policies will not be easy. And there will then be a danger that the rate of growth both of output and of productivity will slow down in comparison with what will be happening in those countries which have always relied on enterprise investment.[28]

The tragedy is that in the long run the total costs of the series of 'patches' to keep a backward plant in being may well exceed the costs of a newly installed very much more productive unit. This may be considered one aspect of 'Treasury-style Saving', of the penny-wise, pound-foolish policy sketched in Chapter 4, section 2; carried out on a large scale, it may affect the whole investment strategy adversely, leading to concentration in dying or slow-growing industry, and to holding back potential growth elsewhere. Moreover, large sections of a modern economy are interdependent, and so are their rates of growth. Thus the slow growth and indeed decline of British motor manufacture held back the modernisation and expansion plans of British steel. Slow growth also slows down amalgamation or rationalisation, the long-delayed reduction in the number of models in order to get longer runs among British motor manufacturers again forming a well known example. It should also be noted here that many of the comparisons made and published, purporting to show that British workers using the same capital equipment produce less than workers abroad, take account only of actual machinery installed and frequently ignored the costs involved in having to work with an irrational lay-out in cramped, old and non-purpose-built premises, with inferior ancillary equipment like cranes or works canals, and with an inadequate public transport system and other imperfect items of the British infrastructure which are the result of 'patching'.

There is also a more technical point: normally the higher the rate of gross investment, the higher the 'net', i.e. the completely new capital component in it. The lower the investment rate, also, the older the average age of equipment, and the poorer the power of adaptation. The power of raising output per pound invested is usually (though not invariably) greater for new rather than replacement investment.[29]

To this have to be added the growing obstruction by the trade unions to innovation, sometimes delaying the use of new equipment by years, or insisting on overmanning it, and the less than full enthusiasm on the part of managers for increased output, both of these, as we have seen, the long-term result of Treasury policies. More direct government actions such as regional policies, the withholding of Industrial Development Certificates in prosperous areas and the relocation of new motor works to unsuitable areas like Merseyside, among others,[30] have no doubt been taken with good intentions but did not help British capital goods to achieve their potential productivity.

In view of all this, it would have been a miracle if British investment had yielded as much output as investment elsewhere. Miracles, alas, happen but seldom, though much of the Treasury's policy seems to have been built on the assumption that we can count on them.

Some critics have sought to diminish the role of investment by pointing to other important elements in successful growth: but that confuses investment as a necessary and as a sufficient condition. No one would pretend that the right quantity of investment alone will guarantee growth at all times and in all places. Moreover, like food in our earlier analogy, it is certainly not true that *any* new capital equipment will do: in order to have its effect, it must be the right equipment, in the right industry and the right place. What is at issue is that in Britain the other ingredients, such as an enterprising capitalistic spirit, technical knowledge, sufficient savings, etc., were all available, eager and waiting, at least at the beginning of the period, but were held back by deliberate policy which operated on investment. What is implied is merely the negative assertion that while capital alone will not guarantee growth, its throttling back will guarantee stagnation. That is what happened in Britain, especially when its after-effects and long-term consequences are also taken into account:

There is not always a consistent, automatic relationship between the level of investment and the rate of economic growth; in most instances, however, insufficient capital investment is a major cause of slow economic growth. A weak investment rate makes for a relatively slow growth of the capital stock and for a relatively rapid obsolescence of this stock.[31]

One final objection remains to be dealt with. It derives from certain econometric techniques, based in turn on such formulae as the Cobb-Douglas production function, which purport to allocate mathematically the 'sources' of economic growth to such components as additional capital, additional labour input, certain pre-defined effects like economies of scale, and an unexplained 'residual', which may then be taken to be largely the effect of technological improvement.[32] When these relationships are tested against actual data, it appears that the differences in growth rates between one country and another which can be derived from the quantity of capital invested are minor, and the largest differences are due to the residual, the technology.

This may be read as another example of the extra advantage derived by the fast grower: a small increase in investment beyond that of the slow grower will bring a very high return in output by some unexplained 'technological' effect. In fact, however, it is based on a logical fallacy, the fallacy that the new capital and the new technology are two different things. The truth is that the additional technology cannot be separated from the capital in which it is incorporated. To install something technically superior is usually the purpose, and generally a by-product of new investment, and conversely there is normally no way of introducing technical innovation except by investment. This is so both in the case of replacement and in net investment, and it is largely for that reason that gross investment (which contains both) is normally taken as the operative quantity, quite apart from the fact that in practice it is not nearly as easy to separate out net from gross capital formation.

A high level of investment and rapid technical progress go hand in hand and it is not practicable to answer the question what would happen to the one in the absence of the other. It is a more useful approach to regard technical progress and investment as different aspects of the same process, namely the application of new ideas to industry and the adaptation of industry to a new environment . . . Most firms emphasize the difficulties of classification. For instance, replacement is seldom replacement in the strict sense as there are usually elements of improvement which result in cost-saving and often also in expansion of capacity. Investment for expansion also usually leads to a reduction in unit costs of products, since the new plant is likely to incorporate some technical improvements compared with the existing plant.[33]

The whole process on which progress and economic prosperity depend is thwarted completely when the government decides to cut investment in order to help it out in some temporary monetary or trading crisis.

## 3  The Illusions of Grandeur

There is a further set of causes frequently put forward for the British *malaise*: the pretensions of successive British governments to Great Power status which the country could no longer afford, and the consequent economic damage imposed in order to keep up political appearances. Unlike some of the other causes discussed in section 1 of this chapter, this one was real enough.

There are at least two fields in which these pretensions operated. One was the Sterling Area as a framework within which other countries were given privileged access to the London money market, and more recently this has been continued in the guise of large aid to certain members of the Commonwealth. Motives here were mixed, containing both political and economic elements. The cost to British prosperity is impossible to estimate since we cannot know what alternative policies would have looked like, though it was undoubtedly large. Aid to poorer countries, in any case, has a justification of its own.

The costs of the other pretension, the politico-military megalomania, while they are less easy to condone, are easier to estimate, at least as an order of magnitude. To get at the real costs we have to multiply the actual expenditure several times, because the restrictions and cut-backs of growth that the authorities imposed in order to wipe out the deficits caused by government overseas spending were several times as large as the deficits themselves. The costs were so large that from one point of view, the government's pursuit of its illusions of grandeur has rightly been seen as the sole cause of the unbalances and therefore ultimately of the decline of the British economy. In that view, no other explanations are necessary.

Let us recall that until the middle 1970s, when inflation began to take over as the official obsession, it was the foreign balance of payments that was the chief, and often the sole, cause of the restrictive policies which so damaged British industry. The official view was that 'the British economy' was living beyond its means by habitually importing more than it exported. But the economy falls into several distinct sectors, and it is useful to divide it into at least two: government transactions and all others. The picture indicated by Table 6.4 emerges.

This result may be astonishing to some eyes. There was in these critical years (and, of course, in the years before and since) no balance of payments problem at all in the British 'economy'. The economy was in a very healthy surplus, and in fact the surplus was greater than that achieved by Germany or Japan in the same years. If it had been allowed to accumulate, it would have doubled British foreign assets abroad, wiped out the problem of the 'Sterling Balances' and itself contributed, year by year, to further payments surpluses to boost further foreign investment, as it did in the heydays of the *Pax Britannica* in the nineteenth century. But instead of being allowed to benefit Britain in that way, it was squandered by the government in its own transactions.

Such a way of putting it might seem unfair. After all, some government expenditure must be incurred by all civilised countries, and

**Table 6.4:    The British Balance of Payments, 1958–69**

|      | Private Balance (£ million) | Official Balance (£ million) |
|------|-----------------------------|------------------------------|
| 1958 | + 558 | − 410 |
| 1959 | + 367 | − 479 |
| 1960 | + 76  | − 533 |
| 1961 | + 605 | − 541 |
| 1962 | + 625 | − 611 |
| 1963 | + 584 | − 691 |
| 1964 | − 78  | − 666 |
| 1965 | + 425 | − 677 |
| 1966 | + 706 | − 754 |
| 1967 | + 332 | − 793 |
| 1968 | + 387 | − 785 |
| 1969 | + 1,362 | − 942 |

Source:  W.A.P. Manser, *Britain in Balance* (1971), p. 29.

in any case, the apparent positive private balance was in part boosted by the official expenditure: thus some exports may have been induced only by the presence of British troops abroad or by the granting of foreign aid. But even if all possible deductions are made on those accounts, there is still a substantial negative balance left, which, as we have seen, has to be multiplied several times to get its true effect. Perhaps the full extent of this can best be appreciated by comparing the British balance with that of other similar countries (see Table 6.5).

It is clear that Britain's conduct of affairs was in a class of its own and bore no relationship to her economic or political position in the world. The only comparable example was the United States, who actually spent less in relation to her national income[34] but at least traded in for it the political leadership over a large part of the world. All the good the British did with their expenditure was merely to weaken the economy year by year to the point that the country's political influence was ebbing *because* of the enormous drain abroad.

The negative balance caused by government action tended to rise over the period. The cause for this was that while British expenditure was constant, the offsetting positive payments on government account fell off as others, but not Britain, adjusted to a peacetime world. The largest items of expenditure were military costs and foreign aid, the latter having a tendency to grow relatively, and the servicing of foreign loans taken up because of earlier deficits.

**Table 6.5:   Foreign Balances of Government Payments and Receipts, Nine Countries, 1966**

|  | (in $ million) |
| --- | --- |
| USA | − 6,385 |
| UK | − 1,288 |
| Belgium/Luxemburg | − 46 |
| Sweden | − 45 |
| Netherlands | − 42 |
| Italy | − 9 |
| France | − 1 |
| Japan | + 315 |
| Germany | + 339 |

Source:  W.A.P. Manser, *Britain in Balance* (1971), p. 31.

It is not difficult to see why Britain alone should have drifted into this dream world of Walter Mitty, Great Power status in the postwar years. There was not only a long and successful history over two centuries to look back on, but also the self-flattering way in which the victory in World War Two was interpreted by crediting it to national superiority rather than to the Channel and some powerful allies: 'Britain had helped to win the war: once more it looked as though British were best.'[35] Politicians and generals have never been very perceptive about the extent to which their power and victories depended on the economic strength of the nation they represented, and the British were no exception: not for them the cutting of the imperial mantle according to their cloth.

In one way, this whole issue raises political questions outside our range. A decision to spend resources on defence may be just as rational as to spend them on opulence. But how far should a government expect the economy to meet any burden they are pleased to place upon it? It is part of our theme that the choice was made with frightening carelessness, and that governments entered into commitments without any apparent idea of the actual cost, let alone the total cost to the national economy when the multiplier of frustrated growth and inhibited technical development is taken into account. This light-hearted disposal of the country's economic, and thereby political and military, future is nothing else but an aspect of the rake's progress that is the theme of this book: an insistence on immediate satisfaction no matter at what damage to the future. It may be argued that without expenditure on defence there might not have been a country or an economy left to prosper, and it would be out of place to examine this view in detail for every occasion of military intervention or politically motivated subsidy. All one can say is that other countries, with a more lively sense of the importance of their economic and industrial infrastructure, not only survived by a more economical form of government housekeeping but ultimately did so with benefit to their political position and military credibility. In Britain the two arms of policy reinforced each other.[36] It is at least arguable that after each intervention a special effort should have been made to repair the damage to the engineering and capital goods industry to allow Britain to compete on even terms in world markets. The Korean venture especially was understood to have immensely damaged British industrial power compared with others who had a smaller urge to defend Western positions in the Far East; it raised defence expenditure from 6 to 10 per cent of GNP — or by two years of growth. But the vulnerable industries, after having been clobbered in war, were picked out time and again as victims of financial policies in the peace years that followed.

The irony of these events, and it is not the first to appear in these pages, will not have been lost on the reader. Here is an economy which not only makes ends meet, but shows an enormous and healthy surplus in relation to the rest of the world; and here is a government spending gaily without any apparent concern as to what the country can afford, and when its extravagance causes an overall deficit to appear, it reacts to it by measures which every time weaken the ability of the economy to make ends meet next time round. At the end of the day, the Minister presiding over this wasteful damage, the Chancellor of the Exchequer, then feels called upon in and out of season to lecture the rest of the population (i.e. that part which has produced the surplus) on the need to restrain their demands, cease living in cloud cuckoo land and learn to live within their means.

If this was all there was to it, we should have had to put reckless government spending beyond our means into the centre of our picture. There is, however, another point to the devastation brought about by this 'imperial hangover'.[37] It does not follow that even the spendthrift and irresponsible way in which politicians undermined the economy in their quest for grandeur need have brought the havoc to Britain that it actually did. After all, Britain still had basically enormous economic strength at the end of the war. The example of France shows that it was possible for a very much weaker economy to spend vast sums on colonial wars, to build up its own nuclear force and in general to show other symptoms of *folie de grandeur*, yet foster its own industrial and economic growth and emerge at a level not very different from those who ploughed their own furrows without troubling too much about the figure they cut in the world. Although there is no telling to what further adventures after Korea, Suez, Kenya, or Cyprus British governments might have been tempted if their home base had been stronger, there is no reason why in spite of them a positive, instead of the actual destructive, economic policy at home could not have protected the economy sufficiently to keep it in step with other advanced countries.

The 'might-have-beens' of history can be taken too far. Without lavish government spending abroad, for example, the Treasury might have found no cause periodically to disrupt the British economy — though it is also possible that it might, for trade finds its own level and there might still have been the odd deficit year which might have given the throttlers their chance. All we can say is that the squanderings for politico-military ends abroad would have caused only temporary set-backs, had economic policy at home been less destructive. Both the government spending spree and the Treasury's policy were causes; but from our point of view, the overseas spending was not the active, but only one of the permissive, causes. We must now turn to examine some other significant permissive causes of the British economic failure.

## Notes

1. Lord Kaldor, Letter to *The Times*, 28 January 1980; also his evidence to the Radcliffe Commission, vol. 3, p. 151; report in the *Guardian*, 25 October 1979.

2. In the case of France, all the traditional reasons, such as the social system, the poor scientific education, the stranglehold of the bureaucracy, etc. would have pointed to industrial backwardness — until the post-war surge proved them all wrong. Rondo Cameron, 'L'économie française: passé, présent, avenir', *Annales E.S.C.* no. 25 (1970), pp. 1418–33. Also J.-J. Carre, P. Dubois and E. Malinvaud, *French Economic Growth* (French original, 1972).

3. E.g. Donald N. McCloskey, *Economic Maturity and Entrepreneurial Decline: British Iron and Steel, 1870–1913* (1973); *idem* (ed.), *Essays on a Mature Economy: Britain after 1840* (1971).

4. It is also often circular reasoning: management is poor because the 'culture' of British managers was less propitious to change and development than elsewhere. E.g. E.H. Phelps Brown in Sir Alec Cairncross (ed.), *British Economic Prospects Reconsidered* (1971), p. 121.

5. S. Gomulka, 'Britain's Slow Industrial Growth — Increasing Inefficiency versus Low Rate of Technical Change' in W. Beckerman (ed.), *Slow Growth in Britain* (1979), esp. p. 186; T. Nakase, *Some Characteristics of Japanese-type Multinational Enterprises Today* (Osaka, 1980), Appendix. But see Keith Pavitt (ed.), *Technical Innovation and British Economic Performance* (1980).

6. E.g. T.W. Hutchison, letter in *The Times*, 4 February 1980.

7. Nicholas Kaldor, *Causes of the Slow Rate of Economic Growth'* (1972), p. 3.

8. The most persuasive study is C.P. Kindleberger, *Europe's Post-War Growth, The Role of Labour Supply* (1967); also the main argument of Francis Knox, *Governments and Growth* (1976).

9. Stout, 'De-industrialisation', p. 176.

10. R. Wragg and J. Robertson, *Post-War Trends in Employment* (1978), p. 50.

11. John Cornwall, *Modern Capitalism* (1977), p. 91.

12. Kaldor, *Causes of the Slow Rate of Economic Growth*, p. 25; P.J. Verdoorn, 'On the Empirical Law Governing the Productivity of Labour', *Econometrics*, no. 19 (1951). For a critique, see P. Stoneman, 'Kaldor's Law and British Economic Growth 1800–1970', *Applied Economics*, no. 11 (1979), pp. 309–19; R. Rowthorn, 'What Remains of Kaldor's Law?', *Economic Journal*, no. 85 (1975), pp. 10–19; and N. Kaldor, 'Economic Growth and the Verdoorn Law', ibid., pp. 891–6; T.F. Cripps and R.J. Tarling, *Growth in Advanced Capitalist Economies* (1973), pp. 22–3, 31–3.

13. E.g. W.E.G. Salter, *Productivity and Technical Change* (1960); Wilfred Beckerman, *The British Economy in 1975* (1965), pp. 26–33; also Chapter 2, section 2, above.

14. Knox, *Governments and Growth*, pp. 132–3; Kaldor, 'Economic Growth and the Verdoorn Law', p. 895.

15. Consider the following by (Sir) John Hicks: 'It is really nonsense to suggest that the phenomenal growth in productivity which has been attained in Germany during the 1950's could conceivably have been attained in a country such as Britain, if only our policies [monetary or otherwise] could have been different, and [especially] if capital investment had been increased. What has been happening in Germany is that consumption *and* investment *and* exports have all of them been expanding vastly. This has only been possible because the opportunities for expansion were ready made.' Quoted in T.W. Hutchison, *Economics and Economic Policy in Britain, 1946–1966* (1968), p. 157.

16. E.g. A.P. Thirlwall, 'The UK's Economic Problem: a Balance of Payments Constraint?', *National Westminster Bank Quarterly Review* (February 1978), pp. 29–30. His paper, 'The Balance of Payments Constraint as an Explanation of International Growth Rate Differences', *Banca Nazionale del Lavoro Quarterly Review*, no. 128 (1979) shows that elasticity of demand for imports was rather lower in Britain than the typical European elasticity from 1953 to 1976 (p. 51).

17. Cf. also Paul Streeten, 'The Objectives of Economic Policy' in P.D. Henderson (ed.), *Economic Growth in Britain* (1966), pp. 61 and *passim*.

18. G.F. Ray, 'Labour Costs in O.E.C.D. Countries', *National Institute Economic Review*, no. 75 (1976), p. 58.

19. Michael Beenstock, 'Taxation and Incentives in the UK', *Lloyds Bank Review*, no. 134 (October 1979), pp. 1–15. For a recent study of the incentive to work, see A.B. Atkinson and J.S. Flemming, 'Unemployment, Social Security and Incentives', *Midland Bank Review* (Autumn 1978), pp. 6–16.

20. Robert Bacon and Walter Eltis, *Britain's Economic Problem: Too Few Producers* (1976). The idea that in the British context more investment would only create unemployment is, of course, widely contested, e.g. *Barclay's Bank Review* (February 1977), p. 13.

21. For a good survey, see Michael Stewart, *The Jekyll and Hyde Years* (1977), pp. 195–6; Francis Cripps, Wynne Godley and Martin Fetherston, 'Public Expenditure and the Management of the Economy', *Evidence to 9th Report of the Expenditure Committee: Public Expenditure, Inflation and the Balance of Payments*, H.C. 328 (1974), esp. p. 2 (para. 6), p. 5 (paras. 15–16), p. 13 (paras. 2–3).

22. Especially Colin Clark, *Growthmanship: a Study in the Mythology of Investment* (1964), pp. 135 ff.

23. J. Carrington and G. Edwards, *Financing Industrial Investment* (1978), p. 86.

24. Table 2.3 and p. 26 above. Also A. Maddison, *Economic Growth in the West* (1964), p. 28; J.-P. Mockers, *Croissances économiques comparées: Allemagne, France, Royaume-Uni 1950–1967* (1969), p. 238; E.F. Denison, 'Economic Growth' in Richard E. Caves, *Britain's Economic Prospects* (1968); Kaldor, *Causes of the Slow Rate of Economic Growth*, pp. 15–16.

25. E.g. *The Economist*, 11 October 1975, p. 15; J.R. Sargent, *Out of Stagnation* (Fabian Tract 343) (1963), *Midland Bank Review* (February 1977). pp. 10–17; Sir Alec Cairncross, 'Concluding Reflections' in *Britain's Economic Progress Reconsidered*, p. 220; Stout, 'Capacity Adjustment', pp. 104, 113.

26. A. Lamfalussy, *The United Kingdom and the Six* (1963), p. 94.

27. *The United Kingdom and the Six*, pp. 105–6; and *Investment and Growth in Mature Economies* (1961).

28. *Investment and Growth*, p. 185.

29. Lamfalussy, *United Kingdom and the Six*, pp. 75–80; David K. Stout, 'Capacity Adjustment in a Slowly Growing Economy' in Beckerman, *Slow Growth*, pp.107–8; B. Moore and J. Rhodes, 'The Relative Decline of the UK Manufacturing Sector', *Economic Policy Review* (March 1976).

30. Society of Motor Manufacturers and Traders, *The British Motor Manufacturing Industry* (1979), p. 65. But this is denied in Economic Development Committee for Motor Manufacturing, *Regional Policy and the Motor Industry* (1969), p. 3.

31. Sima Lieberman, *The Growth of European Mixed Economies 1945–70* (1977), p. 218.

32. The classic example is E.F. Denison, *Why Growth Rates Differ* (1967).

33. T. Barna, *Investment and Growth Policies in British Industrial Firms* (1962), pp. 1, 31. Abo Sir Roy Harrod, *Towards a New Economic Policy* (1967), p. 6; N. Kaldor and J.A. Mirrlees, 'A New Model of Economic Growth', *Review of Economic Studies*, no. 29 (1962), p. 174.

34. The USA spent a larger proportion of her national income on 'defence' than Britain, who came second among the Western countries by a long lead, but Britain spent relatively more in foreign currency.

35. Uwe Kitzinger, *The Politics and Economics of European Integration* (1963), p. 189.

36. E.g. D. Lomax, 'What Attitude to Growth?', *National Westminster Quarterly Review* (February 1974), pp. 28–30.

37. Roger Opie, 'The Making of Economic Policy' in Hugh Thomas (ed.), *Crisis in the Civil Service* (1968), p. 70. 'They seemed convinced', the author goes on, 'that we are still, in some unspecified way, terribly important in the world and that although we can no longer enforce international good behaviour (i.e. what suits our interests), on others, we can shame others into it.'

# 7  PERMISSIVE CAUSES

## 1 The Economists

Historical events, like accidents, are the result of the simultaneous occurrence of several causes. However, not all of these causes carry the same weight or work in the same way. A rough and ready classification would be to divide them into active and permissive causes. To the direct action by the Treasury we must add other circumstances that allowed the damaging consequences to take place in the way they did. Our first such permissive circumstance is the peculiar position and attitude of the economics profession in Britain.

It is at first sight surprising that policies as damaging as those of the British Treasury should have been permitted to continue for such a long period without determined and sustained protests by the economics profession. This is now large and influential. The Establishment at the top, consisting of the leading government advisers, financial journalists, university teachers and directors of research may be expected to monitor and criticise policies and to devise alternatives; and they could count on an educated public opinion at polytechnics and colleges, even in schools and in numerous market and other research bodies, to judge theories and policies on their merits. Why has there been no rebellion from their ranks? Moreover, while it could be argued in the 1950s that there were few economists in the key Ministries and that no one listened to them, this changed in the 1960s. In 1967 there were 110 professional economists in Whitehall plus another 300 administrators with economics degrees; and by 1975 there were 352 professional economists alone.[1] Why was there no one amongst them to stop the grievous damage done by the government to the economy?

It is true that anyone offering a solution out of line with the thoughts of mainstream economics runs the risk of being dubbed a crank. Economics is a subject plagued by cranks, which tells us a great deal about economics; but it is well known that many cranks are later canonised as far-seeing pioneers, and surely after the experience of the last thirty years, 'anything which is the systematic opposite of the highest common denominator of conventional wisdom has a particular presumption in its favour.'[2]

The failure of the economists to halt the British decline is all the more remarkable since British economists are generally considered to be among the best in the world. The greatest advances in the subject, including those rewarded with the Nobel prize, have been made almost exclusively in America and Britain, with important contributions, appropriate to their smaller numbers, from those abroad who habitually use the English language for their learned work, particularly the Dutch and the Scandinavians. By contrast, the genius of the people of Germany, France, Italy, even Japan, the countries with the finest post-war economic record, has not so far made much impact on mainstream economic theory.[3]

There is a simple answer to this apparent paradox: it was this febrile brilliance in the field of economic theory itself that inhibited good advice from the profession. Economic theory, as it has developed in the Anglo-Saxon world, turns out to have been a handicap rather than an aid to good policy. It is worth examining, if only all too briefly, how this has come about.

At the heart of the failure lies the tragedy of economics that it is neither quite an art nor a science. It is near enough to a science to be able to absorb a full range of scientific trappings, including complex computer programmes — yet it has to allow for so many non-quantified outside influences that true prediction becomes impossible with present means. The range of possible errors in every theoretical construct is always wider than the possible policy options, and thus wholly useless for policy-making, yet it is intellectually satisfying enough to be worked over, discussed — and taken seriously. As the subject has progressed, theorems have become ever more elaborate and internally consistent but no closer to reality. The attempts to bridge the gap by econometric studies have normally made matters worse, for they usually have even fewer variables, cruder measures (or only proxy measures) and, if anything, greater dependence on the stability of functions which in the nature of economic and historical reality tend to change in unpredictable ways.[4] The preoccupation with theoretical economics has turned into a most powerful training in the search for intellectual perfection while underrating the need to conform to the real world.

A single example of that pervasive intellectual disease must suffice. It concerns the definition of the subject itself. Anyone who observes what economists do might be forgiven for thinking that their subject is concerned with such matters as man as a working, social animal, with relations expressed in money, with material welfare, or with wealth and poverty. But that is not how the profession sees itself. Its own preferred definition is that 'Economics is the science which studies human behaviour as a relationship between ends and scarce means which have alternative uses.'[5]

It cannot be denied that that is an interesting and intellectually stimulating definition, opening up various new vistas. At the same time, it is clear that it does *not*, in fact, define what economists concern themselves with. One would look in vain, for example, in the literature for discussions on how a conductor fills his limited programme time, or an artist his spacially limited canvas; but at the time when the definition first appeared, in 1932, the world was overflowing with surpluses of every conceivable commodity, a matter with which economists were very much concerned. To put 'scarcity' at the centre of the definition in those conditions was an insult and a mockery to the forty million unemployed workers and perhaps hundred million peasants in the world who were told that no one wanted their labour and their produce. The profession, it seems, was not troubled about the contradiction between this definition and reality: the *Essay* elaborating the above definition was quoted for decades with approval in every standard textbook.

There is clearly a certain intellectual fascination in following through the implications of rational unreality; it requires skill and training which courses in economic theory are designed to foster. The game has certain rules, including the rule that the premises must be realistic even though inadequate;[6] but overall the emphasis, and the glory within the profession, rests on elegance rather than verisimilitude. Paradoxes that bewilder the general public, such as the oft-quoted statement that price rises are necessary to curb inflation, are definitely part of the game. When one noted economist says of some others that 'I have long been puzzled that distinguished economists should have been willing to work from a model as unrealistic, over-simplified, and arbitrary as. . .'[7] his puzzlement is misplaced, for these qualities are of the essence of current economic theorems. Neo-classical economic theory, the kind taught in recent decades, may therefore be an excellent training of the mind, but it is among the worst possible preparations for giving advice on practical economic policy decisions. It was precisely that training in which Britain excelled.

Let us repeat wherein the weakness lies: it lies not in the internal logic, which may be faultless, but in the unreal or inadequate premisses. As a result, economic textbooks and theoretical articles will be found to agree widely, and to be similar the world over; but the advice given by economists will be contradictory. It is highly significant that nowadays economists specify carefully that they are considering the 'real economy' on the rare occasions when they do so, instead of the world of symbols in which they usually move. At best, economic theory may be considered a necessary, but never a sufficient, ingredient of practical advice.

In the present context, this lack of contact with reality shows itself very clearly in the failure to see what the reckless decision to 'cut back temporarily on investment', so easy to carry out when conducted in algebraic symbols representing the whole of a country's capital formation, actually means on the ground:

> once inside the boardroom, investment is no longer an economic abstraction. It is real money that has to be sweated and negotiated for: real money that will disappear into a green field and re-emerge as plant and buildings; real money will be lost, and lost for ever, if the new factory does not make a profit. At the back of all the cogitation and planning in private, risk-taking business, lies the threat of bankruptcy; with the loss of employment and income, and break of career for all concerned. Give a firm a long enough period, then, of shrinking markets and uncertainty, and the philosophy of investment will be 'when in doubt, don't'. This philosophy will tend to persist after good times have been restored. After all, it is always safer *not* to invest. . .And so, over the whole economy, a multitude of company decisions, for good business reasons, adds up to slower growth for the economy.[8]

It would not be too much to say that a great deal of the teaching and training in economic theory serves to hide just such realities. Only thus is it explicable that in the key years of the 1960s, the government devastated the British motor industry, one of the most vital centres of economic life in the country, by changing taxes and HP regulations every ten months on average for 'macro-economic' reasons, without, it seems, even having an inkling what massive damage it was doing to Britain's industrial and economic future. These

> government demand management policies imposed severe cost penalties on the motor industry. They had a detrimental effect on the industry's profitability and planned investment programmes and led to a serious erosion in the UK's competitive position in

world markets. Fluctuations in the level of demand also gave rise to problems of industrial relations and manufacturing efficiency, for suppliers as well as vehicle manufacturers, and were a disincentive for productivity improvement.[9]

Nor does it seem to have struck our policy makers that economic 'resources' are real things that cannot be switched at a moment's notice: that the resources of the building industry, for example, cannot just be converted into export manufacture.[10] Just as they fail to see the real and permanent costs of measures inflicted for temporary reasons, they also fail to recognise that people will learn and will become suspicious of government action and anticipate and counteract it next time round. It is frightening to hear even first-year economics students talk glibly of 'deflating the economy' or of 'switching resources', without evidently the faintest idea what may be involved in costs, dislocation and permanent discouragement: it is like seeing a six-year-old 'repairing' one's favourite watch with a hammer. The Procrustean economics of stretching and hacking the sleeper, instead of adjusting the bed, is taught to our economists from the beginning, and is confirmed with every course in theory they take.

The result of this quest for elegance instead of realism has been that economics as a subject, and economists *as* economists, have been useless as guides for policy making. Lest this should sound too harsh a judgement, let us consider four of the major policy issues on which the advice of economists has been sought, and which have in fact preoccupied many members of the profession, and see what advice 'economic theory' has been able to give.

The first important issue was the depression and the unemployment in the inter-war years, truly a task worthy of the best efforts that economists were capable of. What happened was that the leading academic economists and the Treasury had one set of policy prescriptions; Keynes and his followers had another. We do not need to decide between them: suffice it to say that the advice proffered by half the profession was considered by the other half to be disastrous and counter-productive. How was the country to choose between them? A second major area of interest, mainly since the war, has been advice to developing economies. Here also there is an enormous literature, but nothing of use to the developing world, for every concrete piece of advice given by one economist will be contradicted by another. Thus for every one urging the use of high-intensity technology, there is another urging primitive technology; for every one stressing agriculture, there is another one stressing industry; for every one stressing development on a broad front there is another demanding uneven development; for every one stressing a leading export industry there is another insisting on import substitution; and so on throughout the whole range of options. Our third example concerns the likely effect of joining the Common Market. The question was put to economists and leaving out political and other considerations, was simple and clear-cut: would Britain stand to gain or lose on balance by joining? The reply of the British economists was equally clear-cut: almost exactly half said that we would gain, and the other half said that we would lose. And not one guessed that the French would not permit us to join anyway.

The fourth issue is the theme of this book, British post-war economic policy. In that period, it is true, economic performance has outclassed the inter-war period, and there has been a higher level of employment and a faster rate of growth than ever before. Some economists have not been slow to claim the credit for this, on the grounds that now, at last, they have a 'workable scientific theory'.[11] The fact, however, is that Britain's policies were such that on the very Keynesian assumption which allegedly informed her economic advisers, they should have plunged the country into a depression akin to that of the inter-war years.[12] She was rescued from such a fate only because the rest of the world, particularly that part that did not enjoy the advice of Anglo-Saxon economists, was being propelled forward by a massive secular boom which transmitted itself even to Britain, and the worst out policy makers could do was to reduce the potential growth rate of 5 per cent to an actual one of 2–3 per cent. Exports, rising at the rate of two-thirds of world demand, helped to pull up home manufacturing output.[13] Full employment and its benefits were thus achieved because of rising exports and a higher investment rate than pre-war, but certainly not because of any government policies.[14] Now that the impetus of world buoyancy has been waning, the results in Britain begin to look very much like the characteristic features of the Great Depression of the 1930s.

There is therefore no reason for British economists, basking in the acknowledged superiority of their own theorising, to wonder how it is that the benighted Continentals, without benefit of Keynes, managed to do so well in comparison with Britain and the USA: 'something more is evidently required than a knowledge of techniques. On the continent of Europe during the period immediately following the war, the Keynesian message was not generally accepted.'[15] Indeed, 'the economic performance of countries such as Germany and France, in their years of superiority, probably owed little to the economic steering of their authorities. If anything it was achieved despite their efforts.'[16] But that assumed that the only possible policy of government is Keynesian-type 'steering'. The policy actually adopted by the top French advisers in their first post-war plan was to give overriding priority to massive investment in five sectors, coal-mining, electricity, iron and steel, cement and agricultural machinery and transport. Such a plan would have been much beneath the dignity of British economists, trained to think in macro-figures: they would have left such tasks to hacks and to East Europeans. Yet it turned out to be the first step on the road to France's miraculous modernisation. The French plan arose out of concrete answers to concrete questions for which the theories with which British economists are weighed down are of little proven worth. Nor do the latter seem to have done much good in 'one of their most important roles [in Government service] to react critically to the spontaneous, naive and often inconsistent theorizing of politicians and civil servants'.[17]

This is not to say that economists cannot, or should not, give advice. On the contrary, they are among the most able people in the country thinking about policy issues, they have a great deal of practical experience and close knowledge of problems and mechanisms, and unlike other sources of advice, they usually have no private axe to grind. It is just that their corpus of theory gets in the way, and it is much stronger and more deeply rooted than in other countries. If 'the economist is treated by the public rather like a quack doctor',[18] this does reflect the similarity with pre-scientific, say eighteenth-century, medicine. Medicine then was based on entirely erroneous theories; treatment used the most painful or unpleasant methods imaginable, and while it seldom did anything towards a cure, it frequently did greater harm than the original ailment.[19] Anyone with a flair for statistics could easily have worked out that the calling in of medical advice always enhanced the chance of a fatal termination of the illness. Yet people called in doctors in the eighteenth century, rightly, and for the same reason that they employ economists in Britain in the twentieth: their practical experience and common sense often allowed them to provide useful advice, in spite of the pseudo-science with which their minds were addled. The prestige of economics derives not from the aptness of its answers, but from the frequency with which people ask its questions.

It is significant in this context that British economic advisers in government are frequently found to see problems from the 'administrative' point of view, while the official administrators see the 'economic' point of view in mutual discussion.[20] This is a role reversal unimaginable in the case of real scientists in government service, say medical advisers or research chemists, and highlights the role of economists as common-sense people, and not as trained scientists.

Very few economists, as indeed very few other professionals, break out of the assumptions and the framework of their science: there are very few real 'structuralists' as distinct from 'tinkerers'[21] active in the subject today. Still less can such fundamental reconsideration be expected from even the most able and most critical journalists who work within tight schedules and therefore have to take their ideas from elsewhere within the profession.[22]

Here, then, is one permissive cause of the British economic failure: the economics profession has proved incapable of dealing with a problem that can be solved not by devising better theories, in which British economists excel, but by altering the premises and the possible range of variables within which policy can operate. Lesser mortals, less proficient theoreticians, have been able elsewhere to change course and might have been able to do so here too, but it was the tragedy and the failure of the British economic profession that it was too refined for the earthy problems besetting the British economy in recent years.

## 2  The Treasury and the Civil Service

Up to this point we have used the Treasury as a synonym for the economic decision-makers, and it is time to admit that this does not strictly represent the facts. Nowadays the Bank of England has much influence, as have the opinions of the professional economists scattered in other Ministries; there are the independent research teams and their computers and forecasting programmes; there are the politicians in and out of the Cabinet, there is the political climate, and there is even pressure from abroad. 'The formulation of advice takes place in a climate shaped by prevailing orthodoxies, newspaper comment, lunch-time debate, and all that goes to make up current controversy.'[23] Yet in all this, ultimately the Treasury's view prevails, for the Treasury is not only a centre of thought about policy, but above all a centre of power.

The question is why that power should have been used consistently in the direction of throttling back and damaging the productive part of the economy in order to rectify unbalances on the monetary side. Part of the answer is to be found in Chapter 4, where we have seen that the Treasury's macro-economic power was, for historical reasons, wedded to responsibility for one narrow segment of the economy, namely its foreign exchange and currency balance. In the inevitable strain of loyalties between single-faceted responsibility but multi-faceted power, it is not entirely surprising that the Treasury's own tasks took precedence over the long-term interests of the country as a whole, that it refused to engage in medium-term planning, and that 'what has passed for policy has consequently consisted of reaction to short-term crises'.[24]

There was also a second reason. It is to be found in the traditional job of the Treasury, which is to keep down the expenditure of the other government departments. Expenditure is therefore traditionally seen as the enemy, the evil to be kept down; the actual efficiency of the expenditure in terms of the social or economic good it might do, or the comparative efficiency of two competing claims, are completely outside the Treasury's traditional range: 'The time-honoured Treasury attitude to spending is summed up by candle-ends' — the phrase used by Gladstone to describe minute saving of detail, and a former Economic Secretary, Nigel Birch, found that

> [t]he Treasury can argue for months on end with all the subtlety of Duns Scotus about what a day's subsistence allowance ought to be for Bogotá, but when really large sums are at stake there tends to be a certain withdrawal of interest.

'Instead of worrying about candle-ends', said one Treasury Minister, 'they should have asked themselves the question "in what sense should Britain still be a great power?"'[25]

This blindness to economic reality, as distinct from departmental accounting, was particularly disastrous in the failure to see the difference between current expenditure and productive investment. In times of stress they were treated as equally worthy of cuts — indeed, capital expenditure was generally treated as more easily dispensable, since it offered fewer toes to be trodden on: 'Few Civil

Service jobs are at stake and there are no awkward negotiations with unions or large redundancies.'[26] Similarly, when actual cuts had to be imposed, the tendency was for the burden to be shared out equally between the departments: the exercise was therefore a political rather than an economic one, which would have been to minimise the economic or social damage of the cuts. One could go further and say that the Treasury function as the nation's watchdog over public expenditure was altogether seen as a political task, geared mainly to the power a Minister could pull in the Cabinet, or to the influence of a particular Permanent Secretary as against another. It was as far as it possibly could be from the economic logic of looking at the government's activities as a whole, which might well at times require an increase of expenditure in certain directions, even in tight times, and a more than proportionate cut elsewhere.[27] It was this kind of approach, and only this kind of approach, which made it conceivable for the Treasury to react to all crises with the standard formula: 'produce less and eat up your seedcorn.'

Attempts were made from time to time to develop positive and growth-oriented counter-poles to the Treasury's 'cost- and needs-oriented'[28] economising stance. The most significant of these were the Central Economic Planning Staff of 1947, the NEDC ('Neddy') of 1962, and above all the Department of Economic Affairs (DEA) of 1964. Of these, the CEPS, under the Minister of Economic Affairs, fell under the control of the Treasury partly by accident, since the Minister, Sir Stafford Cripps, had to take over as Chancellor at short notice after the Budget indiscretion by Hugh Dalton. In 1953 the Treasury took over the Economic Section of the Cabinet Office and in 1958 the function of the dissolved Planning Staff. Neddy never had much chance of wielding any power. The nearest that any outside organisation ever came to undermining the dominance of the Treasury over policy occurred at the foundation of the DEA under George Brown:

> It envisaged a wholly novel form of national social accountancy to replace the orthodox financial accountancy by which the Treasury has always dominated British life. [It arose out of the Labour Party's belief in 1963–4 that] the economy was being held back, that unemployment was being kept high, that all sorts of barriers were being erected to keep down industrial activity, by reason of the orthodox financial policy of the Treasury. Out of this thing grew the idea that it would be better to have an economic depart-

ment, which (as I always saw it) would be superior to the Treasury
in determining the country's economic priorities.

Within two years a clash had become inevitable:

> We [tried]. . .to get the whole economy running ahead; the Trea-
> sury was constantly damping things down. . . Repeated doses of
> vast deflation were forced upon us — which was simply the old
> Treasury remedy still being applied in order to maintain the
> fiction that the pound was worth X numbers of dollars.

But, almost inevitably, 'The revolution failed. . .orthodox financial
control won.'[29]
What is particularly interesting from our point of view is the widespread belief that, had the new Economics Ministry been put under
the Treasury, or at least staffed by leading Treasury officials, it
might have been allowed to survive and try a run of its policies.[30] In
other words, the fatal opposition of the Treasury was not so much
directed against different economic approaches, but was part of a
battle for power.
The Treasury's power no doubt derives in part from the native
talent of Treasury men; but very largely it rests on the solid fact that
it holds the purse strings and acts as the personnel department for the
whole Civil Service. What we have therefore is a department standing on three legs. By the fateful constellation of historical development and of its own inherent talents, its most important leg, overall
economic policy, is poisoned by its second leg, the direct responsibility for currency and exchange matters, but is made dominant by
the third leg, the control over the Civil Service.
Planning in the real sense, the direction of private citizens, the
apparatus of *étatisme* were more foreign to the British Treasury and
Civil Service[31] than to the traditions of the Continentals and even of
the Japanese. Not that the range of functions of the modern British
state was any less — according to some critics, it was even greater —
but in the absence of a tradition and of a willingness to recognise the
modern reality, it was *ad hoc*, less co-ordinated, it made less sense
and it was less effective. It was generally left to the politicians in
charge, less well versed in financial matters but more aware of the
general social implications, to force the permanent Treasury officials to think in sensible economic cause and effect, rather than
departmental accountancy and internal politics terms: the famous

incident of Winston Churchill's misgivings over the return to gold in 1925 has been repeated many times since.[32]

Beyond the Treasury itself, the character of the whole top layer in the Civil Service also played a part in permitting the unchallenged pursuit of disastrous policies without change over thirty years. It is difficult to believe that a group like the French civil service elite, with their mathematical-technical training and their relative independence from the politicians, or the American top appointees who come in with each new administration and are therefore less tied to previous policies, or indeed any group less sure of itself would not have acted differently in the same external circumstances.

As matters now lie in Britain, the 'harsh' choices will be at no cost to the Civil Service. While

> The governments which have followed the [consensus, or Whitehall] policies — especially 1964, 1970, 1974 and 1979 — paid a heavy price in electoral terms. . .those who furnished the briefing for the Ministers concerned have continued in power, subject only to the normal wastage occasioned by retirement at 60.[33]

Essentially what counts is the Administrative Class. Within it are to be found all the officials who co-ordinate the actions of different Ministries with or without the consent of the politicians nominally at their head, who provide and select the advice submitted to Ministers, and who can exert direct personal influence on the Ministers themselves. The Administrative Class of the British Civil Service is without doubt an intellectual elite, devoting itself to its tasks with honesty and dedication; but it is also a social and power elite. It is part of the British 'Establishment' and the selection process with all its variants and variations since the war has zig-zagged between the twin poles of a bias towards intellectual ability and bias towards the 'right' background of class and upbringing. It had produced a group overwhelmingly from the professional and managerial middle classes, from the public schools and the ancient universities, with a training overwhelmingly in the humanities. In all these respects, the bias of the direct entrants has been even greater than that of the entrants by internal promotion (see Table 7.1).

By initial training, therefore, most of them are unprepared for the task of administering a complex economy, and while the numbers trained in economics, statistics or accountancy are growing, they are still pitifully small within the overall totals. Add to this the tradition

**Table 7.1: The Administrative Class of the Civil Service, 1960s**

|  | All Entrants (per cent) |  | Direct Entrants (per cent) |  |
|---|---|---|---|---|
| Class origins: |  |  |  |  |
|   Professional and managerial | 67 | ⎫ | 79 | ⎫ |
|   Working | 19 | ⎬ 100 | 11 | ⎬ 100 |
|   Other and unknown | 14 | ⎭ | 10 | ⎭ |
| University, of those whose University was given: |  |  |  |  |
|   Oxford and Cambridge | 70 | ⎫ | 76 | ⎫ |
|   London | 10 | ⎪ | 8 | ⎪ |
|   Scottish | 10 | ⎬ 100 | 8 | ⎬ 100 |
|   All other English, Welsh, Irish and Foreign | 10 | ⎭ | 8 | ⎭ |
| Subjects studied[a]:   Arts | 71 |  | 77 |  |
|   Social Sciences | 28 |  | 27 |  |
|   Natural and Applied Sciences | 13 |  | 9 |  |
|   All others | 2 |  | 1 |  |

Note: a. Adds up to more than 100 per cent since some entrants studied more than one subject.
Source: Fulton Committee, *The Civil Service*, Cmnd. 3638 (1968), vol. 3 (1); A.H. Halsey and I.M. Crewe, *Social Survey of the Civil Service* (1969), pp. 19, 26, 27, 55, 84, 91.

of a different posting every two or three years, and the taunt of amateurism will not appear misplaced: in particular, even top administrators often lack a mathematical sense and a feel for quantitative relationships, preferring to trust their own alleged sense of values. Sometimes, as revealed for example in the Bank Rate leak investigation of 1957, this kind of decision-making is little removed from frivolity. 'Our whole national life is permeated with easy-going self-satisfaction, and the toleration of incompetence.'[34]

The further training within the departments which is part of the working life of the young top civil servant essentially teaches him two things. One is the manner of proceeding. Here he quickly finds that what is rewarded is the ability to write good papers, the ability to compromise and the skill to avoid treading on too many toes; major innovative thoughts are not encouraged, particularly in junior administrators, and habits acquired then tend to stick. As far as the subject-matter itself is concerned, he learns by the time-honoured method of 'sitting next to Nellie', or learning by doing what the others have done before him.[35] It would be difficult to think of a system more designed to perpetuate the basic policies carried on to date and to inhibit their questioning. The occasional secondments to formal training periods, though valuable in themselves, cannot be a substitute for the grasp of overall principles which alone provides the power and self-assurance to question transmitted assumptions.

This is not to impugn the ability of the top echelons: on the contrary, it may well be argued that the power and prestige attached to higher Civil Service jobs has drained too much of the nation's intellectual elite into the Administrative Class. What is at stake is the misapplication of so much brain power. It is precisely because of their innate ability, fostered by the peculiar skills developed in the service, that leading officials have been able for so long to defend the indefensible;[36] one can only wish that an equal effort had gone into devising policies that would not need to be defended because they were successful. It is not even clear that the British Civil Service, with all its weaknesses, is in any sense inferior to that of the more successful countries. It may just be that it is placed in a setting in which both its virtues and its failings work in the wrong direction.

How far do the permanent officials, particularly those in the Treasury, actually influence policy? The constitutional position according to which they provide impartial advice on all the possible options, let the politicians decide, and then loyally carry out the decisions arrived at by the politicians, is clearly little more than polite fiction. The real position is much more complex, and indeed impossible to summarise satisfactorily, not least because it differs so widely according to the personality of the Minister and his top advisers, the standing of the Minister within his party and his Cabinet, public opinion and many other factors.

The fiction of the completely obedient and colourless service has persisted for a long time in part because neither side had an interest in exposing it: no politician with further ambitions would be likely to admit that he could not control his own department, and no top administrator would be so foolish and indiscreet as to advertise his hidden unconstitutional power. Now that the lid has been blown in a series of sometimes sensational revelations, opinion has perhaps swung too far the other way. The ease with which the Conservative administration of 1979 changed economic policy provides a ready proof of the primacy of the politicians[37] though, as we shall see, the change was in fact much smaller than has been made out.

Certainly, one of the more remarkable aspects of the economic policies with which we are concerned is the speed with which leading politicians change their tune when they enter office, and in particular those who were loud in their critique of restrictiveness and concern for symbols become voices of orthodoxy.[38] It may of course be argued that the conversion is a result of having responsibility, rather than a result of Treasury influence, but it would be difficult to separate out these two factors in the 'harsh process of education'.[39] Conversely, it has often been observed how frequently 'departmental policy' remains the same even with a new incoming Minister, but changes when a top civil servant goes — particularly in the Treasury.[40]

The ways in which top civil servants are able to impose their own policies over the preferences of politicians are many and varied. They are anchored on the fact that officials are permanent, whereas politicians come and go and may be moved between departments even within the lifetime of one Parliament. Thus the permanent staff have their own interdepartmental network which may be used to alert other departments who could then put up their Ministers to oppose in Cabinet what the permanent staff has failed to prevent in their own. Further, they largely control the 'framework within which questions of policy are raised' and the information that reaches a busy Minister, who could not possibly himself read and keep abreast of the gamut of outside and alternative opinion. Unwanted options are thus sifted out, leaving the Minister perhaps with only one possible 'choice'.[41] The Treasury is particularly prone to such actions and, once having converted its own Ministers, is virtually unstoppable even if it has a majority of the Cabinet and official party programme against it. Under Mr Callaghan, it is alleged that the Treasury Ministers, together with the top officials of the Treasury and the Bank of England, formed a cabal which not only met in secret, but whose very existence was being kept secret from the rest of the Cabinet:

> Treasury submissions to Cabinet on economic policy (which would often be agreed in advance by the Prime Minister) only rarely tell the truth as the Treasury sees it. Normally, these documents are designed to limit discussion and to ensure that the Treasury line wins the day.

Moreover,

[t]here have been a number of examples in recent years where the

Cabinet has felt itself 'bounced' by a combination of the Chancellor, Treasury and Bank of England. . .into approving at the last minute decisions which have already been irreversibly taken.

No wonder that it has been held that under these conditions Cabinet responsibility 'was a sham' and 'there is no such thing as Cabinet Government in economic matters. Ministers basically do what the Treasury and the Bank of England tell them they have to do.'[42]

In these circumstances the civil servant's sense of loyalty becomes confused and naturally turns towards his current Department, within which he will have to continue working and within which he wants to be promoted. This may go as far as withholding information or even misinforming rival departments in the course of interdepartmental jockeying.

The second loyalty, with almost equal intensity, belongs to the Treasury, and for similar reasons:

All the civil servants I worked with were imbued with a prior loyalty to the Treasury and felt it necessary to spy on me and report all my doings to the Treasury whether I wanted them kept private or not. There was nothing I could do, no order I could give, which wasn't at once known to the Treasury, because my staff were all trained to check with the Treasury and let it know in advance exactly what each of them was doing. . . No doubt this is explained in the case of ambitious young men and women by the fact that the Treasury is the prime source of promotion. Without Treasury support they can't get on. But there are other senior people. . .who just feel the Treasury is their natural boss; and whereas the Treasury and the head of the Civil Service are permanent, the Minister changes once every three years on average. Why should they worry about giving any particular loyalty to me?[43]

The Treasury, a relatively small and elite group, is particularly prone to almost automatic loyalty to its colleagues — and a corresponding contempt for outsiders.[44]

Having made, defended and supported a certain policy over a period of time within the Treasury, its officials are necessarily committed to it; the means then become an end, the defence of past policies a policy object itself. Moreover, Treasury officials not only give advice to their Ministers, but also brief them on how to defend it. A united front then becomes more important than the pursuit of

the best policy, and it can hardly be expected that in such circumstances the views of critics will be conveyed to the Chancellor or
other Treasury Ministers with quite the same enthusiasm as the
defence of the Treasury's past line.[45] Once more, the whole system is
geared to maintain current policies and to inhibit any major changes
in direction.

The British Civil Service has many virtues and was in many ways
an ideal instrument for the later Victorian and Edwardian era; this is
particularly true of the Treasury. Even today it can be relied on to
complete a set task with admirable dedication and reliability. But the
very virtues become faults in the light of the present need to look
with fresh eyes at the role of Britain in the world, and the need to
realign fundamentally the course and premisses of economic policy.
The peculiar strengths and weaknesses of the Civil Service, and of
the Treasury in particular, form a powerful contributory cause of
our decline.

## 3 Other Permissive Causes

Among other outside factors that made possible the peculiar British
fate of starting off with a destructive policy and then being unable to
change it, we must include the political system, and its development
in this period into a genuine two-party system in which both parties
hold office for comparable periods of time. Had there been something like the inter-war sequence, with a near continuous rule by one
party, we might have seen the whole basis of policy questioned. As it
was, both sides were equally guilty of sacrificing the future to the
present, and the topic could therefore not become a live political
issue. The issue on which party debates did take place, such as
nationalisation, tax incentives, the social services or the Common
Market, were all issues with only marginal connections or none at all
with the issues of growth and decline. Only the Tribune group on the
left of the Labour Party offered a policy with alternative priorities,
making heavy investment in the nationalised industries and in others
to obtain a measure of state ownership, together with protection,
into their chief priority in place of stable currency or stable
exchanges. As far as the two sets of governments were concerned, on
all real economic policy issues they were engaged in a sham fight.[46]

Nor was the absence of a genuine alternative policy the only ill
effect of the particular British party constellation. There were at

least two others. One was the tendency to risk long-term strategy by a give-away Budget before elections, leaving the incoming administration, of whatever colour, with the task of doing considerable damage to the economy in order to bring it back on course. It is true that in each of the 'election Budget' years, and particularly in 1955, 1964 and 1970, there were other possible grounds also for an easing off of the brake, but it is hard to believe that the actual recklessness shown was not connected with electoral prospects.[47]

A damaging result of another kind arose from the actual periodic change of the party in power. Here the traditional obligation on the opposition to oppose as part of the normal sham fight had meant a general objection to prevailing policies on the part of the incoming party, even though at heart it would have done much the same thing when in office. The result was the introduction of new policies merely for the sake of being different,[48] and the need to rescind them in due course after they had done their damage — the famous 'U-turns'. The abolition of incomes policies after the elections of 1970, 1974 and 1979 are cases in point, though at the time of writing the 1979 abolition has not yet been reversed, except for civil servants.

Finally, among the permissive causes affecting the British economy adversely is the frequently discussed weakness in applied science and engineering. The low status of these subjects has its roots in history, and in so far as it implies a preference for 'gentlemanly' Arts subjects in the training of entrepreneurs, such as we have seen also to exist in the training of top civil servants, it may be considered a part of the historical weakness of entrepreneurship discussed in Chapters 5 and 6. However, the influence of this factor on economic growth in Britain has been much misunderstood.

Comparisons of educational facilities often fail to note that institutions which are classed abroad as universities might be polytechnics or technical colleges here, and the inclusion of these institutions would very much improve the British showing. There has in any case been a considerable increase in the numbers studying these subjects in recent years, though a further increase would seem to be necessary if the country is to have any hope of catching up with Europe.[49] To date there has not been any suggestion that the quality is inferior: British inventiveness, the number of British Nobel prize-winners in science, the successes in high-powered technology, such as Concorde, show that for the time being, lack of proficiency or originality in technology cannot be blamed for British economic shortcomings. Expenditure on research and development as a proportion of national income was higher in Britain than incomparable countries over much of the period. The difference was that a much larger part of it was devoted to military purposes in Britain, allowing such countries as Germany, Japan and the smaller economies of Europe to steal a march on British industry in useful and productive technology.[50]

The essence of the British problem lies in the inability of the engineering profession to reach in any number the highest echelons of power, in private industry as well as in the government.[51] This affects the decision-making process in a marked and negative way. Untrained directors and managers often fail to see the possibilities of a new process; moreover, there is a natural tendency for technicians to go for the best method, while there is a tendency for non-technicians to prefer balance sheet safety, and thus a vital upward impetus to technical innovation is lost. The general lack of drive towards modern high-technology methods[52] also tends to put a brake on those firms and industries which are capable and would be willing to move forward.

Ultimately, engineers also learn by doing. Engineering training of the best kind 'can only be achieved by involvement of the trainee in projects which call for the exercise of skills at or beyond the bounds of existing experience'.[53] Originality and the drive to innovation depend on opportunity to use these qualities. A country that cannot provide first-class engineering projects in sufficient numbers will lose its engineers of first-class ability. In the longer term, the downward, throttling policies of successive governments will demoralise the engineers and technologists as it has demoralised the entrepreneurs and trade unionists. The weakness in engineering and technology is an effect of Treasury policies, as well as being a permissive cause of further decline.

## Notes

1. Plus 42 qualified in Agricultural Economics. Michael Stewart, *The Jekyll and Hyde Years*, (1977), p. 93; Sir Alec Cairncross, *Essays In Economic Management* (1971), pp. 191, 198; Vernon Bogdanor and Robert Skidelsky (eds), *The Age of Affluence 1951–1964* (1970); pp. 75–6, 119; A.E. Booth and A.W. Coats, 'The Market for Economists in Britain, 1945–1975: a Preliminary Survey', *Economic Journal*, no. 88 (1978), p. 444; Peter Hennessy, 'Union panel studies role of government economists', *The Times*, 8 April 1980.
2. Peter Jay, *Employment, Inflation and Politics* (1976), p. 26.
3. OECD, it has been alleged, had 'so many mainstream British economists on its

staff that it [was] sometimes known as "the British Treasury in exile" ': Samuel Brittan and Peter Lilley, *The Delusion of Incomes Policy* (1977), p. 18.

4. There are now eight models of the economy in operation, including the Treasury model. They not only diverge greatly from each other in their predictions, but testing the best of them against the simple assumption that things will continue as they are produces only marginally better results: anyone with a feel for the market in the next 6 or 12 months could probably beat the computers. J.C.K. Ash and D.J. Smyth, *Forecasting the United Kingdom Economy* (1973); Patrick Minford, 'The Nature and Purpose of Macro-economic Models', *Three Banks Review*, no. 125 (1980) pp. 3–26.

5. Lionel (later Lord) Robbins, *An Essay on the Nature and Significance of Economic Science* (1935 edn), p. 16.

6. A somewhat harsher judgement is that they are either non-verifiable or wrong. N. Kaldor, 'The Irrelevance of Equilibrium Economics', *Economic Journal*, no. 82 (1972), pp. 12–38.

7. Jacob Viner, *International Trade and Economic Development* (1953), pp. 30–1.

8. W.A.P. Manser, *Britain in Balance* (1971), p. 151.

9. Society of Motor Manufacturers and Traders, *The British Motor Manufacturing Industry. A Students' Guide* (1979), pp. 6.1 and 6.2. Also see p. 103, footnote 3, and p. 116, footnote 50.

10. E.g. OECD, *Economic Survey of Denmark* (1955), pp. 14–17.

11. Cairncross, *Essays*, p. 59.

12. E.g. Samuel Brittan, *Steering the Economy: the Role of the Treasury* (1969), p. 116; Roger Opie, 'The Making of Economic Policy' in Hugh Thomas (ed.), *Crisis in the Civil Service* (1968), p. 66.

13. N. Kaldor, 'Comment' in F. Blackaby (ed.), *De-industrialisation* (1979), pp. 20–1.

14. R.C.O. Matthews, 'Why Britain had Full Employment since the War', *Economic Journal*, no. 78 (1968), pp. 555–69 and discussion in *Economic Journal*, no. 80 (1970), pp. 165–76; C.J. Allsopp, 'The Management of the World Economy' in W. Beckerman (ed.), *Slow Growth in Britain* (1979), pp. 146–7.

15. Andrew Shonfield, *Modern Capitalism* (1965), p. 65.

16. Brittan, *Steering*, p. 314.

17. J.F. Wright, *Britain in the Age of Economic Management. An Economic History since 1939* (1980), p. 142.

18. C.F. Carter, quoted in T.W. Hutchison, *Economics and Economic Policy in Britain, 1946–1966* (1968), p. 187.

19. E.g. Vanessa Doe (ed.), *The Diary of James Clegg of Chapel en le Frith 1708–55* (1978), vol. I, p. xiv: 'Clegg regularly used blistering both as a stimulant and as an antidote to pain. . .when he blistered himself in March 1723, he was barely able to walk afterwards although the original cause of his illness, a quinsy, had gone.'

20. Cairncross, *Essays*, p. 202; Alan Peacock, 'Giving Economic Advice in Difficult Times', *Three Banks Review*, no. 113 (March 1977), esp. pp. 20–1.

21. Robert Bacon and Walter Eltis, *Britain's Economic Problem: Too Few Producers* (1976), p. 1.

22. For a good example, see William Keegan, 'Britain's Three Economic Options', *Observer*, 15 January 1978.

23. Cairncross, *Essays*, pp. 199–200.

24. Letter by V.H. Woodward, *The Times*, 17 March 1977.

25. A. Sampson, *Anatomy of Britain Today* (1969), p. 297.

26. Peter Riddell, 'Cutting back just to stand still', *Financial Times*, 7 October 1979.

27. The classic accounts are Thomas Balogh, 'The Apotheosis of the Dilettante: the Establishment of Mandarins', reprinted in Thomas, *Crisis in the Civil Service*, and

Hugh Heclo and Aaron Wildavsky, *The Private Government of Public Money* (1974). Also Dudley Seers, 'The Structure of Power' in Thomas, pp. 94 ff; Lord Diamond, *Public Expenditure in Practice* (1978).

28. Nick Bosanquet and Peter Townsend (eds.), *Labour and Equality. A Fabian Study of Labour in Power 1974–79* (1980), p. 10.

29. George Brown, *In My Way* (1971), pp. 95, 96, 113, 119. Also see Jacques Leruez, *Economic Planning and Politics in Britain* (1975), pp. 48–9; Roger Opie, 'Economic Planning and Growth', p. 171.

30. E.g. *In My Way*, p. 97; Opie, 'Economic Planning and Growth' in Wilfred Beckerman (ed.), *The Labour Government's Economic Record 1964–1970* (1972), p. 171, and his 'The Making of Economic Policy' in Thomas, *Crisis in the Civil Service*, pp. 61 ff.

31. E.g. Shonfield, *Modern Capitalism*, Chapter 6: 'Britain in the Post-War World: Arm's Length Government'.

32. E.g. Brittan, *Steering*. p. 161.

33. Dr Bernard Donoughue, quoted in *The Times*, 2 April 1980; Tony Benn, *The Case for a Constitutional Civil Service* (1980), p. 7.

34. Balogh, 'Apotheosis', p. 32; Dudley Seers, 'Structure of Power', p. 96; and in general, Fulton Committee Report, *The Civil Service*, Cmnd. 3638 (1968).

35. Duncan Smith, 'Why the Government must come to the aid of the Civil Service', *The Times*, 20 December 1977.

36. For an amusing and not at all untypical episode illustrating this, see Michael Davie, 'The Paradise of Houdini Barnett', *Observer*, 7 March 1976.

37. It was boosted by Mrs Thatcher's practice of holding up the promotion of civil servants with economic views differing from her own. Report in *The Times*, 14 February 1980.

38. See, e.g., W. Beckerman, 'Objectives and Performance', in *Labour Government's Economic Record*, pp. 59–60; S. Pollard, *The Development of the British Economy 1914–1967* (1969), pp. 476–7, 484.

39. W. Keegan and R. Pennant-Rea, *Who Runs the Economy?* (1979), p. 72.

40. Seers, 'Structure of Power', p. 92.

41. Benn, *Case*, pp. 6–13; Keegan and Pennant-Rea, *Who Runs the Economy?*, pp. 86, 107–8; Seers, 'Structure of Power' pp. 87 ff; Opie, 'The Making of Economic Policy', pp. 71–2; Cairncross, *Essays* p. 205; Michael Meacher in *Guardian*, 14 June 1979; Alan Booth and Sean Glyn, 'The Public Records and Recent British Economic Historiography', *Economic History Review*, no. 32 (1979), pp. 303–15; 'When it's No Minister! How the battle is fought out behind closed doors', *The Times*, 15 April 1981.

42. Report in *The Times*, 17 March 1980; Keegan and Pennant-Rea, *Who Runs the Economy?*, pp. 63, 99.

43. Richard Crossman, *The Diaries of a Cabinet Minister. Volume One: Minister of Housing 1964–66* (1975), pp. 615–16.

44. Opie, 'The Making of Economic Policy', p. 64; Brittan, *Steering*, p. 26; letter by Adrian Ham in *The Times*, 18 February 1977.

45. Alan Budd, 'Disarming the Treasury' in IEA, *The Taming of Government* (1979), pp. 95 ff; Opie, 'The Making of Economic Policy', p. 72.

46. Samuel Brittan, *Left or Right, the Bogus Dilemma* (1968) and *The Economic Consequences of Democracy* (1977), pp. 251 and *passim*.

47. E.g. Michael Pinto-Duschinsky, 'Bread and Circuses' in Bogdanor and Skidelsky, *The Age of Affluence* pp. 65, 74.

48. Stewart, *Jekyll and Hyde Years*, pp. 241–4.

49. *Engineering Our Future. Report of the Committee of Inquiry into the Engineering Profession* (Finniston Report), Cmnd. 7794 (1980).

50. E.g. C. Freeman, 'Technical Innovation and British Trade Performance' in Blackaby, *De-industrialisation*; Lawrence A. Krause in Richard E. Caves and

Associates, *Britain's Economic Prospects (1960)*, p. 219; Merton J. Peck in ibid., pp. 448 ff; but also see Caves, ibid., pp. 302–3.

51.  E.g. letter by General D.G. Moore in *The Times*, 6 February 1980; G.F. Ray in Blackaby, *De-industrialisation*, p. 76.

52.  E.g. G.C. Allen, *The British Disease* (1976); K. Pavitt (ed.), *Technical Innovation and British Economic Performance* (1980).

53.  R.T. Severn, letter in *The Times*, 17 January 1980.

# 8 CURRENT OUTLOOK AND FUTURE PROSPECTS: SOME CONCLUSIONS

## 1 The Thatcher Years: Monetarism Rampant

There is in operation, we have noticed above, a law of the deterioration of British economic policies. Like the 'average' Russian harvest ('worse than last year's, better than next year's'), every government seems to have done more damage and to have succeeded in fewer things than the preceding one. With Mr Healey as Chancellor, we seemed to have reached the lowest possible plateau and it was reasonable to suppose that no one starting with similar opportunities could have done worse. Alas, the old law still holds. Under Mrs Thatcher as Prime Minister and Sir Geoffrey Howe at the Exchequer, the present government has done more damage more rapidly than any previous administration, or indeed than could have been conceivable even two years ago.

There is no important area of economic life in which the state of affairs is not such that it would have been regarded with horror or as impossible only a few years back. Unemployment at the level of half a million was then considered the absolutely tolerable upper limit, while today we have 3 million and are contemplating a level of 3.5 million with apparent calm. Inflation at 5 per cent was an occasion for public beating of breasts — today we are inured to fluctuations between 10 and 20 per cent. Whereas a Bank Rate of 7 per cent was considered to be crisis level, nowadays the range of MLR is 12 – 17 per cent. Manufacturing industry alone is losing jobs at the rate of several hundred thousand a year[1] and the import penetration of foreign goods rises daily. Only the pound stays high — and that is a feature neither desired nor intended. Here indeed is a surprise, for the economists' chorus of support over the years for the grievous damage done to the British economy in the past in order to keep up the value of the pound sterling is matched by a similar chorus of complaint now that it is up, and wishing it to come down.[2] Facts have confounded both sets, for despite the high pound coupled with a world recession, exports, even in real terms, refuse to collapse as predicted. They stay up, among other reasons, because Britain at last can deliver some of the goods, and they thus cast further doubt on the British obsession with currency manipulation as the major instrument to rectify the balance of payments.

Meanwhile the oil bonanza continues to boost the exchanges and it is estimated that North Sea oil revenue will rise from the present £3.8 billion (1980) for the Exchequer to well over £5 billion in three or four years,[3] or enough to cover at any rate a large part of the Public Sector Borrowing Requirement (PSBR). Such a windfall would have put any other European country on its feet, but in Britain, as we have seen, it served merely to make much of our productive industry unremunerative and to provide markets for foreign makers. Since October 1979, when all controls over foreign investment were removed, capital has been able to flow abroad freely, and the oil now provides not only work and income for foreigners, but also boosts their real capital equipment while spreading industrial dereliction in Britain.

For its part, the government seems to have ransacked the archives to come up with precisely those policies, from the Geddes Axe to Bruening's deflation package of 1930, which did the most damage and provided the least benefit in the depressed inter-war years. The one thing that can be said for them is that they are simple, not to say simple-minded, and follow faithfully the advice given by the 'monetarists' led by the American economist Milton Friedman. They form a strategy that may be viewed as operating in six steps. Its sole objective is to bring down the rate of inflation (step 1). The key mechanism for doing that is to reduce the quantity of money (2). In turn the reduction in the quantity of money, or at least its rate of increase below the inflation rate, is to be achieved by the two parallel methods of high interest rates (3a) and a cut-back in government spending (3b); this will create more unemployment (4) and incidentally thereby weaken the unions. With less money and credit available firms will have to reduce their price and cost increases (5) and in particular will have to resist the unions' wage demands, on pain of bankruptcy. Once the inflation has been 'squeezed out' of the economy, healthy growth without inflation may then be expected (6). The prescription will have worked.

Although forming a rigid mental framework for the toughest economic policies yet seen since the war, there is no timetable attached to this programme. The key relationship in the monetarist canon, the time which it takes for an increase (or for that matter, a fall) in the supply of money to work through to affect prices, has been variously given as 6 to 18 months and up to five years,[4] itself vague enough. For the time span for the medicine to take effect in stage (6), there is no official guidance at all. The original timetable which was going to allow for a promised substantial drop in income tax in 1980 has long since been jettisoned. Sir Keith Joseph 'hoped' at the time of the 1980 Budget that the rate of inflation would start to come down in two years' time, substantially down in three years, and 'dramatically' down in four, or by 1984: the meaning of these terms is not clear, but the last one might well mean an inflation rate of only 7–8 per cent such as the government inherited when it came into office in 1979, or five painful years of monetarist destruction to get back where it started. The recovery of output is estimated to take much longer: for the whole of the five-year period it was expected to grow in total at no more than 1 per cent a year after an initial fall, and, according to the Chancellor, 'even a decade might be needed before the economy was really strong again'.[5]

There is at any rate common ground among critics and the Treasury about the nastiness of the medicine. Jobs have been disappearing at the rate of 100,000 a month, unemployment at the time of writing, in May 1981, is already at 2.5 million and most forecasts agree that it will go up to 3–3¼ million and stay there for some time,[6] though the government, for understandable reasons, has been reluctant to publish one of their own. The authorities' earlier guesses were, as usual, wildly wrong, one forecast of the London Business School, close to them, estimating as late as mid-1980 that unemployment would rise to only 1.8 million in 1981.[7] There will also be a further fall in real output estimated at 2½–3½ per cent. Where views differ is on whether these calamities will constitute a necessary prelude to recovery, or the start of a further cumulative downward spiral. It is doubtful (if not improbable) whether each or indeed any of these six steps will work in the way assumed; they are much more likely to be counter-productive and meanwhile certain to be highly damaging. Let us look at them in turn.

The starting-point is the fight against inflation as the sole aim. Everything else, the implication seems to be, will come right once prices stop rising.

As a matter of fact, in Sir Geoffrey Howe's first Budget of 1979, inflation did not quite enjoy top priority. A still higher priority was given to two other goals. One was the redistribution of income from the poor to the rich, a typical Conservative move, by the lowering of income tax rates with a compensating drastic increase in VAT from 8 per cent and 12 per cent respectively to 15 per cent. As that measure was estimated to have added at least 4 per cent besides imparting an upward dynamic to the price level, it was clearly considered more important than the price level itself.

Not that, in the economic disasters which followed, the rich and the not-so-rich were able to enjoy these tax-concessions for long. By the time of the 1981 Budget, the average married man's income tax had risen by 45 per cent, while his earnings had risen only by 42 per cent, and the total tax burden had jumped from 40 per cent in 1978–9, the last year of the Labour government, to an estimated 47–48 per cent in 1981–2. It has also been estimated that the petrol price increases of that Budget would add 3–4 per cent to transport costs and thus drive prices up still further.[8] The other high priority was enjoyed by defence and by law and order expenditure, where very large pay increases to the forces, the police and prison warders were brought forward, and overall defence expenditure raised in an otherwise diminished budget. There was also a high priority for the principle of a free market, to which any hope of a prices and incomes policy was sacrificed.

With the aid of all these policies combined, the rate of inflation rose almost at once from 8 per cent to 18 per cent. Only the sterling gain of between 10–20 per cent on the foreign exchanges, which kept down the costs of imports, prevented it from rising still further, though within the year inflation was to rise to over 22 per cent, to which government cost and price increases may have contributed directly 6–8 per cent.

As one caustic critic remarked, 'If you are aiming to reduce the rate of inflation as a prerequisite of your attempt to improve the economy's industrial performance, it is somewhat unfortunate to start by presiding over the doubling of the inflation rate.'[9] However, it may be that these were once for all changes, and that henceforth the thrust of economic policy will be concerned above all with reducing the rate of inflation.[9]

Any reader who has followed the argument of this book to this point will not need to be told once more the full import of the government's priority given to inflation. It means that those who make our policy are prepared to tolerate the full horror and misery of mass unemployment, and the human suffering and frustration and the social evils that follow from it; they are prepared to see desperate needs of housing and health service unmet; they are willing to see us remain poor and backward, to stand still and even drop back while other countries at our level, like Italy, Spain and Greece, are making rapid strides to catch up with Europe; they are willing to see whole industrial landscapes devastated, skills lost, enterprise and originality thwarted and stifled — all for the sake of bringing down price rises to levels which in the 1960s, when we enjoyed them, did nothing to halt the relative British decline. Improvement, it seems, is no longer even on the programme. While only a few years ago it was still widely felt that 'simply to turn off the tap would have been a double disaster, not only putting millions out of work but also ringing down the curtain once and for all on Britain's career as an industrial and trading nation;'[10] that is precisely what the new government now proposes to do. As one Treasury Minister put it: 'We're a nation in retreat.'[11] We have here the distilled and undiluted quintessence of the whole of the post-war period: symbols before reality.

The government's line of attack on prices is to limit the money supply[12] by methods which inevitably cut employment and output. It has not even considered the alternative of holding money growth steady and increasing the flow of goods and services, though that would have exactly the same effect on price according to its own quantity theory of money, and at the same time it would increase instead of damage material prosperity. Nor is it perturbed that the fall in output and incomes envisaged will for the same reason itself raise prices, since it is the same money chasing *fewer* goods. If you live in a world of symbols, if prices alone matter, then you operate only on the side of the symbols, on money.

Unfortunately, these are no longer the days of Charlemagne. 'Money' is not only coins minted, or even paper printed, by government. Human ingenuity has devised a large variety of credit instruments, generated extremely flexibly in the market.[13] As a result, there is confusion among the monetarists as to which they are actually limiting — M1 (currency and current accounts), M3 (a variety of liquid assets) or some other sum; and confusion as to methods, such as special deposits, bank 'corsets' or limitation on government borrowings.

The private enterprise creation of money need not generate, but may only accommodate, higher prices and will naturally continue through a multitude of channels, whatever the government is doing. There is

the velocity of circulation, round-tripping, soft-arbitrating and window-dressing by the banks to keep within the 'corset'. What about the many other kinds of money? Did life come to a standstill in the Irish Republic when the banks closed for many months?

The 'corset' has been evaded with ease by the clearing banks on every occasion on which it was used. Indeed the Bank apparently keeps an unpublished and adjusted measure of 'sterling M3' which takes into account those channels of lending which have been used to evade the 'corset'. It is comforting to know that the Bank is aware of the mirage it has been creating.

No wonder that even the Prime Minister had to admit in her Guildhall speech that 'new financial techniques interfere with money management.'[14]

The 'corset' has been phased out, and M3 became the next quantity to which government policy was locked, but the leading monetarists in the government seem to be unaware that its central policy is resting on a mirage. One senior Treasury Minister, John Biffen, does indeed recognise that 'There is no mechanistic and·succinctly demonstrable link between a movement in money supply and a subsequent change in inflation,' and other factors which affect the latter include the level of international trade, domestic business activity and 'the many social traditions that affect individual and corporate economic behaviour'.[15] However, in the surrealist world of monetarist policy making this did not deter him from pursuing the damaging measures that he recognised as being of doubtful efficiency, nor did the rest of the Cabinet or even the Governor of the Bank of England[16] see anything remarkable in his admission. It is no doubt possible to envisage a system of massive detailed control, a mesh of regulations and an army of inspectors that would make sure that only the government created any form of M, but the conversion of the corset into such a strait-jacket would go right against the basic philosophy of the government by restricting the workings of the market and, worse still, restricting the chances of making money. Certainly the City has no stomach for it.[17] It would also show up too clearly the basic logic of monetarist solutions: it is the logic of curing a boil by cutting off the leg.

There is some irony (yet another one) in the fact that almost as soon as M3 was fixed as the target quantity, it began to shear out of line, and instead of dropping, as it should have done and as some other indicators did, it rose from a + 8 per cent rate in 1979 to + 12 per cent in 1980 and + 21 per cent in early 1981. The nimble foot-work of Treasury Ministers to explain away that misbehaviour because of special reasons in 1980 and to fasten on some other indi-cators[18] came as no surprise to those who had been watching the Treasury at work over the years.

Of the two ways of limiting the money supply (stage 3), the more traditional Keynesian method of high interest rates acts by limiting the demand rather than the supply of loanable funds. They are also a way of coping with inflation, since without them the negative returns suffered by savers would be greater still. On the other hand, high interest rates as they affect mortgage rates on houses, for example, have an inflationary effect on pay demands and push up costs. Moreover, by making long-term borrowing less attractive, they tend to *increase* the recourse to the banks, and thus tend to *raise* the sterling M3 which they were intended to bring down.[19] Meanwhile, it was easy to foresee that

> as the effects of last November's rise in minimum lending rate to 17 per cent work their way through the system, [w]hile rising labour and raw material costs continue to put pressure on com-panies' financing needs, the expectation is that the flatter trend in consumer spending now apparent will quickly be followed by sub-stantial destocking and cuts in production schedules.[20]

Not to put too fine a point on it, there will be massive losses of jobs and of incomes, and widespread bankruptcies — and they appeared exactly as forecast.

High interest rates also affect our foreign economic relations. They keep up the value of the pound, attracting foreign speculative sums on which high annual payments have to be made. The total effect of high rates 'will be in the medium term exceptionally severe and the long term permanently debilitating',[21] and they will hit small businesses hardest of all.

We now come to the other line of the third stage in the strategy: the cut-backs in government spending which are to be instrumental in achieving a reduction in the money supply. On the face of it, public expenditure as such is not a sensible category to single out for cuts: it is rather like a policy of cutting down the consumption of commodi-ties of a red colour in order to allow greater consumption of yellow, green and blue commodities: 'There is no occult evil in the nature of public expenditure which is not equally inherent in the other elements of aggregate demand.'[22] The public sector consists of a large number of widely differing economic activities. Among the most important in a by no means exhaustive list are: (a) transfer payments; (b) the provision of free goods and services; (c) the provision of goods and services against payment by individuals; (d) investments in infrastructure like roads and harbours and in directly productive equipment like coal-mines and post office sorting machines; and (e) the costs of administration itself. The consequences of cuts for an anti-inflationary strategy will be very different on each of these — and on others still, not enumerated here.

Cutting (a) transfer payments will have no predictable effect on inflation at all, but it will affect the distribution of incomes. The assumption no doubt is that such cuts will benefit the richer citizens at the expense of the poorer; but they will do nothing for the price level.

Cutting (b), free provisions, will affect incomes and prices, but the exact effects will depend on what is done with the resources freed. If we start with the previous year as datum line in which certain goods and services were produced and consumed within the economy and then impose a cut, say on education expenditure, then *either* we do it to deploy the resources freed by the cut elsewhere, or we leave them idle. If we choose the latter, we are that much the poorer, having unemployed teachers, larger classes, but no compensating benefit elsewhere to show for it. If, on the other hand, we convert the resources to other uses, and, for example, turn schoolrooms into workshops and teachers into tourist guides, it will be a matter for debate whether the new bundle of goods and services produced is more desirable than the old, but it will have nothing to do with inflation, which will be unaffected. This is more evidently true still in the case of (c), goods and services paid for: there is no *a priori* reason why a cut-back that would provide a poorer postal service or a reduction in the supply of electricity in order, say, that more clothes can be bought should be of advantage to anyone. If there is a cut-back but consumers do not spend more on anything else, the country will have worked less and produced and consumed less. Finally, if there is a cut-back on the part of the state, but it is made up by higher prices to consumers, the country will be poorer *and* have higher inflation.

The reduction in capital spending (d) has traditionally been the most common form of 'saving' and it still is. It is also the most destructive.[23] Cuts in capital expenditure prevent the lowering of real costs in the following years, and thus keep up prices; but above all they confirm and worsen the declining trend in the British economy. Anyone can keep alive, for at least a season, by eating up his seed-corn, but it is a rake's progress policy, leaving in its wake a trail of damage to the future. What monetarists forget is that the real division of the nation's expenditure pattern is not between the public and private sector, but between consumption and productive investment.[24] Lastly, we have (e) costs of administration. Here cut-backs without a loss in administrative efficiency would represent genuine savings and a real contribution to national welfare: but that is saying that increased efficiency is a good thing. It certainly is, but not only in the public services:

> There is waste in public expenditure, no doubt on a large scale, but this is an argument not against public expenditure in general but against incompetence in particular. There is plenty of waste in private spending too, all the way from energy consumption to the prodigal use of packaging materials.[25]

Yet at bottom, with the exception of some extremists, the argument by our policy makers does not seem to be that any of this expenditure is wasteful as such, but that in total it exceeds income and therefore forces the government to borrow with inflationary effects.

As a matter of fact, not all government borrowing is inflationary: where the sums borrowed would otherwise have been saved but not used elsewhere,[26] the borrowing may in fact prevent actual deflation rather than causing inflation. With 10 per cent of the labour force and even more of the national capital unemployed, generating incomes is much more likely to boost output than fuel inflation.

> To curtail public investment because the PSBR has been inflated by dole money and by dear money is a recipe for disaster. . .a public investment programme would have a net cost far less than the amount committed to it. . .nor would increased investment be inflationary,

as *The Times* leader commented on the 1981 Budget.[27] That part of government borrowing which goes to investment, particularly in the public corporations, is likely to benefit production, and would be considered normal and praiseworthy if carried out by a private firm. Moreover, as long as inflation lasts the real national debt burden of interest and repayment is lowered year by year,[28] and its real weight can be kept constant only by topping it up by actual increases in borrowing, though admittedly such borrowing would be part of the inflationary process itself. None of this has been allowed to affect the government's determination to reduce sharply all government borrowing in the shortest possible time (see Table 8.1).

It is hardly necessary to add, in the light of the government's performance in all its sectors, that the PSBR target has so far come nowhere near to being achieved, and was in consequence constantly being shifted to bring it within reach of reality — possibly shedding some light on the Treasury definition (itself shifting) of a 'target', in the process.[29] For 1980−1, the post-Budget forecast of £8.5 billion was exceeded by £5 billion in the actual turnout of £13.5 billion; for 1981−2 the forecasts began with £10.5 billion, made at Christmas 1980, and rose almost weekly to £15.5 billion by February: 'every time the forecasters upped their estimates, Sir Geoffrey [Howe] seems to have increased the amount of misery which he was prepared to inflict on the economy.'[30] Ultimately the Budget of 1981 was estimated to lead to the loss of 300,000 jobs and 2−3 per cent of national output in order to meet the 'target' thus arrived at. It is a wry reflection that the determination of the Chancellor to meet as much as possible of his deficits by taxation will weaken and bankrupt even more of private industry in order to keep public expenditure going — the exact opposite of what the government set out to

**Table 8.1:   Public Sector Borrowing, Strategic Plan 1978−84 (at constant prices, in £ billion of 1978−9)**

|                        | 1978−9 | 1979−80 | 1980−1 | 1981−2 | 1982−3 | 1983−4 |
|------------------------|--------|---------|--------|--------|--------|--------|
| Total expenditure      | 74.0   | 74.5    | 74.5   | 73     | 71     | 70.5   |
| Total receipts         | − 65.0 | − 66    | − 67.5 | − 67.5 | − 69.5 | − 71   |
| Implied fiscal adjt.    | —      | —       | —      | —      | 2.5    | 3.5    |
| GGBR[a]                | 9.0    | 8.5     | 7      | 5.5    | 4      | 3      |
| PSBR[b]                | 9.3    | 8.0     | 6.0    | 5.0    | 3.5    | 2.5    |
| As % of GDP at market prices | 5.5 | 4.75 | 3.75 | 3 | 2.25 | 1.5 |

Note: a. GGBR = General Government Borrowing Requirement, b. PSBR = Public Sector Borrowing Requirement. The difference consists of public corporation borrowing from the private sector and from overseas. For comment, see John Whitmore, 'A highly qualified strategy for the medium term', *The Times*, 27 March 1980.

do. It is for that reason that the CBI asked for an expansion plan of £1.5 billion a year for four years, which (together with some other measures) was estimated to raise the production increase to 3 per cent a year, to reduce unemployment and simultaneously to reduce inflation.[31] Such plans are, of course, the direct opposite of Treasury strategy.

Since the reduction of the annual PSBR has also become an identifiable political aim, it is being pursued with a due degree of dishonesty. Thus some 'savings' are being achieved by shuffling off the burden on to local authorities, or even to private firms, none of which will make any difference to inflation: indeed, in some cases, as in the proposed abolition of local authority jobbing contract work and its transfer to private firms, they will enlarge the bureaucracy and raise total costs[32] — a classic example of 'Treasury Savings'. Because of government 'savings', local rates went up by *c.* 25 per cent in April 1980, and by even more in 1981. Most reprehensible of all, however, is the pretence of closing the gap by selling off government assets; £1 billion of such sales, mostly of BP (oil) shares was included in the 1979 Budget and since then there have been plans mooted for disposing of part of the British Steel Corporation[33] as well as other assets. This, of course, has nothing to do with putting the economy on its feet and, as far as the government is concerned, represents the selling off of inherited property to meet current bills, the traditional action of the rake and the wastrel. The nationalised industries chairmen meanwhile pleaded to be allowed to borrow in the money market for

> they see an old pattern returning whereby the Treasury regards nationalized industry borrowing, not as an investment for the future, but as a permanent drain on resources. . .pushing up the money supply and crowding out private companies from the capital markets.[34]

The massive cutting back on real productive investment in nationalised industries, in roads and transport and in housing, with which Sir Geoffrey Howe achieved so much of his 'savings' in the 1979 Budget[35] was among the most damaging and heartbreaking features of the new policy:

> The frustration for British Rail [according to its Chairman] is that we are meeting our financial targets and falling short of fulfilling

our capability. The prospects have never been better, but under present financial stringencies we may be forced to contract in an expanding market.[36]

It has, however, a crazy logic of its own: since the government will make sure that there is no growth, we need no improvements in public services either.

Why this elaborate charade? Why the wrecking of such public services as health and education, and the further neglect of roads and other parts of the infrastructure, raising costs, damaging our future and making recovery more and more impossible? Why the relentless persecution of state expenditure, and why pretend to have nominal programmes even tougher than the actual policies put into practice?

There are two overt reasons and two others, also important, of which we hear comparatively little. The first is that expenditure on government provisions is involuntary: the consumer has no say and no choice, while the predilection of civil servants is for creating jobs, promotion and power for themselves by spending other people's money. Since there is no normal sanction of bankruptcy to hold them in check it needs eternal vigilance and pressure from the elected politicians to keep down the appetite of the public maw. We have met the doctrine of the all-swallowing state before: it contains an element of truth, but its exaggeration itself calls for explanation. The second reason given is that state spending is more dangerous than that of individuals, since the state alone has the power to create money;[37] again, there is an element of truth in this, to the extent that the mechanism by which the government raises its own credit helps to lay a base on which others can pyramid their credit creation.

Behind these two admitted and often discussed causes there are at least two others, not less strong for being mentioned but rarely. One, referred to earlier, is the redistributive effect of state spending which a Conservative government can be expected to dislike. Another is the private enterprise philosophy of the new government which sees the profit motive as the mechanism by which goods and services are best produced. It would not be entirely unfair to add that many of its leading adherents tend to see the mechanism the other way round, and tend to view the economy as a productive machinery whose real object is to generate profits. To keep the same machinery running without permitting private profits to be made as in the case of the nationalised industries seems to them a betrayal of their basic tenets.

At any rate, many take it as axiomatic that publicly run industry must be 'inefficient'.

None of this, it will be noted, has anything to do with rectifying inflation, the ostensible justification for the policy of destroying jobs. But it is not the first government in history to have found that objectives of agreed national importance happen to require methods which have other desirable side-effects.

The distress in the short run and grievous damage in the long run that will be caused by this policy and particularly its fourth stage, that of generating unemployment, are a certainty; what is far less assured is that it will also be effectual in its declared object of reducing the rate of inflation. The most serious doubt arises because the policy is largely self-defeating, since with every job lost and destroyed there will be one taxpayer less and one recipient of unemployment benefit more, putting a double burden on the Exchequer and the PSBR. By February 1981 it was estimated that each unemployed single man cost the country £4,835 a year, and each married man with two children £6,006. Averaging only £5,000, it means that for every 100,000 unemployed (the monthly rate by which unemployment has lately been rising) the Exchequer was worse off by £500 million; the total annual cost to the Exchequer since Sir Geoffrey Howe took over is thus well over £5 billion and still rising. 'What swells public borrowing most uselessly now is the payment of unemployment benefit to more and more people who desperately want to work and produce.'[38]

In addition, nationalised industries like steel and coal pay interest to the government, some of which may be lost if they have to carry through closures in order to 'reduce' the government deficit, and private industry pays taxes which would likewise be lost. Each cut will therefore require a further cut to make good the Exchequer losses of the first cut and so on in a progressive downward spiral.[39] Hard estimates of the shape of things to come if present policies are pursued are difficult to come by. According to Sir Bryan Hopkin, formerly Head of the Government Economic Service and Chief Economic Adviser to the Treasury in 1974–7:

> the Government has embarked on a policy of making unemployment high enough, for long enough, to break down the present scale of wage and salary increases and in this way eventually get the rate of inflation down and so change inflationary expectations . . .nobody knows how much unemployment will be required to

achieve any defined deceleration of inflation nor how long it will run.[40]

The actual fall in output as a result of these measures has begun to assume frightening proportions. By January 1981, the drop compared with a year earlier was 11.5 per cent; manufacturing output had fallen even more, by 15.5 per cent, and was falling further at the rate of 1.3 per cent a month. The effect of the Budget will be to increase the fall by 2–3 per cent, so that the total fall will be of the order of 20 per cent at least by 1982. Engineering and other capital goods declined even more than the average, consumer goods very much less.[41] This fall in output was never forecast in the government's own figures, but was foreseen by its critics. It is precisely what helps to drive up the PSBR, which all the government's painful measures were intended to reduce. All this is quite apart from the fact that, as we have seen, less than full capacity working raises real costs in industry while the fall in real wages at a time of heavy unemployment reduces demand and causes further unemployment.

The opposite policy of creating jobs and employing people would, of course, have correspondingly positive effects on the Exchequer. On the assumption of a 30 per cent tax rate, adding £30 billion to national income would wipe out painlessly the deficit of £9 billion — not counting any savings in social security payments. We have seen above that if Mr Healey had preferred full employment in 1977–9 to his policy of creating unemployment, his PSBR of £−8 billion a year would have turned into an annual surplus of £ + 2.4 billion.[42]

It may be argued that North Sea oil will reach the peak of its production by the mid-1980s and will by then bring in its full tax revenue of at least £5 billion a year. This will completely transform the chances of meeting the government's target of a reduction in the PSBR. If true, it would be equally true without the agony and the destruction until then envisaged on present policies.

Whatever the long-term damage, in the shorter term the next and fifth stage in the official strategy is that of 'monetary discipline', which

works essentially though the market process by preventing employers from passing on to customers inflated wage [and other payments] not earned by increases in saleable output. So long as the supply of money is not expanded to enable customers to pay higher prices, 'unearned' pay increases cause unemployment rather than inflation.[43]

It is the terrifying belief, central to the monetarist credo, that cutting off the money supply will simply force firms to pay lower wage increases or go bankrupt. 'Squeezing industry until the pips sqeak is the key component in forcing employers and unions to cut down on pay settlements.'[44] The plan, in other words, is to turn industrial relations into a battlefield, and to do it on some mind-boggling assumptions. One key assumption is that the firms will know exactly where the brink of bankruptcy is and how far they can go, but there is no guarantee that either the market as a whole or individual firms can see that line; the map will be drawn only by mass bankruptcies, with their long-drawn-out agony, each dragging other firms with it. However, long before that ultimate stage, firms under cash restraint faced by strong union demands will sacrifice all else first before enduring destructive strikes, and among the first to go will be the level of stocks and the vestiges of investment plans that may still remain. Improvement and modernisation will, as always, be the prime victims.[45] All this is already well on its way. Bankruptcies multiply, and manufacturing investment, our one hope for the future, has been falling rapidly in 1980 and is estimated in 1981 at 15–20 per cent lower still than in 1980, to be at its lowest level for 17 years.[46] Ultimately this must end in 'dismissals and bankruptcies or takeover by foreign investors who have cash enough to buy our capital at bargain prices'.[47]

It is also ironic that the small firms from which the government expects much of the positive initiative to rejuvenate the economy will be the hardest hit by this strategy: 'The monetarists' axe is an indiscriminate weapon that can kill small companies while merely bruising giants like Ford.'[48] Against this, the help promised them in the Budget was merely cosmetic.

All the worst faults of British economists in ignoring practical problems when in pursuit of their macro-economic models are combined here in the glib assumptions underlying the monetarist mechanism, and nowhere is this denial of reality more evident than in the role assigned to the trade unions. Even its supporters[49] admit that 'monetary policy works most smoothly, with least dislocation, where the economy is flexible and fluid', whereas unemployment 'will last much longer if rigidities are allowed to obstruct the effects of tight money'. No one could accuse British unions of being flexible and fluid: in fact, the whole gamut of economic policies in recent years, including the monetarist strategy itself, may be said to have been called into being because neither Labour nor Conservative governments could cope with the damage inflicted on all their plans by the stubborn rigidities of trade union attitudes. What we have therefore is a policy which relies for its success on the one ingredient whose total absence made the policy necessary in the first place.

It is possible that continued losses of jobs will so cow the unions, or some of them, that they will be merely nursing their rage for the day when better trade will allow them to hit back; or it may be that some of them will be radicalised to hit back at once.[50] Will present policies not show the moderate union leaders to have been wrong, and bring to the fore the very militants whom this government has set out to curb? Will Mr Scargill not be justified by Sir Keith Joseph, just as Sir Keith can claim justification by referring to Mr Scargill? While trade union leaders have behaved hitherto as if the Treasury did not exist, the new strategy means that the Treasury acts as if the unions did not exist; but in reality they will both be playing on the same side, passing the ball to each other, each using the excuse of the other's existence to do maximum damage to the British economy. Meanwhile the fabric of society will receive further irreparable damage, the concept of government by consent be further undermined, the contempt for politicians[51] further confirmed.

Still, perhaps it will not come to this; perhaps the Tiber will, after all, not run with blood. Perhaps it is only bluff: 'one of the main aims of policy is to frighten industry and the unions into believing that the money for inflationary wage claims is not there'.[52] Or else, perhaps it simply will not work. Maybe there is

> a central flaw in the Government's economic strategy which is the mistaken assumption that the labour market will adjust in textbook fashion to a progressively lower monetary expansion. Surely, it is by now obvious that organised labour is preventing the labour market from functioning as a pricing mechanism . . .and that monetary restraint under these circumstances must cripple the real economy long before it restrains nominal wage increases.

> If the Government just sticks to its monetary targets the present unacceptably high wage settlements will simply translate into unacceptably high unemployment in a year's time.[53]

But nowadays unemployment does not lead to a collapse of workers' resistance to wage cuts — and besides, the people who provoke the unemployment by their excessive wage demands are not the people who lose their jobs as a result of it: 'It could create a situation in which small employers, and non-unionists, bear the brunt of the coming recession.' In the end, 'given the monopoly power of powerful unions and big employers, tight money is bound to mean both higher prices *and* increased unemployment.[54]

In those circumstances the government will ultimately give in, as it has done in the only two earlier experiments in which monetarism has been tried out, in the USA and in Chile. Inflation will speed up again, and as in the case of all other post-war restriction periods, further desperate damage will have been done to British output, productivity, capital equipment, industrial relations and the whole social fabric in the process, without any positive achievement to compensate for it.

There is in the writings and speeches of those who direct and support the present policies a kind of unspoken assumption that there is some advantage in closing plants that are 'losing' money, presumably because the resources tied up there would then be put to better use. 'Much of the present unemployment represents a shake-out that can only lead to greater productivity and prosperity in the longer term' is the view of Prof. R.C. Stapleton: but the whole point of the strategy, in contrast with some earlier ones is that there would be no new employment for the newly idle resources, but that they would remain idle.[55] The men and equipment now capable of producing 5 million tonnes of steel that are to be scrapped will then produce nothing at all — a form of salvation by death. Not that this would seem to worry Prof. Stapleton, believing as he does that 'one reason why E.E.C. countries, especially Germany, have outperformed the UK is that they started from a position of almost complete devastation in 1945'[56] — a doctrine unknown to the Swiss, the Swedes, the Americans and the Canadians, among others, who stayed ahead of EEC incomes and output despite their lack of desirable devastation.

So far as the re-allocation of labour is concerned, there is plenty of evidence that in modern circumstances this is made far more difficult when industry suffers from low demand and intense competition than in a boom, because redeployment of labour is more easily achieved when it is voluntary than when it is resisted.[57]

The strategy is not to move resources from less into more profitable lines: the strategy is to make all lines less profitable, and kill off the marginal ones altogether in the process. It is a strategy an enemy might seek to force on us in wartime.

But let us assume that none of this comes to pass, and that the policy, in the face of all the probabilities to the contrary, actually works; and let us assume further that in three years or so the unions and their employers have been battered and demoralised into submission, that the sixth stage is reached, inflation is 'squeezed' out, that there is a vast labour reservoir of the unemployed, and the government gives its blessing for a controlled healthy expansion. What then?

The government and its monetarist supporters seem to have a touching faith that somehow all will come right at that point. No one else shares this faith, neither the Governor of the Bank of England, nor the Institute of Economic and Social Research, nor the Commons Treasury and Civil Service Committee.[58] Nor is there any reason why they should, for no calculations or even estimates exist on the part of the government to show how it might be done. All we have is the utterly blind guesses of the monetarists at the outset of the government's reign of havoc that 'any temporary loss of output is likely at worst to be of modest significance'.[59] They did not know then, and they do not know now. One macro-economic guess from a less biased source is that to put 500,000 jobs which were so easily sacrificed now, back by 1984 would require a fiscal stimulus of £5–6 billion a year, and to return to below one million unemployed — surely still a modest aim — would take ten years.[60]

Two types of result can be predicted with fair confidence. The first relates to labour:

> Must we not expect that pent-up claims will be asserted then, as they used to be in the recovery from the trough of the old business cycle, but this time also with the animus fed by the belief that the trough was inflicted by the Government?

> Our negotiators will continue to do what they are currently doing: obtain the best deal the employer can afford.

In monetarist terms,

the permanent breaking of inflationary expectations is necessary but it is not sufficient. . . One is always bound to be sceptical about the prospect of sea-changes in attitudes and since this change seems to rest mainly on the extreme perils in certain sections of the labour market, cost-push forces may well reassert themselves if real demand, profitability and competitive power cease to be so desperately low.[61]

Or is there anyone in government, anyone in the economics profession anywhere, who believes that the unions will not at once use their newly regained power to try and catch up on the real wages they lost in the years of the deluge, and thus set an inflationary spiral going again?

The other expectation relates to the ability of British industry to carry an expansion in physical terms at that point. If the steel industry has meanwhile been amputated down to a 15 million tonnes size, if British Leyland has been truncated, the engineering industry similarly slimmed down and the building industry decimated, where is the capacity for expansion to come from? Shall we then recall the steelworkers who have just been paid off with redundancy payments of £4,000 – £23,000 apiece? Does no one in the government or among its advisers know that it takes anything from three years upwards to build up the factories, the steelworks and the shipyards that would carry the anticipated upward movement once the bad years are over, and is there no one who urges that these be built up now instead of destroying those we have got? If you 'bleed the company sector for three years and then cut taxes. . .by that time the import propensity will be rapidly approaching 100 per cent'[62] and this will be the case above all in the capital goods sector, so that most of the needed equipment will have to be imported. For a critical period of two or three years there will be a balance of payments crisis of a dimension that not even the oil will be able to cope with — and it is not difficult to guess what the Treasury reaction to that will be.

In this connection the view of the fountainhead of the theory, Milton Friedman himself, is of interest:

while monetary restraint is a sufficient condition for controlling inflation, it is a necessary but not sufficient condition for restoring Britain to full economic health. That requires measures on a broader front to restore and improve incentives, promote product investment, and give a greater scope for private enterprise and initiative.[63]

It is precisely this which, for the next two or three years, the government has set out with desperate earnestness to prevent. Once again, we find that at each step and for each problem, there is the same recipe: cut employment and cut investment, or in other words, work less and eat up your seedcorn.

It is easy to attack the current monetarist policies, not least because the British political tradition dislikes extremes and it dislikes consistency. With the exception of the beleaguered faithful group of monetarists in the economics profession and in the Conservative Party, there is bitter hostility to the strategy across the political and the economic spectrum, and as its results are seen to be more and more damaging without the slightest sign of the hoped-for improvements, the opposition is strengthened. Yet the most important aspect of the new line is not its novelty, but its continuity.

For although they are being justified on entirely different theoretical grounds, the economic policies pursued now are in practice a direct continuation of those pursued by the succession of post-war governments. All are alike in having a primary objective other than the real base of the economy: in the first two decades it was the value of the pound and the foreign payments balance, in the 1970s and still today it is inflation. In each case the first reaction is to attempt to rectify the unbalance at the expense of wages, and on its failure there follows a determination to sacrifice output and employment. Above all, the choice is to take the easy way out by cutting investment, innovation and improvement. Meanwhile the military and political pretensions of the government are not to be trimmed in line with its reduced means, but on the contrary these means are to be even further undermined in chasing the mirage of Great Power status.

The chorus of disapproval which is heard today from Mr Healey and his friends on the one hand, and from the phalanx of Keynesian economists who have had it all their own way for so long on the other,[64] therefore rings hollow: they all did the same thing in their time,[65] and 'a re-elected Callaghan administration would have had to cut back its spending plans'[66] also. The only difference is that when these very same policies brought earlier governments to the brink of disaster as they inevitably and invariably did, the Chancellors shrank back from the abyss and counteracted their own macro-economic measures by a battery of specific aids, by credits and by attention to 'supply-based' policies. They thus had the worst of all worlds, laying the foundations for a repeat from a lower starting-point next time, though they did avoid dramatic catastrophes such as the collapse of

1979–81. The present administration by contrast (so far) do not shrink: their progress down goes on without flinching. One might even say that Sir Geoffrey Howe has shown that he has the courage of Mr Healey's convictions — if it were not for the doubts even about the monetarist's courage: the retreat over the pit closures in the face of the miners' threat in February 1981 and the continued vast subsidies for nationalised industries have made their own supporters cry out in despair.[67] 'We have to walk a tightrope', according to Mrs Thatcher, 'between the need to face economic facts and the claims of common humanity,'[68] which must be taken to mean that beyond a certain point even her government will halt the carnage and reconsider. Indeed, if we look at actions rather than words, then Mr Healey's 1975–6 Budget cuts were far more severe than those of the present administration so far; possibly he was the better monetarist.

## 2 Further Outlook: is Decline Inevitable?

In one sense, all historical events are inevitable, given the immediately preceding line-up, and so on for every preceding moment. Yet, as human beings we constantly want to change, if not the course of history in the past, then the course of events in the future, and from that point of view we have to know which factors are 'inevitable', in the sense that they cannot be changed, and which may be amenable to our influence.

So much that caused Britain's dismal economic performance since the war seems to derive from the dead weight of the past, beyond the power of anyone alive now to alter. Among these we must count the imperial heritage, the victory in the last war, and the (temporary) ascendancy as one of the Great Powers which followed from it, all of which induced Britain to go in for a level of political and military expenditure that helped to cripple the economy. Again, the earlier role as the world's leading international lender and trader made the Central Bank and the Treasury into institutions that neglected the productive potential of the country in contrast to the care lavished on the productive sectors by their opposite numbers abroad. Earlier successes as a pioneer in the Industrial Revolution and the 'workshop of the world' without rival induced technological complacency, while the school system for the ruling classes stressed the qualities that would make good administrators of an empire rather than great engineers. A balanced political system and a traditional standard of living well above the Continental level justified a tradition of devoting all efforts to a redistribution of the economic cake rather than increasing its total size. All this was held together by a social conservatism, above all a survival of a much more rigid class structure than anywhere else in the advanced world because of the absence of any major invasion or revolution in the past three hundred years. There was also a heritage of traditional industrial locations, out-of-date lay-outs and antiquated equipment on the ground to reinforce the social immobility of the country.

It was a formidable, mutually reinforcing historical burden to carry and to overcome. While other countries suffered from some or other of these handicaps also, none had the complete range of adverse factors like Britain. It was no wonder that many observers, looking at the British retardation over the past thirty years, have despaired of getting the social system to accept modernity with the ease with which the North Americans, the Continental Europeans and the Japanese have, in their different ways, been accepting it.

Of course, if we start with Britain's adverse initial factors and historical burdens, she will have a more complete set of them than other countries, but such an approach will neglect the negative aspects found among other countries and in respect of which Britain had the advantage. Among them, from the vantage point of 1945, was a strong social cohesion and no waste of effort in searching out war criminals and collaborators, no loss or change of territory, the psychological boost of victory, immense technological superiority over all others except the Americans, an industrial machine in much better shape, high prestige as a provider of quality exports to world markets, a sound financial system, and traditional links by language and culture with many of the best and most rapidly growing export markets overseas. Looking back, it is not at all evident that the British, given their starting handicap, were bound to fail; on the contrary, in 1945 they looked hot favourites.

The problem then was to hang on to the lead. Today's task is to catch up. Again Britain's position looks highly promising, and far better than the outlook for the Continental economies, let alone Japan, in the late 1940s. Our resource endowment is much better than theirs, and to the traditional unbeatable coal supply we can now add self-sufficiency in oil, at least for a critical decade or two. Our sea communications to get other resources from elsewhere are as good as Japan's and better than those of the Continent.

The quality of our engineering profession is still as good as that of the leaders. There are unevennesses in technology, but this is so in most countries. Similarly, labour skills in manufacturing and the size of the manufacturing sector compare well with those of the main rivals abroad; neither in that field, nor in general education, is there any catching up to be done as has often been the case for other backward economies in their spurt to join the leaders. The financial system, the system of laws, the law-abiding nature of the population — these and similar pre-conditions, the absence of which often forms a formidable stumbling block to rapid progress, exist and are in excellent shape.

The main material problem would be to divert enough resources from consumption to investment, and likewise to expand the capital goods industries to supply the actual buildings and machinery on which economic prosperity must be based. Measured by the wild fluctuations imposed on the British economy in the 1970s, the sums involved are not large: perhaps an additional diversion of 4−5 per cent of national income to investment, and even that need not all occur in one year, but could be fed in part from the production increase that a programme of reconstruction would itself bring in its train. Let us recall that we have at present 3 million people unemployed and, according to some estimates, 25−33 per cent of industrial capacity under-used.[69] Putting it differently, if 2 million of the present 2.5 million unemployed could be put to work on schemes which would, directly or indirectly, modernise the British economy and make it competitive again, it would be sufficient without having to cut consumption. Hitherto we have had one period after another in which the British people have been asked to tighten their belts and make sacrifices for the future: they have always obeyed the call, only to see their self-denial used merely to make them poorer and create more unemployment. It is hard to believe that the same temporary sacrifice, if necessary at all, would not be forthcoming if for once it were to be used, not to cause damage, but to build up prosperity.

It is the nature of the resources required, rather than their quantity in macro-economic terms, that will cause problems. The main victims of the government's destructive actions in the past have been the capital goods industries, engineering and especially machine tool production, steelmaking, building and construction. Although there is some spare capacity, any serious re-equipment of the road and rail system, the factories and the other productive units is likely to come up against a bottleneck in the capital goods industries which itself will take several years to overcome and thus put back a recovery programme by a similar period. The alternative of importing a large part of the capital goods required would, as in the case of North Sea oil equipment, cause a massive balance of payments deficit and besides, some activities like building cannot be imported and have always to be provided largely from home resources.

One other favourable factor deserves mention: the present technical backwardness of much of the British economy and the large gap between best practice and British practice would mean an extremely rapid rate of growth, once up-to-date equipment was installed. We should enjoy the opportunity of the hyper-growth rates registered by Japan in the 1950s and 1960s and by Spain and Greece more recently.[70] One important advantage of installing the latest plant in a backward economy is the opportunity of setting up the unbeatable combination of low wages with high technology until such time as the general level of wages creeps up to the level of other advanced countries with the general transformation of the economy. That opportunity is open to Britain today in view of her present very low wage level and should allow her to recapture very rapidly a large part of her former share of world markets, and particularly markets for manufactures in Britain itself, which in turn would give further opportunities for cost reductions.

As far as the material pre-conditions are concerned, therefore, nothing stands in the way (as nothing has stood in the way during the past decades) of rejoining the advanced countries of Europe by an upward spiral of modernisaton, output rise, cost reductions and the recapture of market shares at a rate comparable with that of other catching-up economies. This would be true whether we envisaged a boom world, like that of the years 1948 – 73, or a relatively depressed world like the years since: both have advantages and disadvantages for the catcher-up. From the resource point of view Britain could easily reach the then European level within twenty years, or say by the end of the century, meanwhile enjoying the invigorating and socially positive aspects that accompany rapid economic growth. Catching up becomes more difficult with every year that passes but, as we have seen, there are some advantages in backwardness at the start, and there is nothing here that other economies have not overcome in their turn.

The problem, of course, does not lie in material possibilities, it lies in attitudes and policy decisions. What is required is a change in attitudes powerful enough to overcome thirty years of a learning process which hammered in the opposite lessons. Thus the simple German post-war solution of encouraging the profit motive by freedom of action and high rewards for entreprise is no longer feasible: after thirty years of being hit on the head British industry will not get up from the ground even when the hitting stops. Even if they are given the right incentives, our entrepreneurs will merely invest abroad or in speculative purchases, as they did in 1972, but not in production at home; they will distrust the promises of British governments to support those who put their money on British industry, for these promises have been broken far too often in the past. The vicious circle of distrust feeding on disappointed hope between British industry, including the nationalised industries, and the British government can be erased only by a similarly long period of faith being kept. Meanwhile we shall have to rely as a minimum on a mixed system in which much of the steering and the initiative is taken on by the state, on the French or Japanese model.[71] The necessary mixture of incentives and directives, of tax funds made available and markets promised, of unqualified support by all Ministries and above all of a firm commitment to keep to reconstruction as the first priority must ultimately derive from the government.

Just to sketch in the outlines of the path which Britain has to follow is enough to be overwhelmed by its terrifying hopelessness. To give it any chance at all would require a change of heart on the part of at least three groups of people.

The easiest to persuade will be the managers in private and nationalised businesses. Their natural instinct is to expand, to become more efficient and to beat the opposition. The amount of investment and technological improvement actually installed in the face of persistent government discouragement gives good grounds for hope that a more favourable official climate will set them quickly enough on an upward course. Nevertheless, the experience of three decades is not easy to shed, and it will require years before the confidence to invest in Britain is restored.

The second group, the trade unions, forms a more formidable hurdle. In their case government policy over thirty years has been able to build on the traditional and almost natural resistance of all professional interest groups to technical progress that will undermine their skill, let alone their jobs. Opposition to innovation or acceptance only under impossible conditions have thus become second nature to our trade union leaders and the havoc imposed by the present government on certain key industries will have convinced the last waverers that it is the duty of all trade unions to oppose progress, for its chief purpose is to make many of them unemployed. It will take years to erase the impression of Sir Keith Joseph and his colleagues from the memories of trade unionists, even under optimum conditions, and these are years we cannot afford.

Moreover, even if the future should show that new technology means better jobs rather than unemployment, this will still be a long way from the widespread conviction which is familiar in other countries, but very rare here, that improvements in pay, except of the most limited and temporary kind, can come only from greater productivity. We are even further away from a positive interest by unions themselves in the productivity of their members. It is therefore hard indeed to be optimistic and to imagine that British unions will allow improvements to be introduced as smoothly here as elsewhere; it is, of course, even more difficult to envisage circumstances in which they would be too weak to oppose them — even if that were desirable.

Lastly, to effect a change of heart on the part of our economic policy makers and the chorus of professional economic opinion accompanying them will be the most difficult of all. As we have seen, this is not basically a matter of theory: nothing said or implied here as to mechanisms or relationships is at variance with the views of at least a large and influential part of Treasury or economic opinion. The difference lies in the view as to what is feasible in the range of possible options and leverage points. The whole of post-war policy has been built on the assumption that whatever else can be manipulated or changed, actual production and investment cannot be and must be left to industry, and that the most the government can do is to set the scene which therefore receives top priority — at the expense of damaging the production and the investment, for the benefit of which the scene-setting is supposed to have been undertaken in the first place. To come round to the opposite view requires no re-learning of economic theory, but it implies an admission that grievous and quite unnecessary damage has been done to the economy for many years and it is hard to imagine a body as powerful and self-confident as the Treasury condescending to such an admission. Still less is there any hope of seeing the present constellation of power disturbed to allow a less tainted Ministry to take over the control of economic policy. The Treasury is there to stay: it will not yield, and it will not change.

There are some who hope for the power of the trauma: the trouble with Britain, they argue, is that at no point have her misfortunes been severe enough to force upon her a fundamental reappraisal. If only we sink far enough, and disaster strikes hard enough, widespread changes in outlook will follow. If that were so, then there is indeed some hope, for the present government is set on course for a devastation of much of Britain's industrial strength that will be far more dramatic than anything we have yet seen. Some vulnerable areas like South Wales have felt the shock waves already, but there will be a more general deterioration of employment, a fall in incomes and output, an obvious failure to reduce inflation or government deficits, and a possible loss of control over the money supply. Clearly, this will not be allowed to happen without strikes and bankruptcies, and political and social debates of increasing bitterness, all of which will do further massive harm to the productive part of the economy.

At the same time, there must be some doubt whether this sort of brinkmanship will really work as a method of concentrating the mind. It is true that when workers are faced with the obvious destruction of their employer, as British Leyland workers were by the end of 1979 and again in March/April 1980, the majority will shrink from administering the *coup de grâce*, even though they may be strongly urged to do so by their shop stewards and by some national leaders, and this particular case was all the more remarkable since industrial relations in that firm had been among the worst in the country, and certainly the worst of any motor company in the world. But here the effect was visible, immediate and directly related to action. By contrast, a national economy can die a much slower lingering death and the responsibility of any small group for bringing it about is very hard to bring home to them. This is even more true of the grim combination of bankers, Treasury pundits and obsessionally dogmatic politicians for whom industry has in any case never been of more than secondary or tertiary importance.

Optimism, then, is difficult. There is a positive side, and it is the basic endowment of the British economy which is such that it could without difficulty launch Britain on a course of rehabilitation to catch up with the advanced world by the end of this century. But against it is set the attitude of mind that has grown up over three decades, by choice on the part of some, as a result of experience on the part of others. Attitudes of mind can be affected by argument. It is to the argument that this book addresses itself.

## Notes

1. One estimate was 750,000 from mid-1979 to the beginning of 1981. *The Times*, 14 February 1981.

2. For a typical approach (though at least healthily critical of the other shibboleths of monetarism) see Brian Gould, John Mills and Shaun Stewart, *Monetarism or Prosperity?* (1981).

3. Report in *The Times*, 25 February 1981.

4. Wynne Godley and Robert Neild, *The Times*, 9 January 1981.

5. Reports in *The Times*, 29 March and 27 February 1980.

6. Reports will be found conveniently in *The Times*, 27 February and 5, 9 and 30 March 1981; *The Economist*, 31 January 1981.

7. 'Economic Outlook 1979–83' (June 1980).

8. *The Times*, 13 March 1981, also Melvyn Westlake, ibid., 3 February and 11 March 1981.

9. William Keegan, *Observer*, 2 March 1980.

10. Peter Calvocoressi, *The British Experience 1945–75* (1978), p. 107.

11. Report in the *Sunday Times*, 5 April 1981.

12. This is now standard. E.g. W.D. McClam, 'Targets and Techniques of Monetary Policy in Western Europe', *Banca Nazionale del Lavoro Quarterly Review*, no. 124 (1978), pp. 3–27.

13. Although fundamentalists will deny their own evidence and maintain that 'inflation is caused solely by an undue increase in the quantity of money and. . .it can and must be prevented. . .only by the restriction of the basic money supplied by the central bank'. (F.A. Hayek, 'How to deal with inflation', *The Times*, 27 March 1980).

14. Letters to *The Times*, Richard Lamb, 15 November 1979, Austin Mitchell, 17 March 1980, Elizabeth Bendle, 3 December 1979. Also Michael Meacher, 'Four reasons why the Budget strategy cannot succeed', *The Times*, 9 April 1980.

15. Report by Michael Jones in the *Sunday Times*, 20 April 1980; also *The Times*, 21 April 1980. This is the burden of the argument of the anti-monetarists among the Economics Establishment. Sir Alexander Cairncross and others in *The Times*, 20 November 1980, P. Ormerod, ibid., 5 June 1980, and the statement by 364 economists reported in the press on 31 March 1981.

16. David Blake, 'Price stability is crucial, Bank Governor says', *The Times*, 21 April 1980.

17. Cf. David Blake, 'Chancellor welcomes slower money supply' and 'Opposition from Treasury and Bank of England to full monetary base system', *The Times*, 21 March 1980; ibid., 31 March 1981; letter by Lord Kaldor, ibid., 17 June 1980.

18. E.g. reports in *The Times*, 20 February 1981, 11 March 1981.

19. E.g. D.A. Bell, *The Times*, 22 September 1980, John Whitmore, ibid., 25 February 1981, Lord Kaldor, ibid., 17 March 1981.

20. John Whitmore, 'A highly qualified strategy for the medium term', *The Times*, 27 March 1980.

21. Letter by Kenneth Baker, MP, in *The Times*, 27 February 1980. Also see the exchanges with Sir Geoffrey Howe in the House of Commons, reported in ibid., 21 March 1980.

22. Evidence of Lord Kahn and Michael Posner to *Public Expenditure Committee, Ninth Report*, H.C. 328 (1974), p. 67, also pp. 76–7.

23. This is one of the main points made by the Commons Select Treasury Committee. Report in *The Times*, 9 April 1981.

24. See the Report of the House of Commons Treasury Committee, *Guardian*, 3 May 1980.

25. Reginald Maudling, 'The one way we could push up our earnings', *The Times*, 31 May 1978.

26. In 1978 about three-quarters of the PSBR came from genuine savings.

27. 11 March 1981.

28. E.g. Anthony Harris, 'Honesty in Government Borrowing' in IEA, *Catch 1976. . . .?* (1976), pp. 25–6.

29. See R.C. O. Matthews and W.B. Reddaway, 'Can Mrs. Thatcher Do it?', *Midland Bank Review* (Autumn 1980), p. 17.

30. David Blake in *The Times*, 19 March 1981.

31. Report in *The Times*, 6 March 1981; CBI, *The Will to Win* (1981).

32. Report in the *Guardian*, 6 November 1979.

33. Reports in *The Times*, 9 February, 11 February 1980.

34. Report in *The Times*, 26 January 1980.

35. Frances Cairncross, 'Why the Governments's public spending clean-up means it will be dirtier by rail', *Guardian*, 19 April 1980.

36. Report in *The Times*, 24 April 1980.

37. 'Public expenditure is financed mainly by raising taxes and to some extent by borrowing from the public, from foreigners and by increasing the money supply, whereas private expenditure is largely financed by earnings, interest or other income and only to a small extent by borrowing from other sectors. The power to levy taxes and to create money to pay for public expenditure is the unique feature of the public sector. Private persons (whether individual or corporate) cannot do either of these things' (*Public Expenditure Committee, Ninth Report*, H.C. 328 (1974), p. ix, para. 9).

38. Leader in the *Observer*, 15 March 1981; *The Times*, 7 and 12 February 1981.

39. E.g. letters to *The Times*, by Anthony Vickers, 11 December 1979; E.H. Woolf, 10 January 1980; Alan Williams and Ray Rees, 6 February 1980.

40. 'Is the Government blundering around in the dark?', *The Times*, 15 April 1980.

41. The *Times*, 12, 17 and 30 March 1981.

42. P. 63 and Table 3.7 above.

43. 'The Private Pocket, not the public purse, is the best defence against runaway inflation', memorandum signed by twenty leading economists in *The Times*, 9 January 1980.

44. David Blake, 'The Budget: a promise of hope tomorrow', *The Times*, 27 March 1980.

45. Andrew Shonfield, *British Economy Since the War* (1958), p. 241.

46. *The Times*, 19 December 1980; (Treasury) *Economic Progress Report* (January 1981).

47. I.F. Pearce in *The Times*, 5 June 1980.

48. *The Economist*, 11 November 1978; also 'Credit Squeeze angers small Firms', *Sunday Times*, 18 November 1979.

49. E.g. the twenty signatories mentioned above, *The Times*, 9 January 1980.

50. 'If we go back to work', said Mr Sirs, of one of the least militant unions in the country at the end of its 13-week dispute, 'it is only to gird our loins so that the next struggle we will be fighting comes over jobs. . .I only hope that the whole of the trade union movement will be prepared to stand and fight as we have been.' Report in *The Times*, 2 April 1980.

51. E.g. J. Alt, *The Politics of Economic Decline* (1979).

52. William Keegan, in the *Observer*, 30 March 1980.

53. Letters by David Heathcoat-Amory, *The Times*, 27 February 1980, and R.S. Dale, ibid., 28 November 1979.

54. Lord McCarthy, letter in *The Times*, 16 January 1980; also B.C. Roberts, 'The Government's Challenge to the Unions', *Three Banks Review*, no. 124 (1979), p. 14.

55. Under earlier restrictions, the fear was that resources not spent by the government might 'go into savings and discourage consumption'. Today that is the intention, and growth will have to wait for three or four years. Christopher Johnson in

IEA, *The Taming of Government* (1979), p. 59.

56. Letters in *The Times*, 2 April 1981 and 25 November 1980.

57. Francis Cripps in F. Blackaby (ed.), *De-industrialisation* (1979), pp. 168–9.

58. *The Times*, 27 May 1980, 31 March 1981 and 9 April 1981; *Financial Times*, 9 April 1981; also R.G. Opie, *The Times*, 1 April 1981.

59. Patrick Minford, 'A Return to Sound Money', *The Banker* (July 1979).

60. Frances Williams in *The Times*, 30 March 1981.

61. Sir Henry Phelps Brown, letter in *The Times*, 5 March 1980; Mr Zeno Opadia-Kadima, ibid., 3 December 1980; Matthews and Reddaway, 'Can Mrs. Thatcher Do it?', pp. 12 and 19.

62. William Keegan, 'Thatcher stands firm', *Observer*, 2 March 1980.

63. 'Monetarism: a reply to the critics', *The Times*, 3 March 1980.

64. E.g. Denis Healey, 'My Plan for Britain's Recovery', *Observer*, 16 March 1980; Nicholas Kaldor, letter in *The Times*, 3 March 1980.

65. E.g. David Blake, 'Worse than our partners', *The Times*, 29 December 1979; John C. Carrington and George T. Edwards, 'Keynesians and monetarists — are they really poles apart?', ibid., 4 December 1979; Paul Ormerod, letter in *The Times*, 5 June 1980.

66. Peter Riddell, 'Cutting back just to stand still', *Financial Times*, 27 October 1979.

67. E.g. letters to *The Times* by Derek Gaulter and Ian Harris, 19 February and 23 February 1981.

68. Reported in *The Times*, 13 March 1980.

69. Lord Kaldor in *The Times*, 17 March 1981.

70. E.g. M.V. Posner, 'Industrial Policies and Growth' in Sir Alec Cairncross (ed.), *British Economic Prospects Reconsidered* (1971), p. 148; John Cornwall, *Modern Capitalism* (1977), p. 114.

71. David Liggins, 'What Can We Learn from French Planning?', *Lloyds Bank Review*, no. 120 (1976), pp. 1–12; W. Keegan and R. Pennant-Rea, *Who Runs the Economy?* (1979), p. 16; Ch. Sautter and M. Baba, *La Planification en France et au Japon* (1978).

# INDEX

America *see* United States of America
Amory, Heathcote 42
armaments production 36
Austria 3, 7, 115

balance of payments 12, 31, 33, 38, 42, 46, 54, 65, 73, 74, 136, 166, 183-4, 188; deficits 44, 48, 50, 51, 56, 122
balance of trade 88
Balogh, (Lord) Thomas 74, 98n7
Bank of England 43, 48, 75, 80, 85, 92, 94, 157, 158, 170, 182
bank rate 40, 43, 44, 45, 165, 171; leak 155
bankruptcies 171, 179
Beckermann, Wilfred 73
Biffen, John 170
Birch, Nigel 151
British Leyland (BL) 11, 81, 83, 100n40, 108, 112, 119n20, 120n23, 183, 191
British Rail 107, 175-6
British Steel Corporation (BSC) 11, 107, 110-1, 175
Brittan, Samuel 50, 74, 98n7
Brown, (Lord) George 104, 152
budgets 36-9 *passim*, 40, 45, 57, 160, 167, 168, 173-5, 178-9
building industry 81, 99n26, 147, 183, 187
bus strike 110
businessmen 102-6 *passim*
Butler, (Lord) R. A. 39, 67n13

Cairncross, (Sir) Alexander 94-5
Callaghan, James 44, 115, 157
Canada 2, 8, 33, 181
capital equipment 23-4, 28; exports 40, 88-9; formation 46, 146; goods industries 81, 82, 187; per head 26-7; *see also* investment
Capital Issues Committee 49
Central Economic Planning Staff 152
Central Policy Review Staff 83
Chancellor of the Exchequer 28, 29, 34, 37, 39, 42, 43, 57, 58, 59, 97, 139, 158, 165, 167, 174
Chief Economic Adviser 49, 94, 177

Churchill, (Sir) Winston 154
City of London 34-5, 87, 88, 92, 97; banks 86
civil service 150-9 *passim*; strike 110
Cobb-Douglas function 134
Common Market *see* European Economic Community
construction industry 81
consumer durables 82, 103
convertibility 32-3, 40
'corset' 169-70
credit squeeze 62
Cripps, Sir Stafford 33, 152
cycles *see* fluctuations

Dalton, Hugh 152
deflation 14, 45, 52, 72, 91, 166
demonstration effect 15
Department of Economic Affairs (DEA) 43, 54, 69n52, 74, 152-3
depreciation 47
devaluation 14, 34, 45, 80
distribution of incomes 12-13
dollar problem 32, 35
Dresdner Bank 11

economic 'miracle' 4-6 *passim*; policy 1, 31, 55; success 1
economics 55, 144
Economics Establishment 36, 63, 76, 92
*Economist, The* 57, 58
economists 29, 143-50 *passim*, 184, 190
energy conservation 93
engineering industry 82, 178, 183, 187; profession 161; strike 111-12
entrepreneurship 122-3
environment 15
European Economic Community (EEC) 6, 25, 66, 93, 129, 148, 181
European Payments Union 36
Evans, Moss 111
exchange rate 80
export promotion 78

Federation of British Industries 43
fluctuations 51, 103, 122
Ford Motor Co. 11, 83, 179